THE NEW LIBRARY OF PSYCHOANALYSIS

The New Library of Psychoanalysis was launched in 1987 in association with the Institute
of Psyc   d
apprecia   g
mutual   es
such as   al
sciences   n
and dev   n
outside,

The   e
psychoa   )–
analysis,   of
Psycho-   o
member   es
internat   al
ethics a   d.
Distingu   1,
Ronald   d
Winnic
Volu   d
Tuckett   e
under t   d
Campbe

First published in 1989 by
Routledge
11 New Fetter Lane, London EC4P 4EE
29 West 35th Street, New York, NY 10001

Reprinted in 1991, 1993 and 1994

Filmset by Mayhew Typesetting, Bristol, England
Printed and bound in Great Britain by Mackays of Chatham PLC, Kent

British Library Cataloguing in Publication Data
Joseph, Betty
Psychic equilibrium and psychic change:
Selected papers of Betty Joseph, –
(New library of psychoanalysis; 9)
1 Psychoanalysis
I. Title   II. Feldman, Michael
III. Spillius, Elizabeth Bott
IV. Series
150.19′5

Library of Congress Cataloging in Publication Data
Joseph, Betty.
Psychic equilibrium and psychic change; selected papers of Betty
Joseph / edited by Michael Feldman and Elizabeth Bott Spillius.
p.   cm. – (New library of psychoanalysis; 9)
"Complete list of the published papers of Betty Joseph": p.
Bibliography: p.
Includes index.
1. Psychoanalysis   I. Feldman, Michael.
II. Spillius, Elizabeth Bott. 1924–
III. Title   IV. Series.
RC504.J67   1989   89–4407
616.89′17 – dc19   CIP

ISBN 0–415–04116–3 (hbk)
ISBN 0–415–04117–1 (pbk)

NEW LIBRARY OF PSYCHOANALYSIS
9

General editor: David Tuckett

Psychic Equilibrium and Psychic Change

SELECTED PAPERS OF BETTY JOSEPH

Edited by

MICHAEL FELDMAN and ELIZABETH BOTT SPILLIUS

LONDON AND NEW YORK

To the past and present members of my seminar
— which has evolved into a workshop —
with whom the ideas in this book were developed

Contents

Preface

The strength and vitality of scientific ideas can be judged by their growth and the developments which arise from them. Freud's own ideas changed and developed to the end of his life. They also gave rise to many different, sometimes divergent or even controversial developments, and I do not mean such 'dissident' developments as those of Jung or Adler, but those genuinely based on Freud's own work and his work in various phases of his own development, some followers pursuing more his early work, some the later.

Of those pursuing Freud's later work, Melanie Klein is probably the most significant. Like Freud's, her own work developed, bringing in new ideas and changes of emphasis, till the end of her life. That development continued in the work of her pupils. Her central ideas of the importance of early stages of development and the paramount role of the interplay between unconscious phantasy and reality and that of the shifts between the paranoid-schizoid and depressive positions inform the work of all her pupils. Technically, the importance she attaches to the transference is a constant in their work. On the other hand, they pursued their researches in different directions — for instance, Bion and Rosenfeld into the analysis of psychotics — and her various followers developed different styles of work with different emphases.

One of Klein's late concepts — that of projective identification — of which she gives only a few lines in her paper 'Notes on some schizoid mechanisms' (1946) generated research which has resulted in rich contributions to both theory and practice. In particular it contributed to the understanding and uses of countertransference — an area unexplored by Klein herself. It was also one of her concepts which has gained world-wide acceptance among psychoanalysts of various orientations.

With the group of analysts who particularly investigated the implications of that concept for daily technique and clinical approach to patients, in recent years Betty Joseph's work is a particularly important development. It is unspectacular and developed step by step, and it is only slowly that it started to gain increasing importance, particularly among Kleinian analysts, but becoming gradually also more generally accepted not only in Great Britain but also arousing a great deal of interest abroad, including the USA.

I first met Betty Joseph when she came to London as a candidate in 1945, but began to know her only in 1949. She was just qualified, having started her analysis with Balint in Manchester and having followed him to London. After qualification she started an analysis with Paula Heimann, and it was at the time of this transition that she came to me (I was just starting as a training analyst) to discuss some of her cases. It always surprises me that I actually remember one of her patients and a dream he brought. He was a shoe fetishist and was particularly interested in high heels, especially those known as stiletto heels. He dreamed that he threw a knife under a cupboard, and I remember telling her that his picture of the phallic woman was based on his projection of his *own* penis into her. It says something about the vividness and conviction with which she presented this material that I remember it to this day. I also remember it with affectionate amusement, considering how much I have learned from her about projective identification in later years.

Betty Joseph started in the classical Kleinian way prevalent then, but by the 1970s it became clear that she was developing her own increasingly distinctive style. It is characterized by the way in which she listens to her patients with ever-increasing attention to the minute-by-minute psychic changes occurring in the patient's mind, related to, and linked with the constant interplay between analyst and patient and its effects on the transference and countertransference.

Some years after becoming a training analyst in the mid-1950s, like many of us Betty Joseph started conducting a postgraduate seminar. This seminar also underwent an evolution. Starting as so many other clinical graduate and postgraduate seminars led by a 'teacher', it has changed in character to become a real workshop, giving rise to creative group work under her leadership. Like her own work, this workshop is concerned with describing in detail exchanges between the patient and the analyst in the session and looking at the clinical implications of every intervention, describing details of technique in the moment-to-moment interaction. But in the process of so doing, the members of the workshop are also hammering out a theory of technique with, I think, wider theoretical implications than they themselves are aware of. It is also significant that this work together does not produce a monolithic technique, and its members have their own individual styles.

I have worked closely with Betty Joseph for nearly forty years, and in such a relationship it is difficult to sort out who learned what from whom. I know that in the work of my contemporaries I was influenced most by Bion and later, though maybe not to the same extent, by Betty Joseph. I, and others, have learned from her particularly to pay much more acute attention to the subtler and continuous acting in of the patient in the session and its effect on countertransference. This is an area, however, in which there are individual differences among Kleinian analysts. These differences concern the technical problem of how and when to interpret explicitly the unconscious phantasy and infantile experience which is being enacted in this interplay between patient and analyst. There is general theoretical agreement that such linking should be done only when it is emotionally meaningful to the patient, but in practice analysts vary in their assessment of when the right moment has come. For example, my impression is that I myself put more emphasis on the need to link the interplay in the session with the infantile context than Betty Joseph does.

In her own work what strikes me most is a rare combination of very fine intuition with great intellectual and technical rigour. There is no self-indulgence in that work. The careful attention to detail, which also characterizes her work, gives a very full picture of the patient, the analyst, and the exact interaction between the two in the psychoanalytic process, and this is why I think her papers, though dense and difficult, are understandable and appealing to analysts not otherwise familiar with the Kleinian approach.

Hanna Segal

Acknowledgements

I would like to thank the editors, Dr Michael Feldman and Mrs Elizabeth Bott Spillius who have organized these papers, and, with great patience and understanding, attempt to introduce them to the reader.

Among many other colleagues I particularly wish to thank Dr Hanna Segal, who has over years mulled over, discussed, and always constructively criticized the majority of the papers in this volume.

I also want to thank the following for their kind permission to reproduce copyright material: *The International Journal of Psycho-Analysis* (Chapters 1, 2, 3, 7, 9, 10, 11), Jason Aronson Inc. (5), Caesura Press (6), the *Bulletin of the European Psychoanalytical Federation* (8), International Universities Press (12), *Psychoanalytic Psychotherapy* (13), and *The Psychoanalytic Quarterly* (15).

Betty Joseph

General introduction

Michael Feldman and Elizabeth Bott Spillius

Until recently Betty Joseph's work, which represents a particular development within the Kleinian tradition, has been little known outside a comparatively narrow circle of British psychoanalysts and Kleinian psychoanalysts abroad. It is the purpose of this book to collect her various papers together so as to make her seminal ideas more readily accessible. The aim of this General Introduction is to outline the main themes of her work. The papers themselves are divided into four sections, each of which has an introduction of its own which links the particular papers of the section with the main themes described in the General Introduction. The papers are reprinted in the order in which they were written, which sometimes differs from the order in which they were published.

Joseph's psychoanalytic technique and her way of conceptualizing the processes involved have evolved over many years, particularly in relation to the intensive and prolonged analysis of a number of difficult and resistant patients. These patients confronted her with subtle technical problems which have become a major interest of hers and which she addresses in the papers collected in this book. Although the patients with whom she was working could be classified as narcissistic, borderline, or perverse, the technical and theoretical issues with which Joseph has been concerned are of very wide application within psychoanalysis.

The type of patient with whom Joseph is particularly concerned in these papers is the sort of person who comes to analysis because consciously he (or she) wants to change, but who appears to be unwilling or unable to do so, even though his feeling about analysis and his analyst is usually basically positive. Joseph sees patients in a rigorously maintained

1

psychoanalytic setting in which patients are seen five times a week and are expected to use the couch, except of course in the case of child patients. Within the framework of this setting she attempts to provide a precise working out of the way the patient's ideas and feelings, conscious and unconscious, about himself, his analyst, and the analytic relationship are lived out in the session. She argues that the way in which the patient consciously and unconsciously structures the analytic relationship makes apparent the nature of his internal world, which itself is the product of his complex history. Increasingly she has moved away from making global, explanatory interpretations towards making more limited and precise descriptions to the patient of how, at a given moment, he sees the analyst, himself, and what is happening between them. She tries to follow carefully any shifts in behaviour, feeling, and atmosphere that occur in the session. In her view such immediate interpretations, even though apparently so limited, offer the best hope of working towards psychic change. This Introduction attempts to describe how she came to this view and the conceptualizations that lie behind it and developed with it.

Joseph's papers are like her interpretations: precise, sensitive, and detailed. A not infrequent experience on reading her papers for the first time is for the reader to be overwhelmed by the complexity of clinical detail and to find it difficult to formulate for himself the paper's central theme, even though the writing itself is deceptively clear and simple. Closer scrutiny reveals several important themes, themes which gradually become more and more clearly and confidently propounded and elaborated in successive papers. Inevitably there is repetition in these papers, but each repetition adds something new to the earlier formulation.

With Bion, Segal, and Rosenfeld, Joseph has been particularly involved in exploring the therapeutic use of Klein's concepts of unconscious phantasy, projective identification, and introjective identification. All four authors work with, and have in various ways further developed, Klein's concepts of the paranoid-schizoid and depressive positions (Klein 1935, 1940, 1946). The anxieties, object relationships, and defences of the paranoid-schizoid and depressive positions are fully described and discussed by Joseph in many of the papers of the present collection. Although the interests of Bion, Segal, Rosenfeld, and Joseph have differed to some degree, each has adopted an approach in which very close attention is devoted not only to the verbal contents of patients' communications but also to their use of words to carry out actions which have an effect on the analyst's state of mind. It is this tradition of work that Joseph has particularly contributed to and extended.

There are three or four major themes in Joseph's work, so intertwined and closely related that it is difficult to describe them separately. The first is emphasis on the patient's need to maintain his psychic equilibrium. The second is psychic change and the factors that militate against it and those that foster it. The third is Joseph's particular way of focusing on transference and countertransference, on patients' acting out in the transference, and on their attempts, usually unconscious, to induce the analyst to join in the acting out. And the fourth is her avoidance of what one might call 'knowledge about' in favour of 'experience in'.

The first theme, the patient's need to maintain his equilibrium, is present in Joseph's earliest papers, in which she describes a particular constellation of defences against persecutory and depressive anxiety. Similar constellations of defence are elaborated and refined in successive papers. In spite of their conscious wish to change, the patients she describes mobilized their system of defences in the analytic situation in order to maintain their existing state of equilibrium. At first Joseph developed her use of the concept of equilibrium when working with patients who were clearly very seriously ill and difficult to treat, patients who were narcissistic, psychopathic, perverse. Indeed, she has always been interested in patients who are persistently destructive and self-destructive — dominated, in Melanie Klein's usage of the term, by the death instinct. But gradually she began to recognize the relevance of the concept of equilibrium in work with *all* her patients, so that she now thinks it likely and natural that any patient will respond to an insightful interpretation, even an interpretation that he accepts emotionally, with some sort of attempt to restore his slightly disturbed sense of balance.

Of course this emphasis on patients' need to maintain psychic balance is not new. What Joseph adds to the usual discussions of defence and resistance is the idea of a *system* of defences which is used to maintain balance, combined with the detail, precision, and depth of her clinical explorations of the manoeuvres and shifts that take place in the immediate to-and-fro of sessions as patients struggle to reconcile the new analytic experience with the old system of maintaining balance. In particular, she gives very telling examples of the complex way in which patients use projective identification with the analyst to avoid having their psychic equilibrium disturbed. A sado-masochistic patient, for example, may say things in such a way that the analyst finds himself making slightly punitive interpretations which confirm the patient's masochistic expectations. Or a patient may for a time behave as if he has lost his capacity for thinking, understanding, or desiring anything, all of which then become the problems of his analyst; by this means such a patient protects himself from the pain and anxiety which would result if he were to accept responsibility for these mental functions himself. Joseph believes that if the analyst fails to recognize this state of affairs he will be likely to make interpretations which may sound 'correct', may even *be* correct, but which will be ineffective because the crucial transference/countertransference issue is the patient's projection of thinking capacity into the analyst.

Joseph's emphasis on psychic equilibrium is closely linked to her preoccupation with psychic change, a theme which runs through all her papers. She became aware early in her work that with a number of patients, interpretation of the verbal content of the material, the wishes, anxieties, and defences which it revealed, often proved ineffective in producing any lasting movement. Further, with several patients she felt that the analysis looked as if it was progressing satisfactorily but at the same time she had no feeling of emotional contact with her patient. She was led to examine the reasons for this lack of contact, reasons which she began to think lay both in the patient's intrapsychic structure and in the dynamics of the analytic situation. It is in this willingness to be curious about patients' emotional inaccessibility and failure to improve that Joseph's particular strength lies. Whereas it would be easier to fit in with the patient's defences, to give up, or to condemn the patient as unsuitable for analysis, Joseph has made this type of difficulty her special focus of interest and research.

She found that patients who failed to improve in analysis were more than usually insistent on maintaining their psychic equilibrium. While the patient may appear to attend carefully and to make use of the analyst's interpretations, Joseph suggests that this may simply be a form of accommodation, and that what takes place in the session is in fact being used to support the pre-existing state of balance and thus to avoid change. Or a movement may occur in a session only to be succeeded a little later by a restoration of the status quo. There may be several reasons for the patient to avoid change in this fashion. He may resent the analyst's capacity to understand and to help him because it threatens his belief in his own independence, self-sufficiency, or narcissistic superiority; in brief, it may be an expression of envy or, even more likely, a form of defence against having to be aware of feeling envious. As part of a belief in his own self-sufficiency, a patient may be caught up in forms of destructiveness and masochistic self-destructiveness that he feels to be much more exciting than being dependent on an analyst and on his own constructive capacities. He may discover that change, even a small change, threatens him with anxiety and inexplicable psychic pain. Or he may feel, consciously or unconsciously, that changing his present defensive system would plunge him into psychic chaos and disintegration. Thus he acts as if he fears that change will lead him into even worse experiences of anxiety than he already knows.

How, then, can psychic change take place at all? It is Joseph's view that

4

if the analyst attends first and closely to the psychic reality of the inter-action between patient and analyst, the patient may be able to make a shift, a small change of his defensive system, even though it may be followed by a return to the status quo. 'Long-term psychic change', she says, 'is based on, and is a continuation of, the constant minute shifts and movements we see from moment to moment in the transference' (from 'Psychic change and the psychoanalytic process', Chapter 14 below). Embedded in this simple statement is a wealth of clinical experience and conceptual formulation.

First, Joseph stresses that if one wishes to foster long-term psychic change, it is important that the analyst eschews value judgements about whether the shifts and changes in a session are positive or negative. Following Bion's (1967) ideas on the contaminating effect of 'memory' and 'desire', she thinks that value judgements about changes distort the work. The moment-to-moment changes need to be recognized and accepted as the patient's unique way of dealing with his relationships and his anxieties. Nor should we be concerned with change as an achieved state; it is a process, not a state, and is a continuation and development from the 'constant minute shifts' in the session.

Second, like other Kleinian analysts, Joseph thinks that the interpreta-tions that are most likely to lead to psychic change are those that are anchored in the transference and countertransference; that is, in the analytic relationship as it is experienced by patient and analyst. This reliance on the transference interpretation as the primary, perhaps the sole, agent of therapeutic change is part of the Kleinian conception of transference, which differs from that of other schools of thought, especially from that of ego psychology (Payne 1947, Zetzel 1956, King 1973, Hinshelwood 1989). Moreover, in the Kleinian view, transference is not regarded as simple literal transfer on to the analyst of attitudes from whole 'primary' objects (mother as remembered, father as remembered, and so on). Rather, following Klein's emphasis on the 'total situation', transference is seen as a complex pattern of unconscious thoughts and feelings (unconscious phantasy, in Kleinian terms), expecta-tions, anxieties, and defences which the patient brings into the analytic situation as into any other situation (Klein 1952a; Heimann 1956). To quote Joseph herself:

> the transference is full of meaning and history ... everything of importance in the patient's psychic organization based on his early and habitual ways of functioning, his phantasies, impulses, defences and conflicts, will be lived out in some way in the transference.
>
> (From 'Transference: the total situation', reprinted below in Part 4, pp. 164 and 167)

5

In this way, what happens in an analytic session is regarded as the product of interaction between an immediate reality and the patient's view of this reality, which is derived from his unconscious phantasies rooted in his history. The patient's history, in other words, is in his inner world. It is through observing and experiencing the pressure to live out aspects of this unconscious internal world in the immediate transference relationship that the analyst comes to know his patient and his history.

Joseph relies on countertransference to understand the transference experience of the patient. It is important to note that throughout her work Joseph uses the term 'countertransference' in the broad sense; that is, to include not just the feelings of the analyst that come from his own psychopathology, but *all* the feelings and potential responses aroused in the analyst by his experience with the patient in the session. This particular broadening of the concept of countertransference was initiated by Heimann (1950), and is further discussed by Money-Kyrle (1956), Segal (1977), King (1978), Brenman Pick (1985), Spillius (1988, vol. 2), and Hinshelwood (1989).

Joseph describes her use of countertransference as follows:

> Much of our understanding of the transference comes through our understanding of how our patients act on us to feel things for many varied reasons; how they try to draw us into their defensive systems; how they unconsciously act out with us in the transference, trying to get us to act out with them; how they convey aspects of their inner world built up from infancy — elaborated in childhood and adulthood, experiences often beyond the use of words, which we can often only capture through the feelings aroused in us, through our counter-transference, used in the broad sense of the word.
>
> (From 'Transference: the total situation',
> reprinted in Part 4, p. 157)

The idea that patients unconsciously induce the analyst to act in a way consistent with their internal world is taken up in somewhat different language — 'role actualization' and 'role responsiveness' — by Joseph and Anne Marie Sandler (J. Sandler 1976a, 1976b; J. and A.M. Sandler 1978).

Hence what is crucial for Joseph's purpose is her view that it is the patient's ability to live out his defensive system in the session, his attempts to draw his analyst into it, and the ability of the analyst to feel and to recognize the pressure without acting it out, which creates the opportunity for analyst and patient to reach a basic understanding that can make change possible.

Gradually Joseph has become convinced that these experiences of psychic reality in the session, however uncomfortable for analyst and patient, should come before intellectual links are made with the patient's remembered past or the 'facts' of his life outside analysis. It is her view that attempts to 'explain' the patient's defensive system may be more comfortable for patient and analyst, but are less likely to lead to psychic change than staying with the material of the session; on the contrary, they are likely to bolster up the patient's existing defensive system. They are 'knowledge about' rather than 'experience in'. (Compare Bion's views on 'being like' as contrasted to 'being'; on 'having knowledge' versus 'knowing'; on 'minus k' compared to 'k'; Bion 1962, 1963, 1965, 1970.)

In a paper on differing conceptions of transference, Pearl King gives a description of one way of using the transference which is fairly close to Joseph's method of work; King says that this way of using transference involves focusing primarily on the 'here and now', the rationale being that focus on past relationships may defuse the intensity of the patient—analyst relationship (King 1973). In common with a number of other Kleinian analysts, Joseph is sometimes accused of being too exclusively concerned with transference and countertransference to the neglect of the patient's history and current life situation. Even among Kleinian analysts there are differences on this matter of the 'here and now' and reconstruction. A few Kleinian analysts do indeed focus almost exclusively on the here and now. Others, perhaps the majority, refer to the past and engage in reconstruction whenever they feel it to be relevant; they do not think that this will necessarily result in a loss of emotional immediacy. Still others, including Joseph herself, think that the here and now should be clarified first, before explicit links are made with the past. It is clear, however, that Joseph's understanding of the to-and-fro of the analytic relationship is affected by her knowledge of the patient's past experiences; there is thus a distinction between awareness of the past in the analyst's thinking and what he actually finds it useful to say to a patient at a given moment. Joseph also thinks that during the session the analyst's knowledge of the patient's past should not be allowed to become too prominent and obtrusive in his thoughts. If such awareness is kept in the back of the analyst's mind, it is possible that the patient and analyst may be able to rediscover the past in a new way. If awareness of the past becomes too obtrusive, however, the analyst runs the risk of seeing in the patient's material only what he expects to see — another instance of Joseph's agreement with Bion's strictures about the damaging effect of 'memory' (Bion 1967).

It is clear that many of the factors that contribute to psychic change need to be understood in greater depth, and Joseph is not dogmatic on this matter. She feels that her method is the one that has proved to be most effective in her own work, but she does not claim that hers is the only way of achieving psychic change.

Nor does she claim to have developed a comprehensive theory of psychic change. In her work she found herself trying to link certain themes, all of which had a bearing on psychic change — transference, countertransference, patients' attempt to maintain their equilibrium, their attempts to get the analyst to behave in ways consistent with their unconscious phantasies. Her own theoretical position on psychic change is based on the work of Klein herself and is very much in the tradition of Strachey (1934, 1937), Heimann (1956), and Segal (1962). Strachey believes that change occurs through the 'mutative' transference interpretation — that is, an interpretation which establishes for the patient a distinction between the actual behaviour of the external analyst and the primitive superego, consisting of idealized and persecutory internal objects, which the patient projects on to his analyst. Through introjection of those aspects of the external analyst that differ from his archaic internal objects, the patient's internal objects may change. Heimann's view is similar, although she stresses the effect of benign introjections from the analyst on the patient's ego rather than on his internal objects. Segal stresses the importance of the patient acquiring insight through analytic interpretation — meaning by 'insight', knowledge, usually conscious as well as preconscious, about his unconscious internal objects and aspects of his ego and their interrelationships.

Joseph is especially concerned with the *method* of achieving these aims, and, as described above, she thinks that it is the moment-to-moment shifts in the session that can become the foundation of the possibility of lasting processes of psychic change.

The papers which follow reflect the evolution of a way of observing and thinking about what is going on in an analytic session, which gives the analyst access to the patient's underlying assumptions concerning the nature of his objects and his object relationships. These will, of course, be continuous with experiences derived from early stages of development, which it may be difficult or impossible for him to express in words.

The issues and problems Joseph addresses will be familiar to most analysts, and her understanding of the transference/countertransference situation with the difficult patients she describes carries a strong sense of conviction. She offers her readers, like her students, a way of thinking about the clinical situation in which they are engaged (and in which they are often stuck) with the possibility of enabling movement and change to take place.

The difficulties and the strain of working in a way which pays such careful attention to the subtle but compelling pressures placed on the analyst are lightly but clearly drawn by Joseph. She describes very well the fluctuations between the sense of movement and development which can occur when something has been understood and properly contained by the analyst and the attacks and regression which so often follow. She points out the necessity of trying to distinguish whether this regression is primarily driven by the patient's envy, by his inability to tolerate an unfamiliar experience of unbearable pain, by his fear of disintegrating, or by the *analyst's* difficulty in sustaining a particular contact with himself and with what is taking place within the session. Thus, while she leaves us in no doubt about the difficulty of attending, thinking, and working in the ways she describes, there is also a feeling of excitement, of challenge, and of hope in the rigour and precision of the approach she offers.

PART 1

Beginnings

Introduction

Michael Feldman and Elizabeth Bott Spillius

Several of the themes that were to become central in Joseph's work are evident to some extent even in her earliest papers. In an unpublished paper of 1953, for example, she stresses the importance of observing what the patient *does* in the transference as well as attending to what he says. In the two papers reprinted here, 'An aspect of the repetition compulsion' (1959) and 'Some characteristics of the psychopathic personality' (1960), she introduces the theme of equilibrium, balance, and the patient's need to maintain it even when he or she consciously wants to change.

In the first paper reprinted here Joseph is concerned with those patients who experience themselves as being passively and repetitively subjected to unpleasant treatment at the hands of others. She suggests that this passivity often in fact involves a very active deployment of defence mechanisms, primarily to protect the patient from overpowering anxieties linked with the experience of dependence. The patient she describes presented as a woman who needed no one, though everyone, she said, liked and needed her. She complained that she could not love anyone because they would let her down. She had very little feeling, positive or negative, about analysis or her analyst, though she gave her analyst the impression that she wanted her to think that she was different from other patients, more insightful, more accommodating, more helpful. Gradually it emerged in the sessions that the patient was splitting off the needy aspects of herself and projecting them into other people around her, including her analyst. Simultaneously she idealized the good aspects of her analyst and other important people in her life, had taken these aspects into herself unconsciously, and had become identified with them. She *was* them, and she had no awareness of the origin of the idealized qualities she felt herself to possess. Projective and introjective identification were thus being used simultaneously to avoid dependence and to avoid the resentment and envy that she might have felt if she had been able to value her objects more. But in this patient dependence aroused unbearable guilt as well as persecution, for it emerged in her analysis that she had a conviction that her ambivalence had caused immense damage to her primary object, her mother and her mother's breast, so that unconsciously she felt this primary object existed inside herself in an extremely perilous condition which she could not face.

We have repeated the description of part of Joseph's analysis of this patient's defensive system — a combination of splitting, projective identification, idealization, and introjective identification — because it is a particularly clear exemplification of the views Klein put forward in her analysis of the paranoid-schizoid position (especially in her 1946 paper) and later in her work on *Envy and Gratitude* (1957), as well as Bion's development of some of these ideas in his paper 'Attacks on linking' (1959). In her subsequent papers Joseph returns to this combination of defences again and again, elaborating the system and its interdependencies which she encountered in a number of the patients she describes, and which were important to them in maintaining their psychic equilibrium.

In the analysis described in this paper on repetition compulsion, Joseph interpreted to the patient both her active attacks on external and internal good objects and the projective processes she was using to avoid dependence and guilt. In the subsequent development of her technique and ideas, however, Joseph becomes much less convinced about the therapeutic value of making immediate and direct interpretations of motive, such as envy in the case of this patient, or mental mechanisms such as projective identification. By contrast, as we shall see, in her later work she focuses first on the immediate situation in the analytic relationship, especially on the way in which the patient perceives the analyst. She may point out, for example, that following a particular interpretation the patient seems to be seeing the analyst in a certain way — as crushed, let us say, or self-satisfied, or left out. But she does not immediately assume that she knows the motive for this perception or, even if she could guess the motive, that it would be useful to point it out to the patient before having more evidence about it from the patient himself. She has also become more cautious about making explicit to the patient the parallels between the patient's relationship to the analyst and his current and past relationships to other people in the outside world — all in the interest of promoting psychic change by keeping the interpretive work as immediate and emotionally relevant as possible.

In the next paper, 'Some characteristics of the psychopathic personality'

(1960), Joseph continues her exploration of a different group of patients, those who function in a psychopathic way. In spite of the different psychopathology, she found that the pattern of defences was similar to that of the preceding patient. But here the patient, an adolescent, was troubled by having a very limited capacity to tolerate anxiety or frustration; indeed, when forced to do so he felt threatened by feeling that he would go mad, fall apart. He approached activities and people in a greedy way, but his greedy desires stimulated in him feelings of intense envy, which led to his spoiling and devaluing what the other person could give him and thus led to his feeling deprived and greedy once again — a vicious circle of desire and attack.

The patient described in this paper was using omnipotence, projective identification, and introjective identification defensively to maintain a precarious state of mind in which guilt, depressive anxieties, and overwhelming persecutory anxieties were constantly evaded. His psychopathology and the quasi-delinquent acting out which he engaged in were part of the means by which he evaded a deep sense of guilt; he got himself accused or punished 'for the wrong things', as it were. When this system was disturbed, either within the analysis or outside, he felt a threat of catastrophic fragmentation and psychosis. When these manoeuvres were not completely successful, there was a brief emergence of some depressive pain, which seemed to be connected with an intense fear of the destruction of his good internal objects. In her later papers Joseph explores the emergence of this kind of pain in much greater detail.

In these later papers, too, she explores more fully the way in which the patient's psychopathology is enacted in the transference, and the often very subtle countertransference pressures brought to bear on the analyst to fit in with this so as not to disturb the patient's equilibrium. But one can also see, even in this early paper, Joseph using a method which was to become very important in her later technique; namely, a close tracking of the patient's responses to interpretations with detailed observation of what happened when the interpretations disturbed the patient's equilibrium.

1

An aspect of the repetition compulsion

This paper was first read at a meeting of the British Psycho-Analytical Society on 7 May 1958, and was published in the *International Journal of Psycho-Analysis* 40 (1959): 1—10.

In this chapter I want to discuss one aspect of the repetition compulsion which Freud first introduced in 1920 (Freud 1920). The question of the repetition compulsion as a whole has been discussed in a number of papers. I would refer especially to those of Kubie (1939), Hendrick (1947), and Bibring (1943).

Freud (1920) showed how neurotics, and, as he put it, 'some normal people' could be seen to be constantly, as if under pressure of a compulsion, re-experiencing situations in their lives which brought them only unhappiness, and the repetition of which therefore seemed to 'override the pleasure principle'. He spoke of such people as giving the impression of being possessed by a daemonic compulsion, adding, however, 'but psycho-analysis has always taken the view that their fate is for the most part arranged by themselves and determined by early infantile influences'; however, later in the same paragraph, he adds the following interesting point:

> This 'perpetual recurrence of the same thing' causes us no astonishment when it relates to active behaviour on the part of the person concerned and when we can discern in him an essential character trait which always remains the same and which is compelled to find expression in a repetition of the same experiences. We are much more impressed by cases where the subject appears to have a passive experience, over which he has no influence, but in which he meets with a repetition of the same fatality. (p. 22)

It seems to me that we all, in our analytic practices, see a number of patients who show a marked tendency again and again in their lives to go through repetitive unhappy experiences, apparently passively. In this communication I am going to limit myself to considering this one aspect of the repetition compulsion. It will be remembered that it was the discovery of the repetition compulsion that was one of the factors that led Freud to put forward his theory of the death instinct. In my concluding remarks I shall try to make a very tentative connection between the apparently passive repetition compulsion and his theory of the death instinct. In this chapter I shall isolate and consider one group of patients who show markedly this type of repetition, that is, those patients whose repetition is blind, unconscious, very compulsive, apparently passively experienced and not provoked by them and almost invariably unpleasant in its results; it is very noticeable in their history and in their current relationships when they come into analysis.

Freud, it will be remembered, started his discussion of the repetition compulsion with a consideration of its pathological manifestation in traumatic dreams and in the impulse to repeat seen in children's play, from which he concluded, 'we are therefore left in doubt as to whether the impulse to work over in the mind some overpowering experience, so as to make oneself master of it, can find expression as a primary event and independently of the pleasure principle'. I am suggesting in this chapter that patients of the type I have just described are dealing with unconscious anxieties that are felt by them to be potentially overpowering; that the anxieties relate primarily to problems stimulated by dependence on the primary object or part object, the mother or her breast; that the mechanisms which are compulsively used to master these anxieties consist of a specific combination of splitting, projective identification, and introjection, which deeply influences their behaviour and personality structure. I shall try to show how these methods of mastering anxiety are linked with the achievement of a particular balance between destructiveness and love, and how the very nature of this balance in itself can lead to no progress, but only to a blind compulsion to repeat.

I shall start by describing certain elements from the history of a patient in whom the working of the repetition compulsion could be very clearly seen. I am not here going to discuss the factors underlying these fragments of history, and I am only introducing those which are immediately relevant to my theme of passive repetition. I start with A.'s relationships to men, since it was here that in her analysis we first saw the repetitions emerging so markedly.

When A. came into treatment it soon became clear that from late adolescence onwards up to about the time of her marriage there had been a series of relationships with men of a very similar type, in which the men were deeply devoted to her, she much less attached to them. The relations always went wrong. The men very much needed her and depended on her, but she did not fall in love with them, believing that she was afraid of becoming too dependent on anyone for fear of being let down. As the analysis proceeded, it could slowly be seen that the relationships were patterned on elements of a very difficult relationship with her father and with a young brother. A. felt very disturbed by her father who had a bad relationship with the mother, criticizing the latter to my patient whom he openly preferred. He wanted A. to go on holidays with him and generally be with him. A. found his company extremely embarrassing. When she was in analysis he used sometimes to visit her, and would sit almost silent looking at her, she felt, adoringly and finding it pathetically difficult to leave her home. A. had herself connected her difficulties with men with her relationship with her brother. As a young child she had bullied and dominated him, believing that she did so because her mother was so inept with him. Subsequently he became increasingly dependent on her, desperately wanting to get at her, trying to break into her room, constantly disturbing her. She was unaware of doing anything to foment this behaviour. Subsequently, I learned about relationships with various uncles and cousins, showing a similar quality. They were a closely knit, lower-middle-class family from the North of England. One after the other, they appeared in the analysis as particularly devoted to my patient and needing her. One eccentric uncle, for example, could not manage unless she visited him daily after school; another talked freely only to her, and so on. By her they were felt mainly as a burden, but one which she shouldered.

As she described these relationships, the factor that began to stand out was the sense of devoted need these various people felt for her. During analysis I began to see that new men were being added to the list; if she had to see a professional or business contact, such as a solicitor or doctor, it would very quickly appear that this man began from her point of view to establish a very special relationship with her, would keep her chatting after the professional interview was over, would tend to turn into a family friend rather needing her family for companionship, good food or similar needs; she did not know how this happened. Linked with this we saw that if for any reason A. had to change doctors, lawyers, and so on, she would feel very guilty at leaving them. Only slowly as the analysis proceeded did she begin to realize that she was convinced that they needed her for some reason — for example, that her case was interesting, that they would miss her fees if she went. One aspect of this pattern emerged very clearly, that is, A.'s intense rivalry with her mother and myself — as shown, for example, in her unconscious need to be preferred by the men, her father, brother, and the current professional contacts. But it was only when this aspect had to some extent been worked through that certain other aspects, those which it is the main aim of this chapter to discuss, emerged behind the more obvious Oedipal material. Indeed, as I shall later try to show, genital Oedipal material was often stressed as a defence against the recognition of earlier failures in development.

Turning to A.'s relationships with women, it was striking that so many of her close women friends were gifted, quasi-homosexual people who valued and stuck to her, but whose relationships eventually became irksome, as they appeared to exploit or overwhelm her. This became apparent as a current problem with her maids and nurses who emerged as needing her and her family, being rather burdensome, often hardworking, moody, and somewhat martyred. We began to recognize an earlier version of this story, the history of which is this. In my patient's childhood her family had been, and indeed still were, very poor. An orphaned girl cousin many years older than my patient came to live with the family at the time of A.'s birth, acting as nurse and mother's help. She was a strange character, very ugly, had no life of her own, and was utterly devoted to my patient, but increasingly felt by A. to be like a ghastly shadow over her, always around doing things for and with her. She believes that she always wanted the mother to get rid of her, but the latter did not do so. There is, however, an Achilles' heel to this story. The mother has told my patient that when she, A., was a tiny child she would crawl or toddle around the house after this cousin, calling after her to be with her, as if not able to let her out of her sight. This is not remembered at all by my patient. Underlying this relationship with the cousin, however, was a very unhappy relationship with the mother. A. described her as being a mother who saw that the children's material needs were well satisfied, but who was herself always restless and on the go and would never sit down quietly with them. The mother seemed forgetful of the children, my patient and her two brothers — and apparently especially of my patient, whom she would often forget to serve at meals when visitors were there, or would fail to call for her from parties until long after all the other children had been fetched. It seems that she breast-fed A. for three months, after which her milk failed. As A. described the problems of her childhood one felt emerging a picture of resentment and hostility, and an awareness that something was lacking in her home and in her relationship with her mother that she wanted; but sadness and affection or conscious longing for affection from any of the family were markedly absent, and the resentment and a determination to be independent of the mother, a pattern apparently repeated with the cousin, were very much in the forefront. One slowly gained the impression that what was available emotionally in the home this child could not use. It seemed that there must be a connection between A.'s later inability to love men, as she thought, lest she should be let down, and her early need to make herself independent of her mother, whom she felt to be too unreliable to trust.

I should add one further piece of compulsive repetition which belongs to the general pattern. A. invariably found herself burdened by her friends; her house was constantly full of people who were passing through London, who wanted help or money. She felt overwhelmed by their needs, and there seemed little time when she and her husband could be alone without disturbance. When my patient came into analysis in her early forties, she had no idea that these were repeated patterns, nor that she was involved in any way in bringing them about. She only felt herself to be universally popular with friends and relatives of various ages. In these respects, although my experience of this type of patient is limited, I think that A. can be said to be typical of a particular group of people who come to us for treatment.

Although A. seemed to have lived through so many of these relationships apparently passively and without wanting these relatives and friends, nevertheless, as I have stressed, she had a sense of disappointment that something she wanted from her home was missing. But she was not aware that something was basically wrong about her own capacity to love and to accept goodness. Again, currently in the transference she would appear to appreciate that something was lacking in her feelings; for example, she would compare herself with friends who, when they were being analysed, seemed so much more involved emotionally in the treatment, happy about it, upset by it or missing it, none of which she felt. She did not miss it, or me, during breaks and seemed quite unaware of any feelings about myself, my consulting room, and so on. Superficially she gave the impression of being a well-organized and co-operative woman; but I soon began to get the impression that she was unconsciously needing to convey to me a sense of being different from my other patients, more adult, insighted, helpful to me in my work both analytically and practically — as, for example, fitting in with times that I might need, with no complaint. Slowly I saw I was destined to become one of the professional and business group who was soon to find her specially indispensable to me, both financially and as an interesting case — as I have described would occur with her doctors, lawyers, and so on, standing for the relatives of her childhood.

I shall now give some material from this patient. We had been working on her denial of feelings, especially feelings of dependence and rivalry connected with myself. She came on a Monday saying that she had again been very much concerned with a problem that she had spoken about in the previous week, that was whether she should spend the next weekend away from home in the North, with her husband who had to be away

20

for some weeks on business. It would mean leaving her three children, including the youngest, a boy of about thirteen months, with the maid. Should she do so? She had approached various friends for advice. It was then becoming clear that my advice was being sought, and I thought that she wanted me to say that she should go. She went on to tell that she was angry with herself for getting so involved in difficulties with the maid. She gave a long-drawn-out description of an argument with the maid over the first name of a particular actor whose surname was the same as A.'s own married name. Having described the incident she quickly explained it, saying that she supposed that she got so upset because the maid twisted the argument and always had to be right and know best, and that this was what she herself did in the analysis. She then told about the second difficulty. The maid had complained about a bad back; my patient arranged for her to see a doctor, but found herself very much hoping that the doctor would say that the work was too heavy and that the maid should leave. But then, what would happen to the maid, she had no other friends, she was always around the house, even on her day off, she so much needed the family . . .?

I am here condensing her material and my interpretations. But broadly I interpreted this material in terms of her inability to tolerate her own needs both for myself and for her husband in the weekends. It is not she who wants to go to him, it is the husband who needs her, it is not she who voices even this, but her friend who says she should go for the husband's sake; and if she does go, it will be because I tell her she should. I think that this is the meaning of the discussion with the maid on the first name of the actor. They both agree on the surname. Here I, standing for the mother, am reduced to the maid and the argument foreseen is about the identity of the actor — who is it that wants whom? She or her husband? I think that what she unconsciously fears is that I shall show her her own unconscious knowledge that the name of the person with the needs is her own name, not the husband's nor mine. Secondly, I am to be the maid in the sense that, as she experiences it, I indicate by my constant interpretations about myself, always bringing myself into the picture, that I am the person who is neurotic, ill, who is in the way, but who needs her, her family, and her money to keep me going. At the same time, she, by her swift interpretations of her own material, shows that at the moment of putting the ill, needy person into me (and the husband) she has taken into herself my analytic skill and has become the analyst.

I shall now give a further fragment of material from a session two days later. She started by speaking about a minor physical complaint of her own, but the doctor had said there was nothing wrong, and the maid still had a bad back. Then her tone changed, and she described how well the

21

children were doing now, there had been no need for the doctor for any of them for months; but there was one difficulty; she found herself so distressed by her eldest son's appearance, he was losing his first teeth and there were such gaps between them, he looked so ugly; of course, it wouldn't last forever, she knew .... She paused to query why on earth whenever she was talking of something that made her happy, she had at once to go back to her worries, adding in a voice as if interpreting that perhaps it was because of her anxiety about what to do about the weekend, and whether she should leave the children, and it was easier to worry about something like the teeth that didn't really matter than about something that did. Here one could see the constant shifts between a growing awareness of her own needs for help from the doctors, the husband and myself, and her denial of them, as well as a growing awareness and a denial of the importance of gaps in time, the weekends. I thought that she saw in her son her ill self, the self with the gaps — splits in her own personality — and the point connected with this that I particularly concentrated on was the damage that she did by constantly making gaps in her own analysis. I instanced how she had just been giving the interpretations about her worries herself, but seemed to have left a great gap between that and the last sessions, so that no insight or understanding derived from the analysis appeared to have been carried over from one session to the next. She agreed that it did seem odd, as she had found the sessions so important at the time. I showed her that she had turned against and bitten great holes into what I had to give and had become identified with the bitten-up analyst, fundamentally the bitten-up breast. And she had at the same time taken over the analysis herself, making her own links, her own interpretations, she had identified with myself and become me, the mother, doing the feeding herself. She went on to describe something at home that had made her angry and that she could not understand. Her little son kept crawling around the house after the maid, calling out her name and wanting to be with her. The maid was delighted, but my patient found herself intensely irritated by this, but did not think that it was just a matter of her being jealous of the maid.

I agreed with her that it did not seem to be primarily a question of jealousy of the maid; and indeed her jealousy on the Oedipal level was much more conscious and by now comparatively easily recognized and accepted by A. I therefore suggested that this description of her difficulty about her little son seemed to be an explanation of why she could not keep the connection between the sessions and had to make these gaps, since keeping the links meant links between her own insight and my previous interpretations, between herself and me, and this was tanta-mount to allowing myself and my work to be loved and valued, and it was too painful; it was like allowing me to be as important as to be worth crawling after and caring about in the the way her son did to the maid; and I reminded her that the description of her son's behaviour was exactly the same as that of her own behaviour, now completely forgotten but described by her mother, when she as an infant tried to keep hold of the cousin. So it was clear that here, her little son was standing for her lost childhood and infant self — the self that used to experience emotions of wanting and loving, towards the cousin, and one can suggest, originally, towards the mother — but these emotions had very early on been split off, and now to see this self in her son was very disturbing.

The point that I am particularly stressing here is that one could see in all this material the patient's struggle against being dependent on me and my work, or on her husband or in the past, the cousin, and behind the cousin, the mother. She had always assumed, as I have previously shown, that her wish to be completely independent was based on her fear of being disappointed and let down. But now it was becoming increasingly clear that the problem was not primarily one of being let down; indeed historically the cousin who was toddled after was a most reliable and always present person and the mother, despite her restlessness, continued always to live with the children. It seemed rather to be a problem associated with the rivalry and resentment that would be stirred up if I were to be valued and depended on, and this problem prevented her using what was available in her home. This I shall illustrate more fully in a moment. Here I only want to remind you of the way in which she seemed to evade the rivalry problem by doing my work for me, analysing her own worries and, when the sessions were felt to be especially important, destroying them by biting gaps into them so that again they ceased to exist as valuable. Also, as was typical for her, the gaps seemed to have arisen passively.

During this and the next few sessions we gained further understanding of the importance of this aspect of her struggle against dependence. A. described her growing insight very clearly at the end of the same week, when she told me that she had decided to join her husband for the weekend and had been thinking how very enjoyable the few days might be; then this idea became connected with the work we had been doing in the sessions and suddenly, as she described it, all 'the pleasure drained away like sand running through my fingers'. We could see that when she was thinking happily of the weekend, this became a good experience like a good feed, then she saw that the experience, feed, was connected with my work, as if milk was seen to come from a breast which was mine and attached to my body — so she drained it away, could not use it and turned it into sand, like faeces or urine. Here then we could see that the link that she could not tolerate and had to destroy was that between the good work — feed — and myself (this whole problem is discussed in detail by Bion (1959)), and that indeed it was her rivalry with me, standing for her mother, her envy, resentment, and anger that were stimulated when she was dependent on me and I was felt to be helpful; that was the real problem we were up against. Thus, A., in avoiding the unhappiness and difficulties which she associated with needing her mother, lost also the happiness and good experiences of her babyhood.

I am therefore suggesting here that the main anxieties that are being dealt with in this patient A., and in patients of this apparently passive repetition–compulsion group, are anxieties connected with dependence on the primary object; that dependence itself, implying the possibility of experiencing needing, loving, and valuing, at once stirs up intense hatred and destructiveness since it reactivates the earliest envy situation in which the primary object, the breast, in so far as it was valued, was immediately envied, hated, and attacked (as is described in detail by Melanie Klein (1957)). This hatred and resultant ambivalence with its inevitable train of guilt and depression is intolerable, since these patients have, I believe, an unconscious conviction that such ambivalence has somewhere in the past caused their primary object immense damage, and that internally the object exists in an extremely perilous condition, which cannot be faced. This I shall describe in more detail later. What has, therefore, to be avoided is a repetition of dependence which would lead to ambivalence, and in order to avoid it these patients, whenever dependent feelings are felt to be emerging, repeat their particular pattern of defences which I have been illustrating in A.'s material. To summarize this combination of defences, these patients split the self, splitting off the dependent and needy parts, including necessarily much that is good as well as the envious and hating parts, and project them into their object; but at the same moment, the object is split into a persecuting part which, as I have just described, contains the bad and unwanted parts of the self, and an idealized part. What one sees in operation is that the unwanted parts of the self and the persecuting part of the object are constantly split up to lessen their intensity and projected out into a variety of objects. Simultaneously the idealized object is introjected and completely devoured, and the patient becomes completely identified with it, so that the object ceases to have any separate existence either externally or internally.

I shall now discuss in more detail the various elements of this combination of defences, and their effects on the personality of the individual. For the sake of simplification I shall break up this combination of defences into two parts and shall discuss, first, the introjection

24

and maintenance of the idealized object; and, second, the splitting off and projection of the persecuting object and unwanted parts of the self. It will be seen that this is a very artificial type of simplification, since I think that it is, in fact, the very simultaneity of these various processes that makes this combination of defences so effective and so rigid.

Starting, then, with the idealized object — I am suggesting that these patients' main difficulty begins in their being unable to tolerate an external good and needed object because of the hatred and envy that this arouses; but what they succeed in doing is that, the moment any significant external object might be felt as good and needed, it is immediately introjected and possessed to the point of becoming fused with the patient's ego. This means that the object is, in a sense, unconsciously both triumphed over, and yet saved from overt aggression by being devoured wholesale and having no separate existence. Under these conditions it is ideal. The working of this can be seen clearly when, for example, A. devoured me and did my work, as if she were the analyst, at moments when otherwise she would hate me for doing it successfully. At such moments I ceased to exist as a separate analyst. This total identification with the idealized object has a further essential value for the individual. It means that so long as the object is part of, and fused with, the self, it can be kept alive and not lost. I think that this situation is comparable with what Freud described when he spoke of love at the oral stage being indistinguishable from the annihilation of the object. In these patients the object is annihilated as a separate object, but nevertheless maintained. This type of love is of a highly narcissistic nature directed towards the internal object, experienced as identified with the self. It can be seen that this narcissistic condition not only preserves the idealized object and therefore some capacity for love, but also prevents the individual from being overwhelmed by his hatred and therefore by persecution. His narcissism thus protects him from psychosis.

It is clear that this object has to be kept internally paralysed; if it comes alive and is felt as separate and creative and with a life of its own, it arouses great hostility and destructiveness — as happened with A. when she momentarily experienced my help over her weekend problem and 'drained it away like sand'.

Naturally, this type of relationship to the object results in various problems. In so far as it is the idealized object that is internalized — for example, the mother whom everyone needs, or the successful analyst — the patient unconsciously tends to idealize himself. This is, I think, one of the main factors contributing to his omnipotent and superior attitude to his environment. But in so far as the idealized object is introjected, not with love and gratitude but in order to avoid need, separateness, hate, and ambivalence, the object cannot be taken in as good, and therefore no

25

really secure core to the ego and no internal stability and self-confidence can be established, so that behind the narcissism and the omnipotent superiority always lurk great doubts about the self and its essential goodness. The fear of the emergence of these doubts and anxieties is one of the additional factors making for the rigidity of the manic and obsessional mechanisms in this group of patients.

I have so far been discussing the part of the combination of defences concerned with the violent introjection of the object, and have tried to show how, to a large extent, hate towards the object can in this way be obviated; but necessarily what must also be obviated is the possibility of loving with all the risk of loss and depression. This accounts in part for these patients' awareness that something is missing from their personality. They are naturally unable to develop any real capacity for love, and one sees frequently in treatment that experiences which they consider to be deeply loving turn out on further analysis to be methods of actually avoiding real love associated with dependence. I shall give a brief example from B., who did not belong rigidly to the repetition-compulsion group of patients, but who reacted in similar ways when certain specific anxieties were aroused.

B. was a university student. She had had what she considered to be a very important love affair when she was about twenty. It became clear in the analysis that in this relationship she and her partner spent almost all of the 24 hours of the day together; they never thought differently about things, never read different books or had different interests, and were scarcely apart at all. It seemed that in this relationship B. also used very strongly the mechanism of projective identification described by Melanie Klein (1946). She was able to project large areas of herself into her partner, especially any sense of need and all ambition, and she introjected the idealized partner into herself, so that he almost ceased to exist as a real external individual. She felt, for example, that he needed her so intensely that he could scarcely be away from her, but she had no sense of needing him. He was ambitious, but she gave up her career. This relationship was naturally extremely precarious and finally broke down completely, though B. then had the greatest difficulty in letting her partner go. She, like A., was never able to stand a deep and dependent relationship with a really separate whole person, and this so-called love relationship actually enabled her to avoid real loving and dependence.

I shall now go on to discuss the second part of the combination of defences that I am suggesting is pathognomic for these apparently passive repetition-compulsion patients. I stressed that they carry out a simultaneous defensive movement in which the idealized object is introjected — this I have just been discussing — and in which the persecuting object and unwanted parts of the self are projected out into people in the environment. I shall consider now this latter aspect.

First, to give an example of their projective identification — here the expulsion of the unwanted parts of the self. We learned in A.'s analysis that dependence was, in her mind, essentially associated with violent physical possessiveness, greed, envy, and domination. Therefore in projecting out all sense of need she expelled all these parts too, and so her conscious picture of herself was of a nice, likeable, and undemanding person; while on the other hand, her husband was felt to be extremely demanding, possessive, and somewhat childish. But dependence was, also, associated with attachment, and potential affection, and therefore these, so to speak, good parts of the self were expelled as well. I shall return to this point later. Here I am concerned mainly to show how when a patient is using such violent schizoid mechanisms, primarily to rid himself of the bad parts of the self and objects — generally his destructiveness — he necessarily creates for himself an extremely persecuting environment. I shall discuss some of the implications of this.

In the analysis of such patients one is quickly aware of their struggles against becoming conscious of any persecution; this they partially achieve by various denials, avoidances, and splittings. One of their main needs is to avoid massive projection of the unwanted parts of the self into the primary object in the transference, the analyst, which were it to occur would naturally turn the analyst into a too terrifying figure. To give an instance from A. : she would project the envious parts of herself into all her unmarried and childless friends, to such a degree that she was uneasy when with them and invariably had to tell them stories about the troubles and difficulties of looking after the children, in order to placate them and ward off their assumed envy. But she had entirely to deny such feelings towards myself. So long as these projective identifications are split up and spread out over a large enough number of people in this way, these patients can avoid overwhelming anxiety, though they are a prey to constant, petty, nagging anxieties, for which they can find no solution; they cannot, for example, just get away from these people partly because they need them to carry their projections, and partly because — as I briefly mentioned before — these people are also carrying good parts of the self, like affection and attachment. These patients therefore get very much involved with the people whom they use as projectees. They become fascinated by them, and cannot give them up.

In these situations one can see that a precarious balance is achieved both in their own personalities and in the state of their object — a balance between life and death, between love and hate, between splitting and integration, between concern and persecution. These patients keep

27

themselves emotionally as lifeless as possible by so much splitting and projective identification, yet they do not lose touch with the split-off, more alive parts, since they keep up their involved relationships with the people into whom they project. But there the situation gets frozen, since they cannot become more integrated and take back into the self the split-off parts, as they have not enough trust in their love to be able to tolerate the ambivalence that integration would imply. Or, considering this problem from the angle of their objects, they show concern in so far as they keep the people whom they are using for their projections alive enough to keep the good parts of themselves in them alive; and alive enough to ward off their fears of phantastic retaliation — as A. did by giving help and money to her envious and demanding friends — but not alive enough to become really happy and established, since this might reactivate the patient's hostility and rivalry. Thus there is some attempt at reparation, but it must of necessity be stopped before it arouses further destruction; and the very reparation contains much that is in fact of the nature of placating and appeasing.

I have so far been discussing how these patients attempt to master anxiety by spreading out their projections into a large number of people. The more that these projections become focused round one or two important figures, the greater is the accumulation of anxiety. In the transference this can readily be seen, and may, as the analysis proceeds, lead to attempts on the patient's part to stop the treatment. This happened with B., who, as her splitting lessened and she started to work well with her university studies, slowly decided that she should now give up the analysis, her reasoning being that she had not time to study and have treatment. It could be seen that all her rivalry and envy associated with her improvement and dependence on myself was now being projected into me, and she could not tolerate her as yet unconscious fears of my rivalry and my envy of her potentially good examination results and future career. Previously, her envy, jealousy, possessiveness, had been split up and projected into a variety of external figures, especially her boy friend.

In their external relationships these patients' need to avoid such anxiety is very apparent in their constant unconscious attempts to avoid any really close relationships with significant figures in their environment, as for example parents or partners. I have already described A.'s distant relationship with myself in the transference and her actual lack of any close relationship with her mother. I shall discuss this further later. The closer the relationship, the greater is the potential dependence, and therefore the greater is the need to fall back on the specific combination of defences that I am discussing; but in addition, the closer the relationship the more the various split-off parts of the self must be projected into the one close figure, for example, the partner; and then, in coming into close contact with the partner, the patient must necessarily come into close contact with his self, or rather with the unwanted parts of the self that he has so urgently expelled — all now focused in one person, who is necessarily felt to be extremely menacing. I have already instanced A.'s difficulties in being close to her husband, as well as his complaints that they were never alone together; and indeed, when they were together, without the family in the North for the weekend, A. developed a vaginal symptom, felt somewhat ill at ease and overwhelmed by him, both physically and emotionally, and finally managed not to be with him for too many hours on end. I think that it is this need to avoid closeness that is one of the main reasons for repetition-compulsion patients having to fill up their lives with so many people, who not only act as carriers for their emotions, but also act as barriers between themselves and their objects. It also means that, unlike patients who have some, if a limited, capacity to tolerate ambivalence, these repetition-compulsion patients suffer more from closeness than from loneliness. The latter can be evaded by oversleeping and various forms of activity and denials, but closeness cannot.

I have so far been discussing the combination of defences that this group of patients use to avoid aggression and therefore ambivalence and guilt towards their primary object, and thus basically to avoid depression. In so far as these defences are successful, these patients can retain their stability and can often pass as comparatively normal personalities. I am however suggesting that these defences, though they have a long history, have also a pre-history; that there has been a time in the early infancy of these patients when they have been greedily, possessively, and demandingly dependent on the mother and her breasts, and that this greed has stimulated intense hatred and envy of the mother, and has led to violent aggressive attacks on her and projections into her. Naturally, if as in A.'s case the mother is in fact emotionally withdrawn, unstable, or neglectful, this is likely to increase the hatred and attacks. The result has been, in this patient's case, a phantastic inner situation in which the mother has been felt to have been reduced to an extremely perilous condition, as I mentioned at the beginning of this paper, though I would now add that behind this is an even deeper anxiety that the internal object, the mother, has been totally destroyed. It is the repetition of this situation which these patients are forever desperately struggling to avoid, by the use of their combination of defences designed to keep aggression away from the primary object. And it is the facing of this phantastic inner situation which these patients have never been able to manage; they have never been able to tolerate the guilt and depression about this perilous, or destroyed, condition of the object and have never been able

29

to make real reparation and work through the depressive position. Therefore their rigid combination of schizoid mechanisms must be seen also as an attempt manically to control their internal object and thus to ward off and evade these depressive anxieties. Indeed, what one sees is that the internal object is experienced and kept as paralysed, neither dead nor alive; in other words, it is kept, as Melanie Klein has described it, in a state of suspended animation. In order to discuss this further I shall give two examples of this state, one from B. and a fuller one from A.

B. described her internal situation very vividly in a dream in which she opened a cupboard and saw that she had left inside it, without doing anything about it, a cage which contained birds which now appeared to be almost putrefying, and yet moved slightly as if not quite dead. She closed the door quickly lest her mother should see. This dream occurred when we were getting near to her depression. I think that this neither dead nor alive situation is basic to her depressions and has always haunted her; if her objects, the birds — here clearly related to the mother — are revived and free she fears she will attack again, but in the condition in which they are in the dream, they can scarcely yet be faced.

A. dreamed one weekend that she was with X., a man who wanted to have sexual intercourse with her, but she, out of concern and guilt to her husband, refused. There was a second part of the dream, which was something about giving a present to the daughter of a cousin; the present was a fishbone with little bits of fish adhering. Her associations referred to X., who was very fat and flabby; she found such men extremely attractive physically; she had nicknamed him Wolfie, though this was not his name; she had known him well in the past and he had wanted to have sexual relations with her while his wife was ill with polio; X. had much in common both in appearance and background with her father. The girl to whom she gave the present was said to look like A. herself, though A. considered her childish. The fishbone was associated to a visit from an aunt on the day of the dream; this aunt ordinarily spent nearly all her life in bed, though she was not believed to be physically ill. One day the aunt and her husband gave a dinner party and served fried fish bought from a fish shop because the aunt's illness prevented her shopping and cooking.

On the face of it, it looked as if the first part was a typical dream of A.'s in which her sexual impulses were in part projected into X., standing for the father, who wanted her sexually, but on further analysis it could be seen that the father, X., was largely really a woman, fat with flabby breasts; that into this combined parent figure (father — containing the mother — analyst) was projected not just the apparent sexuality but her own oral wolfish impulses. In the dream the patient and X. did not have intercourse because of guilt about the husband. Actually the patient did not have analysis — it was the weekend; and the deprivation was construed by the patient, therefore, as being due to something arousing guilt. In the associations the poor fish meal was due to the paralysed, ill state of the woman. Thus the patient's deprivations were felt to be caused by the ill state of the mother. The same theme is repeated in the second part. The food was given to the girl who represented the childish part of A.'s self. What prevented her getting the good dinner and left her with only an almost fleshless fishbone was the mother seen as bedridden and paralysed. I had had reason in the sessions preceding this dream to point out to my patient her attempts to control and paralyse me as a creative worker and as a woman, when I seemed to be lively and working helpfully. Thus we could see that if my patient felt dependent on me, she attempted to paralyse me externally and internally. In an attempt to ward off this aggressive behaviour, she split off her needy, greedy, wolfish impulses, but now they could be seen to be projected not just into the father, but right into me, as the primary figure, the breast mother who then became wolfish, devouring, and menacing, but who behind that was felt to be paralysed, and unable to feed her children adequately. The internal figure is thus seen to be in a perilous and paralysed condition. The patient is no longer omnipotent, but can only give as a present a fishbone. Now, too, one can see the link between the devouring and depriving internal mother revealed by the dream, and the devouring, exploiting, and needy people in A.'s environment.

I am suggesting therefore that both A. and B. have at depth the same type of internal figure, the one putrefying but not dead, the other paralysed. It is the condition of these internal figures that they cannot face, which is of course evidence of their failure to work through the depressive position. Considering this from the dream material, I think one can see how from infancy and early childhood A. has always been haunted by the internal mother that she has attacked, reduced, and even, as I suggested, fundamentally fears that she has destroyed. But if she brings her alive, the mother will become feeding and creative and will occasion further envious and destructive attacks; but if she lets her die, starvation and the fear of murderous and devouring retaliation and at depth hopeless guilt and depression will be the result. A compromise between life and death is found in the condition of paralysis, of suspended animation. Her object is paralysed, just as she herself is emotionally largely paralysed. What makes the problem so insoluble is exactly that it is only a compromise, a balance between life and death, between love and hate; so there can be no real integration, and no real mitigation of hate by love; therefore there is no progress but only a compulsive repetition.

31

Summary and conclusions

I have tried in this chapter to discuss the apparently passive repetition compulsion. Freud (1920) showed that these repetition-compulsion patients are attempting to master anxiety that would otherwise be experienced as overwhelming. I am suggesting that the anxiety that these patients are struggling against is anxiety associated with dependence; that feelings of dependence and need stimulate intense envy and hatred towards the primary object, and therefore what these patients unconsciously fear is intense ambivalence, guilt, and depression. This they particularly fear since they have an inner conviction that their earliest aggression has reduced their internal object to an extremely perilous or destroyed condition — which they cannot face. Their method of avoiding this depressive anxiety is to avoid the experience of dependence by the use of the splitting, projective and introjective identification combination of defences that I have been describing. These patients therefore get caught in an insoluble situation; they cannot face ambivalence and guilt and so cannot reach and work through the depressive position; they retreat from it by the use of defences belonging to the paranoid-schizoid position, so that they are subsequently faced with manifold persecutions. Their particular method of splitting and fusion with the idealized object protects them from psychosis, but their inability to tolerate ambivalence, conflict, and therefore integration obviates the possibility of normality.

I want now briefly to make a very tentative concluding connection between what Freud said about the repetition compulsion and the death instinct and what I have been suggesting here. Freud postulated that the repetition compulsion was a manifestation of the death instinct at work, describing the death instinct as tending towards the reinstatement of a previous state of existence, in the final issue to an inorganic state. Following this line of thought, I feel that one might consider that these patients do feel most free from anxiety when they can become near to inorganic — that is, free of emotions, and this is, in part, what they aim at achieving by their violent projective identifications, although, as I have suggested, they keep in touch with the split-off living parts of themselves by remaining involved with the people into whom they have put them. In any case, conflict is constantly introduced, as Freud showed, by the life instinct. It manifests itself in a need to love and be dependent, and in the need for relationships with desirable and significant people, of whom the analyst is the prime and most disturbing current representative. Each time these carriers of the life instinct disturb the patients' peace, a situation akin to a trauma arises, and they react in a way which seems aimed at restoring their quasi-inorganic state; they react by their compulsive method of splitting, projective identification, and introjection, attempting thus to restore their peace. Considered from this angle one might suggest that in these patients, in the fusion of the life and death instincts, the life instinct does not sufficiently predominate for the patient to be able to rely on his love being strong enough to mitigate his destructiveness. Clinically we see this in the sense that the patient is never able to make a full relationship with his object nor restore it to full life and creativity, since he unconsciously fears that his aggression would immediately emerge to attack it; he is never able to achieve a full integration of the self, since his hatred would then have to be faced. A compromise is achieved in a state of paralysis, of suspended animation, in which conflict and depression are avoided, in which the object is neither dead nor alive, and where the patient can be seen to be identified with his object, he himself being not dead emotionally nor yet alive.

In conclusion, a note about the apparent passivity of the type of repetition compulsion that I have been describing. It seems that it is due to the fact that the individual is employing against his main anxieties a combination of defences that is so powerful and immediate that he does not appear himself to be actively involved in his own fate, but only to be constantly re-experiencing it at the hands of the people into whom he has projected the unwanted parts of his self. In other words, it seems that he is not, as Freud's description in part suggests, passively experiencing, but rather very actively splitting, projecting, and introjecting, in preference to tolerating dependence, with all its concomitant emotions. Thus it can be seen that the so-called passive repetition compulsion is part of the larger picture of the repetition-compulsion phenomena, and that it consists of a particular combination of very early defence mechanisms of an extremely rigid character, which is likely to be repeated whenever the problems round dependence are reactivated.

2

Some characteristics of the psychopathic personality

This paper was first read at the 21st Congress of the International Psychoanalytical Association, Copenhagen, July 1959, and was published in the *International Journal of Psycho-Analysis* 41 (1960): 526–31.

In this chapter I shall discuss some characteristics of the psychopathic personality. I use the term here in the sense in which it is generally employed in psychiatric and psychoanalytic literature. I cannot, in a paper of this length, discuss the analytic literature on the subject, but would refer particularly to Alexander (1930), Bromberg (1948), Deutsch (1955), Fenichel (1945), Greenacre (1945), Reich (1925), Wittels (1938). It will be seen that my approach to the problem is essentially dependent upon an understanding of the work of Melanie Klein (1935, 1946, 1957).

I shall limit myself to describing and discussing one psychopathic patient whom I have had in treatment for about three years. I shall then draw certain conclusions from this case which seem to me, both by comparison with other psychopathic patients and from a perusal of the literature, to be relevant to the psychopathology of the non-criminal psychopath in general

X. was sixteen when he came into treatment. His family is Jewish. His father is a somewhat weak and placating man; he works in a large industrial concern, but originally trained as a lawyer. The mother, of French origin, is an anxious and excitable woman who looks younger than her age. She started running a small café a few months before treatment started. There is a daughter who is two years younger and is more stable than X. There seems considerable tension between the parents, but both are concerned about X. X. was referred for restless, unhappy, and unsettled behaviour. He could not stick to anything, had no real interests, and was doing badly at school. His mother was anxious about his precocious sexual development and interests.

X. was breast-fed for about two months; he was then put on to the bottle, as the mother had insufficient milk. He cried a lot between feeds. He appeared to have become increasingly difficult with his mother since puberty, but was overtly fairly friendly with the father despite flare-ups. He went to boarding-school at thirteen and in his holidays had one or two vacation jobs but could not stick to them. He seemed interested only in earning a lot of money in the easiest possible way. At sixteen he was moved from boarding school to a cramming college in London in order to come to analysis. At this period he started to mix with a group of restless, near-delinquent teenagers who had no regular careers, training, or jobs, and himself remained just on the outer fringe of delinquency. He and his friends went to endless parties where there was a lot of petting with girls until all hours of the night, and they had virtually no other interests. At college he despised and mocked his teachers, did almost no work, and cut his lectures. His two ideas for his future career were to be a lawyer or to go in for catering (his parents' careers). Soon he added a third, that of being a psychoanalyst! He was extremely demanding and exploiting with his parents, getting everything he could out of them — money, food, training — and then manifestly throwing away his opportunities. About all this he showed no apparent sense of guilt, but was very bombastic, and maintained a picture of himself as being in some way special and unique. He seemed emotionally very labile and impulsive and was apparently easily influenced by his group. He would often talk in a somewhat maudlin and sentimental way. Although he considered himself universally popular, he had in fact no real friends. In appearance he was slim, with a rather effeminate gait.

It seemed to me that X. was in fact clearly a psychopathic personality. His difficulties did not seem to be just those of normal adolescence; he lacked obvious neurotic symptoms; he was not psychotic, and had a severely disturbed character formation. As I have suggested, he was impulsive, had a weak ego, and was apparently lacking in a conscious sense of guilt. His object-relationships were primitive, he was shallow in affect and very narcissistic.

In analysis X. attended regularly, but there were periods when he would become very aggressive, would twist my interpretations, throw them back at me, verbally attack and mock at me, or would argue and cross-question like a sadistic lawyer. At other times he was on the whole co-operative, often very smooth to the point of being placating; but there was a shallow type of response to my interpretations; he seemed consciously to pay little attention to them, would vaguely say 'Yes' and go on to something else, and would not from one session to another show any continuity or refer back to insight he might have gained.

I shall now discuss three interrelated characteristics which I believe to be fundamental to X.'s psychopathic state. First, his striking inability to tolerate any tension; second, a particular type of attitude towards his objects; and third, a specific combination of defences with whose help he maintains a precarious but significant balance.

X. constantly shows his difficulty in tolerating any kind of tension. On a primarily physical level he tears at his skin and bites his nails when he experiences any irritation; he was unable to establish proper bladder control until well into latency. He reacts to any anxiety by erecting massive defences. He cannot stand frustration and tends to act out his impulses immediately with little inhibition. Nevertheless, as I shall indicate later, a great deal that appears to be an uncontrolled acting out of impulses can be seen on further analysis to consist of complicated mechanisms to avoid inner conflict and anxiety.

As to the second point — his particular type of attitude to his objects: X. is, as I have described, extremely demanding and controlling, greedy and exploiting. What he gets he spoils and wastes; then he feels frustrated and deprived, and the greed and demands start again. I want to show how this pattern is based on a specific interrelationship between greed and envy. To give an example: he must have analysis, he must have the sessions at the times he wants, it does not matter how difficult it is for his parents to afford the fees, but when he has it he mocks, he disregards, and he twists the interpretations. As I see it, he knows that he wants something and will grab, almost to the point of stealing, but then his envy of the giver — of the analyst, teacher, at depth the good parents — is so intense that he spoils and wastes it, but the spoiling and wasting lead to more frustration and so augment the greed again, and the vicious circle continues. Melanie Klein in discussing an aspect of this problem says, 'Greed, envy and persecutory anxiety, which are bound up with each other, inevitably increase each other.'

As to my third point, I am suggesting that the nature of the anxieties aroused by this interrelationship between greed and envy leads to the establishment of a characteristic series of defence mechanisms. These I shall describe in more detail, and I shall suggest how they enable X. to maintain a particular type of balance. I shall show how X., despite his greed, exploitation, and impulsiveness, is not a criminal; despite his envious, omnipotent incorporation of his objects, his cruelty towards them, his apparent lack of concern for them, and his resultant inner persecution, he has not become psychotic. The balance that X. achieves is, as I see it, the psychopathic state — a state in which profound guilt and depression, profound persecution, and actual criminality are all constantly being evaded.

The group of defence mechanisms mainly used by X. to keep this precarious balance is centred on the maintenance and actual dramatization of powerful omnipotent phantasies which are largely based on massive splitting and excessive projective and introjective identification. So long as these mechanisms are effective, X.'s balance can be held and breakdown warded off. I have given some instances, such as his inability to visualize any career for himself other than that of his parents or myself. Or, when he was attempting to study economics for his General Certificate of Education, he immediately saw himself as a future writer of textbooks or an economic adviser to governments — not as a beginner student. I have also instanced how, when he was attending college, early on in the analysis, he in fact did no work, cut lectures, and mocked at and derided his teachers as he did myself in the transference. But when faced with the reality of exams he would firmly maintain that he could easily catch up in the two or three weeks that remained.

These defences depend upon a total introjection of, and magical identification with, the idealized, successful and desirable figures — the parents, analyst, writers of text-books. This type of introjection enables him to ward off the whole area of depressive feelings. He avoids any dependence on his objects, any desire for or sense of loss of them. In addition, since he has swallowed up these idealized objects, and in his feelings stolen their capacities, he avoids envy and all competitiveness, including his Oedipal rivalry. He has all the cleverness — the teachers and I are stupid, not worth his while attending to, we are failures. Thus he splits off his wasting, failing self, his failure to make good and use what is available, and projects it into the teachers and myself. He is also magically reparative, can put everything right — for example the exams. In this way, failure, guilt, and depression are completely obviated.

Similar mechanisms are at work in his choice of friends. I have stated how, for a long time, he mixed only with a group of unsuccessful, near-delinquent young people. It became clear that he projected into them his own criminal self — they stole, they lied, not he; thus he avoids actual criminality and the guilt that could result. It is interesting to note, however, that on the one occasion when he did get arrested by the police, along with a delinquent friend — mistakenly, as it turned out — he lived in a state of near collapse for days, confirming that in fact it is the intensity of his fear of persecution that prevents his being a criminal.

A similar method of avoiding actual criminality and persecution and yet living out his stealing impulses by projective identification can be seen in the following type of behaviour. He would give a friend 10s. to hand over to a storeman who would 'lift' a coat from a warehouse and get it round to X. X. is constantly having to evade his inner persecuting figures and superego. These he would project into the police and parents, or, at college, his teachers, and then he allied himself with his delinquent friends against them. At other times he would identify with his inner accusing figures and turn with violent accusations against his erstwhile friends, containing his criminal self. At yet other times he would appear to do a great deal of wheedling, cajoling, and bribing of his internal figures as if constantly trying to prove that his criminal impulses were not what they seemed, as is indicated in the example of the coat 'lifted' by the storeman.

Naturally, the constant use of projective identification to rid himself of the bad parts of the self and inner objects leaves him feeling more persecuted externally. This he deals with either by flight — for example, he eventually could not face his college and teachers at all; or by a manic, mocking, controlling attitude, as I have described in regard to his behaviour with myself and his teachers.

The need to project these various internal figures into the external world to avoid both inner persecution and the possibility of guilt plays a role of great importance in motivating psychopaths to manoeuvre rows, brawls, and fights in their outside environment to get themselves noticed and punished and attacked for apparently petty reasons. X., when his environment did not persecute him and when he seemed to be more settled and happy and to be getting more insight, became noticeably accident-prone. He poured boiling oil on his foot and cut off the tip of his finger as if he now had to play out the role demanded by his slashing and burning internal figures. It was also obvious that he unconsciously felt that such attacks were justified. He managed in a striking manner to neglect his scalded foot. I shall later indicate how such unconscious guilt and inner persecution drove X. into actual stealing and into actually being rejected.

I have so far been trying to show some of the main mechanisms that X. constantly used to avoid guilt, depression, inner and external persecution, and actual criminality. I want now to mention a more extreme defensive process which may occur when these ordinary mechanisms of omnipotence and projective identification fail him, and when he is momentarily faced with psychic reality. This process — a massive fragmentation of the self and inner objects — could be seen at certain periods in the analysis when the nature and need for his omnipotence were being interpreted; then one might get a sense of immediate chaos. X. might become extremely angry and abusive with me, shouting at me for being ridiculous, or he might appear to collapse, yelling 'All right, all right, all right', as if he were falling completely to pieces. In these situations parts of the self and internal objects that had previously been split off and projected out and kept at bay by his holding on to the idealized omnipotent phantasies are, by virtue of the interpretations, brought back into contact with the self. At this moment a new violent splitting and falling to pieces and projective identification takes place, since the patient feels overwhelmed by his impulses and by his emerging guilt and his internal objects; at once the bad — for example, 'ridiculous' — parts, as well as his inner persecuting figures, are projected into the analyst, who is attacked and abused, or is placated in a desperate masochistic manner — as with X. crying, 'All right, all right, all right'. This splitting is now of a diffuse fragmenting type, making one aware of his nearness to schizophrenic disintegration, and his absolute need for the omnipotent defences that prevent it.

In the second part of this paper I shall bring more detailed material to illustrate some of the main points that I have been making — especially the interconnection between greed, envy, and frustration in X. and the nature and functioning of his characteristic defences.

The material I am quoting occurred about a month before a Christmas holiday. My previous patient had in fact just left, but X. arrived early, and instead of going as usual to the waiting room, came straight to the consulting room, opened the door, looked in, realized his error, shut the door and then went to the waiting room.

At the beginning of the session he told a dream, *which was that he was in a place like a bar which also served food; his penis seemed to have come through the zip opening of his trousers. He put it back, but then it was as if he pulled it out again; he thought that people would realize that he was a homosexual, or a pervert. There were other men, perhaps sailors, in the bar.* His associations were to a bar in a village near a town D., where he had stayed during the previous summer holidays. The bars there were closed on Sundays, but everyone went to the bar in the nearby village which was really meant only for travellers passing through. The penis showing through the trouser opening refers to a party the previous weekend when X. got a bit drunk and a boy had his trouser opening showing. X. then described how he went into a public lavatory a week or so before: the notice on the door said 'Vacant', but when he opened the door he saw a man's bag standing on the floor inside, then realized that there was a man in the lavatory saying something to him as if inviting him to come in. X. was alarmed and fled. Briefly, I am suggesting that X. was showing his feelings about the coming Christmas holidays, when I was felt to be the shut bar, and he turned away to the open bar, the homosexual relationships with men, experienced as a drinking and feeding, which I connected with fellatio phantasies. As I was speaking he said that he was just thinking about masturbation phantasies he had had about sucking his own penis. He then seemed to trail off, saying that he had a heavy bag of school books with him, and wished he could leave it here in my flat. I pointed out that he seemed to be turning my flat into the lavatory scene that he had experienced the previous week, for he had started the session by pushing open the door as if maintaining that it said 'Vacant' and was proposing to push the bag in here too.

I shall now bring together the main points that I tried to convey to him and that I want to discuss here. First there is the dramatization of the whole situation in the transference. There is also the avoidance of the frustration and anxiety about my being shut, as the mother, unavailable over the Christmas holiday, by turning greedily to the ever-open bar. But the bar is run by men; he turns to the father inside the mother, my room being a combined parent figure. There is a reference to his greed; last weekend he was a bit drunk; but the greed leads at once to envy of the person who can feed, so he incorporates the feeding penis which is equated with the breast, and omnipotently sucks from his own penis in his masturbation phantasies and will, apparently, feed the other men — the sailors. His trousers then become the ever-open bar. Thus, all feelings of anxiety about loss and possible rejection by the mother are obviated; his need and desire for her are in the men who are split-up aspects of the father. But now the father containing these bits of himself becomes an object of terror, as is seen in the association about the flight from the man in the lavatory. In the dream there is a break-through of persecutory fears; he puts his penis back again, as if afraid of the greed of the sailors. X. achieves his omnipotent solution by becoming homosexual, meaning that he now contains the penis—breast. But the guilt and persecution about the stealing of the breast is evaded, since the actual homosexuality is projected into myself as the father seducing him.

There are two further points I want to make. First, that the homosexual collusion with the men — there are no women in the dream — is mirrored in his placating relationship with his actual father, in which both quietly denigrate the mother. Second, I am trying to show here the depth of X.'s omnipotent phantasies. I have already stressed his need to have both his parents' careers, and he finally chose the one based on his mother's, both her immediate one and her original maternal feeding one. In this material it becomes clear that at depth what X. feels he must have is the mother's breast stolen by the father and fused with the father's penis.

I shall now bring material to illustrate more fully an aspect of what I described earlier as X.'s particular type of attitude to his objects. I shall show some of his ways of avoiding his deepest guilt towards his first object, especially his method of dramatizing a situation in which he is thrown out, and thus punished, for a petty crime, rather than enduring the deeper underlying guilt which would lead him to experience the depressive position.

X. decided to take up catering as a career and by now was able to start in a realistic way; he was accepted at a catering college and found a job in the kitchen of a good hotel where he could get preliminary experience. He was good at the work, and, for the first time since he had been in analysis, very happy in what he was doing. Suddenly, after being there just a month, he arrived saying that the chef had given him the sack, but he did not know why, except that they were cutting down staff. This reason did not convince him. Throughout the session he spoke very restrainedly, kept telling how very helpful and nice everyone had been, the work place, the employment agency, adding frequently, 'I didn't fall to pieces, I didn't fall to pieces', and then went back to everyone's niceness. When I showed him both his belief that the chef had now stolen his job and his potency, and his fear of facing his own despair, persecution, and hate, he suddenly said that he thought that the chef was a crook. He had once overheard a conversation which seemed to indicate that in a previous job the chef had stolen some hams. As he described this X. became panicky, saying 'My anger's coming out', and went back to describing how nice and helpful everyone had been. Right at the end of the session when speaking of his fear of his anger he said, 'It's like when I went to the cinema on Saturday, they showed the film of a plane crash, where fourteen people were killed. Tears came right up behind my eyes — ordinarily you act as if you felt tearful, but this was real, it caught me by surprise, I stopped it, but in a way I was glad the feelings came.'

I want to stress three points here: first, his fear of falling to pieces if the hate, the persecution, and despair were allowed to come through and overwhelm him, just as he seemed to be liable to fall to pieces in the session that I instanced earlier when his omnipotence was being analysed and he was momentarily facing psychic reality. Second, his attempt again to deal with the guilt by projecting the stealing parts of the self (as will emerge later) and the Oedipal impulses towards the mother, and the robbing, castrating internal figures into the chef standing for the father, and at first even denying his fear about him. Third, the profound idealization of the self, being so quiet and constructive, and of the whole outside world other than the chef. But this splitting and idealization is now aimed also at keeping his good objects alive and safe. This can be seen by the emergence of depressive feelings; for example, the strikingly sincere way in which he spoke of the plane crash, and his fear about the crashing of his constructive work, at depth his good internal objects. But he had in fact brought about this partial crash, the loss of the good job. The reason for this emerged more clearly three days later when, in response to interpretations, he said that he thought that he might have been given the sack for stealing food from the hotel. Three times he had taken sandwiches home with him. So the criticism of the chef for stealing became clear. But as I shall now try to show, this petty stealing of the sandwiches which almost certainly got him the sack was, as I suggested at the beginning of this paper, not just an acting out of greedy impulses, but a more complex method of avoiding the deeper guilt and anxiety about stealing by the spoiling of his good object — at depth the mother's breast. This was shown the following day, when he arrived complaining that although he had got a new job he had only been paid one pound to keep him going. 'I can't manage, I have to pay rent, I can't manage, I shall have to borrow. At the hotel the menu is in French and I can't understand it.' I suggested that what he could not properly understand was how he got into all these muddles with money, and I should add that there was an important connection here with the French menu, the French mother's food. He spoke of plans for paying the money back, and went on to say he had had a bad night; his hot water bottle had leaked, the stopper wasn't in properly, and the bed got damp. I suggested that the real problem was that he felt that the money, just like the analysis and his other opportunities, seemed somehow to leak away and not get used properly. He spoke about a difficulty in plans for the day; how to manage about the suitcase he had with him. If he took it to work, the doorman would go through it when he left to make sure he wasn't steal-ing anything, and he would be so embarrassed as it was full of soiled linen. I showed him his anxiety about taking in stuff from me, the hotel, in a stealing way, that is, not to use it himself, for example, to have a good meal but to slip it out secretly and make it into a mess represented by the soiled linen, as he did with the analysis, when the sessions again and again got lost and chaotic. He said that at the previous job it was true he did get three good meals a day, but then went to the lavatory three times a day to defecate.

Thus, the real nature of his guilt, his self-accusations, here projected on to the doorman, concern his turning his good meals at once into faeces, my good interpretations into disregarded stuff, which are then just defecated or leaked out.

There are two points that I want to stress here. First, I believe that it is this type of envious spoiling that is the really critical point of the guilt in these patients, leading in X. to a fear of loss and rejection. This guilt and anxiety he avoids by getting himself actively thrown out of his job for apparently petty, greedy stealing. Second, it is this spoiling and wastage that leaves these patients always dissatisfied, feeling, as they express it, that 'the world owes me something', and this stirs up greed again. Of course, this dissatisfaction is increased by their guilt, which also prevents them from feeling able to use and enjoy what they do get.

42

Conclusion

I am suggesting in this chapter that the psychopathology of X. might be considered to be typical for a large group of non-criminal psychopaths. It seems that he is particularly unable to tolerate frustration and anxiety: that he approaches his objects with an attitude of extreme greed and stealing: that the greed and experience of desire lead immediately to feelings of intense envy of the object's capacity to satisfy him; he attempts to obviate his envy both by spoiling and wasting what he gets from the object, thus making the object undesirable, and by omnipotent incorporation of the idealized object. He is faced with profound anxieties on many levels. He cannot face and work through the depressive position both because of the intensity of the persecution of his internal objects and his guilt; and because he is partially fixated in the paranoid-schizoid position owing to the strength of his envious impulses and splitting. I have tried to show how, faced with these various anxieties and impulses, he manages to keep a precarious balance, avoiding criminality on the one hand and a psychotic breakdown on the other. I have discussed the nature of the defence mechanisms — based on omnipotence, splitting, and projective and introjective identification which keeps this balance going — and am suggesting that this balance is the psychopathic state.

43

PART 2

Breakthrough

Introduction

Michael Feldman and Elizabeth Bott Spillius

In the four chapters in this section the themes of Joseph's work begin to emerge clearly. The fundamental theoretical position remains the same, but there is an important shift in emphasis, evidently arising from her concern to explore the factors which facilitate or impede psychic change. The first chapter is full of important ideas and observations but is very detailed and complex. The second states some of the ideas of the first chapter more simply and directly. The last two are incisively lucid — the ideas have arrived. Psychic change, psychic equilibrium, acting out in the transference, inducing the analyst to fit in — all are now in clear focus.

In the chapter on the analysis of a perversion (1971) Joseph emphasizes the necessity of analysing the way in which the perversion manifests itself in the transference, both because this allows the patient's defensive organization to be examined in detail in the to-and-fro of the session, and because Joseph believes that this is the approach most likely to lead to psychic change.

She describes a highly narcissistic man, a fetishist, who came to analysis because of unsatisfactory personal relations and various other symptoms including claustrophobia and occasional panic attacks. He was apparently uninvolved with the analysis and was indifferent about holidays and weekends. It began to emerge in his analysis that he was splitting off the dependent and aggressive aspects of himself and locating them in the various people around him, including his analyst, while simultaneously appropriating to himself qualities of power and super-iority — again the combination of projective and introjective identifica-tion that Joseph was finding to be such an important defensive combination. One of the consequences of this use of his objects,

47

especially his wife, was claustrophobic anxiety. In phantasy he invaded her with oral and genital desires and then felt in danger of being trapped inside her. Occasionally cruelty and sadism to his wife showed through his conventional politeness and indifference. He treated her body and the marriage itself, for example, as a kind of fetish, something he could get into to avoid the anxieties connected with other forms of human relationship, as well as a means of enviously and sadistically attacking and controlling his wife.

However, it was only when the more hidden manifestations of his sadism could be located and addressed in the analytic relationship that it became possible for Joseph to understand the patient's perverse behaviour in greater detail. Joseph began to recognize that the patient was engaging in a refined form of cruelty; he would repeatedly attack a helpful interpretation or a good session by withdrawing into flatness and deadness. The analyst would be left as the one who wanted or needed something which the patient was withholding in a subtly cruel, tormenting, and excited fashion. As Joseph puts it:

> we, in the quietest possible manner, were locked in a sado-masochistic relationship, in which I was to be excited and tormented, and . . . it was far more difficult for him to give up this gratification and have a real relationship with his analytic material and me as a woman and an analyst than to retreat into his heavy silence, his words, and his theories, which I believe are actually being used as the rubber fetish into which he can withdraw from contact.

We see here a theme to which Joseph returns in many subsequent papers: it is not only that projective identification distorts the patient's perception of his analyst; it is also that projective identification, frequently but not always, is accompanied by attempts by the patient to get the analyst to act in a manner appropriate to his unconscious projection.

The importance of Joseph's chapter on perversion lies not only in her elaboration of the psychopathology of a narcissistic and perverse patient, but also in her description of the way in which she began to attend very closely to the patient's verbal and non-verbal behaviour in the session, observing in detail not only what he said but the *way* in which he brought his communication. This chapter and the three which follow begin to develop the approach which has proved to be Joseph's distinctive contribution, with the careful working out of the dynamics of the transference, and the *enactments* which both patient and analyst find themselves involved in, and which, Joseph believes, if properly understood, can both illuminate the patient's psychopathology and lead to significant and lasting change.

The second paper of this period, 'On passivity and aggression: their interrelationship', written in 1971, makes a more incisive statement of one of the central ideas of the preceding chapter on perversion. In the 'passivity and aggression' chapter Joseph gives a particularly clear description of the way a deeply passive patient was using her passivity as a form of silent attack not only on the analyst but also on the patient's own capacity for self-observation and thought.

The next chapter, 'The patient who is difficult to reach' (1975), marks an important step in the development of Joseph's work and has proved to be highly influential. The important technical and theoretical points which were described in the 1971 chapter on perversion are more clearly and powerfully expressed here and are further elaborated and clarified.

The starting point, once again, is Joseph's concern with finding ways of promoting psychic change in our patients. She began to recognize that with certain patients there appears to be a therapeutic alliance, with the patient behaving co-operatively and the analyst feeling relatively comfortable for a while; but gradually the analyst becomes aware that nothing is changing, indeed nothing is being allowed to change.

She explains this as the result of the way that the needy and potentially receptive part of the personality is split off and projected and/or attacked by an envious and destructive part of the personality. It is thus very difficult for the analyst to make contact with that part of the personality which needs the experience of being understood, and which needs to be more fully integrated into the patient's ego.

In his work on narcissism (1964, 1971b), Rosenfeld has shown how useful it is to recognize that there is often a part of the patient which is caught up in envious, destructive activities, turned against the analytic work and against the more dependent, needy part of the self. Joseph elaborates the ways in which this splitting may become manifest and acted out in the transference. She demonstrates the detailed and subtle ways in which the patient uses his conscious or unconscious perceptions in repeated attempts to disturb, arouse, or provoke the analyst into actions which will militate against the possibility of real understanding or change.

In this chapter Joseph focuses more directly on the patient's methods of communication, both verbal and non-verbal, and the extent to which speech is used as a form of 'acting out'. (Here she speaks of 'acting out in the transference'; in subsequent chapters she often uses the phrase 'acting-in'.) The purpose of this acting out is often to affect the analyst, to induce a certain emotional state, or to put pressure on the analyst to function in ways which do not essentially disturb the patient's equilibrium. Joseph describes the way in which she uses her awareness of the effect of the patient's communications and actions on her, and on the atmosphere of the session, to enable her to focus on what the patient is *doing* through his words or through his silence, so that she can follow and then interpret the way in which the more defensive and destructive parts of the personality function.

The last chapter in this section, 'Towards the experiencing of psychic pain' (1981, but written in 1976), addresses an important problem of technique and theory. Like 'The patient who is difficult to reach', this paper on psychic pain has deeply influenced the thinking of other analysts; it gives a moving and meaningful interpretation of a puzzling clinical phenomenon with which all analysts are familiar.

The starting point is a description of a type of pain which the patient finds difficult to define. It feels almost physical, located near the heart, but known by the patient to be mental. It is connected with loss but is not actually the feeling of depression. Such patients do not describe is as anxiety. They say it is raw pain, incomprehensible.

Joseph suggests that this kind of psychic pain may originally have been the thing that led the patient to seek analysis. She thinks that the patient tries to mobilize his defences in the analysis so as to regain his balance and keep the pain at bay. When, however, he begins to emerge from the equilibrium which his system of defences has achieved, the patient is exposed to the pain which is difficult to endure. Development of capacity to bear such pain, even briefly, with the analyst's help, represents a significant shift. For such patients it is a movement towards accepting the unknown, the new possibility of 'real responsibility for themselves and their relationships and their understanding and their impulses, and we get a real shift towards the depressive position with concern for people'.

Joseph also describes the pressure the analyst may feel under to ease the pain, often by some form of activity (such as answering questions, giving reassurance, or giving explanations) whose tacit meaning to the patient is that the analyst cannot stand the pain either. If the analyst is able to recognize and continue to address the pressures and anxieties with which he is immediately confronted, he may be able to give the patient the experience of helpful containment (Bion 1962), with the possibility of a gradual movement towards greater integration characteristic of the depressive position.

Although Joseph clearly considers the links between the manifest content of the patient's material — what she experiences going on in the session, and the possible infantile origins of these anxieties and defences — she makes it clear that she does not consider it useful to share such ideas prematurely with the patient. On the contrary, she demonstrates in a convincing way in this and many other papers that when she follows the to-and-fro shifts which take place within the session, avoiding the pressure towards premature 'knowledge' about the origins of the patient's anxieties, the responses of the patients are often very impressive and moving.

3

A clinical contribution to the analysis of a perversion

This paper was presented to the British Psycho-Analytical Society on 3 December 1969, and was published in the *International Journal of Psycho-Analysis* 52 (1971): 441—9.

In the literature on perversion, so far as I can ascertain, there is great deal about the meaning of various perversions, the mechanisms involved and similar aspects, but a paucity of detailed clinical reporting. This lack is unfortunate, since my impression is that, while one may deduce a great deal from these patients' symptoms, activities, and history, this is therapeutically comparatively useless unless one can analyse the manifestations of the perversion in the transference. One would expect that the main aspects of the perverse symptomatology will appear in the transference if only one can locate them. This may not appear particularly difficult with more overt sadistic perversions, but can be very tricky with certain apparently unaggressive perverts and fetishists, particularly perhaps those whose material is very repetitive and whose behaviour seems somewhat passive.

I want in this chapter to bring clinical material from the early stages of the analysis of a rubber fetishist to discuss: first, how aspects of the perversion manifested themselves in the transference; and second, how the way in which they emerged enabled me to gain insight into this patient's psychopathology. I think that certain elements in his psychopathology which stand out as particularly important may be of some general significance in the field of perversions.

My plan is as follows: first, I shall describe my patient and his problems, and then outline briefly certain ideas about his character structure and psychopathology stressing those elements that I believe to be specific to his difficulties. Then I shall bring material from the early period of his analysis to illustrate how I arrived at these ideas, particularly, as I have indicated, discussing the emergence of the perversion in the transference. I do not intend to discuss the meaning of the fetish in any detail, since I am more concerned about the underlying character structure.

The patient, whom I shall call B., is a man in his early forties. He has been in analysis for about four and a half years. His complaints were that he felt depressed and that he was not able to make proper relationships with women, although he thought that he wanted to marry and have a family. His sexuality was abnormal, mainly consisting of masturbation, with phantasies of getting totally inside a rubber garment. Early in the analysis we learned about other symptoms, particularly of the sensation of choking at night, occasionally as if something was stuck down his throat or was going down it, so that he would wake desperately trying to cough it out. He also had an occasional acute skin irritation on his arms and legs. The details of the rubber fetish we only learned as the analysis went on. It had, before the beginning of analysis, sometimes been acted out with prostitutes or alone, but it was mainly used as the content of very vivid masturbation phantasies, which were roughly of three types. First, he and a woman, both in rubber, preferably black, would be having sexual intercourse, or the woman masturbating him; second, figures in rubber would come and menace, beat, attack, and almost kill him, he dressed also in rubber; third, he would be dressed in rubber from head to foot and this very often excited the whole of his skin and he might ejaculate. He managed to keep the fetish activities separate from any woman that he cared about, being acted out only with prostitutes, but, after some time in analysis, he became afraid of wanting to involve his wife (he had by then married) and myself in these activities. One of my aims will be to show that unconsciously in his phantasies he actually lived out his perversion in the analysis, and this was the only way in which it could really be understood. For a long time in the analysis he was convinced, and often worried about the fact, that the interest and excitement of the rubber phantasies were far greater than any pleasure that normal sexual intercourse could ever offer. His interest in rubber, mackintoshes, groundsheets, and the like goes back as far as his conscious memory.

B.'s background is as follows: he is the fourth and youngest child of middle-class parents, coming from the north of England. His father, an architect, is said to have been a man with a very violent temper, possibly connected with his having been wounded in the head in the First World War. The mother emerges as a kindly, but probably not very warm, person. She is alive and in touch with her children; the father died a few years ago. There is an older girl and then two boys next to the patient.

B. appears to have been very much attached to the sister in his early childhood, almost as if in love with her, and my impression is that she must have been devoted to him and idealized him. There are indications of a confused and bad relationship with the brother next to him, vaguely sexualized, and B. has the idea that in some way or another his brother was also involved with the fetish. B. had a number of operations in early childhood on his middle ear and there were anxiety dreams relating to anaesthetics, which seem to date from this period, in particular about being inside a globe and nearly falling through a hole in it. We know very little about his early history and he is still unable to ask his mother about this.

First, I want to try to convey this patient's personality as it emerged in treatment during the early period. He is a slim, carefully dressed, intelligent man, with a high administrative position, earning a very good salary, in a large industrial organization. When he started analysis, he was unmarried, and had an almost non-sexual relationship with the young woman whom he married after three years of analysis, largely, I think, on her initiative. He was attached to her, but there was little real love or passion. He had an occasional casual affair with one or two other girls, who meant almost nothing emotionally to him.

His relationship with me in analysis showed the same apparent lack of involvement — he came regularly, he brought his problems and dreams, he listened to interpretations; he responded by saying, 'Yes' and 'How interesting', and they and I appeared to be completely unimportant to him. He would talk round interpretations academically, or become extremely wordy, until the feeling and significance of what I had said were lost. Weekends and holidays were scarcely noticed consciously, but he tended to oversleep and miss the occasional session around the weekends, and started a casual affair with a girl at one early holiday — so it was clear that unconsciously he was trying to deny the positive meaning of the analysis. Though treating me very politely, he was, in fact, arrogant, aloof, and superior in his attitude to me, in a tolerant and unruffled way, and he was very, very passive in the analysis. This behaviour contrasted markedly with the anxieties and panic states — for example, of choking in the night — that he occasionally reported.

It became clear that B. was a highly narcissistic man, who was keeping a none too stable balance by the use of projective and introjective mechanisms. He split off his love, his infantile needs and desires and dependence into his objects, myself in the transference, or his girl friends, and appeared to introject the capacity and superiority of his objects; as, for example, when he received interpretations with 'How interesting', as if we were sharing knowledge about a third person, and he helped to start, and worked on the administration of, a high-grade delicatessen shop. It became clear that he was not going to depend on a woman or analyst, but was introjecting their good feeding and interpretive qualities, while getting rid of his needs into them, and in his environment his women did seem to run after him. Thus he presented from the beginning as a very polite, arrogant, omnipotent person, who needed no one, loved no one, had no reason to envy anyone, or, generally speaking, even to dislike them. I had the impression that the avoidance of dependence and envy and hatred was quite crucial in his pathology. But, at the same time, he had to have people around him who would carry these split-off infantile parts, and he rarely at that stage could spend even one night in his flat alone, or he would panic.

About all this there is nothing at all specific. It is a very usual picture of a narcissistic personality organization (Rosenfeld 1964). What I think is more specific to this man is the way in which he dealt with sexual excitement; and it is this that is so particularly associated with his perversion and his passivity. I shall try to show that B. used projective identification to rid himself of sexual excitement; first, as I have indicated, to get rid of his sexual wishes in so far as they were linked with feelings of dependence on, and love for, a woman, which might lead to envy of her role or lovability. Once these were projected, he was no longer attracted by women, but they were running after him. Second, his excitement had to be split off and projected, and was felt as unendurable, because it was deeply associated not just with aggression, but sadism, which had to be disowned. But, I shall indicate, this projecting of excitement was not only defensive, but was also used as an attack on his objects, particularly at depth, an attack on the calm and stability of the breast, to destroy its quiet and strong feeding qualities. This projection of sexual excitement, of course, made him apathetic and impotent, and it also led to an erotization of the transference of a silent and invisible type.[1]

I shall now go on to discuss and illustrate some of these points about the personality structure of this patient as they emerged during roughly the first three and a half years of treatment. I can best illustrate the nature of B.'s adjustment, as it appeared in the early part of treatment, by describing a dream which he brought after having been in analysis for rather less than two years. He had spent most of the previous night with one of his rare casual girl friends. The dream is in three parts.

DREAM

1. *B. was at the seaside near an hotel on the beach; a woman came with a duck which she had modelled in sand on a tray – she put her hands up the back*

of the neck inside the throat in order to make inside it a more realistic tongue. She painted it in bright colours and put it on a pedestal.

2. *Pat (the patient's regular girl friend, whom he subsequently married) was telling people something about what we 'do when we go shooting'. The patient knew that what she was saying was snobbish, artificial, and untrue.*

3. *B. was in the hotel, looking with anxiety as the wind drove the waves up towards the hotel. Nearby he had left his suitcase; he ran out to rescue it quickly.*

I am not bringing the patient's associations, but simply using this dream as background. I think it indicates how B. uses the analysis and myself to build up himself in his own mind as this brightly coloured duck forever on its pedestal. His tongue is here, I think, equated with a nipple, which he has perpetually in his own mouth and throat, and therefore, instead of having a hungry open beak, he contains his own internal feeding nipple. This is one of the meanings of his constant talking round, as if talking to himself or down to me, that I mentioned before — it is his tongue, not mine, that feeds him. The tongue has got into the interpretations, nipple, and taken over its function. (I shall refer to other aspects of this talking later.) We knew from previous material something of the omnipotent use of B.'s faeces — I think the reference to the sand links here, but I am not going into this. The notion of the duck on the pedestal is supported by the one-sided admiration of the girl friends, particularly the one with whom he had spent the night, and in his childhood, the devotion of his elder sister, whose little duck I think he really was.

But, by the second dream, insight appears about something artificial and unreal going on — not his — but Pat's about shooting. The patient had nothing to be proud of in relation to his sexuality, his shooting, at this time.

By the third dream we can see what dangers threaten if the omnipotence fails and insight takes over; his whole case — I think here his personality — is in danger of being flooded by reality, external and psychic, and by the anxieties that go with it.

I have brought this dream to illustrate, therefore, the narcissistic organization that I have been describing. How B. is living on a pedestal, maintaining that he is loved, omnipotent, and admired, can provide everything for himself, nipple, food, words, so that his infantile needs, oral (the beak) and loving, and feelings of being small or dependent, are split off and projected. So long as this balance held, feelings of resentment, loss, envy, and aggression could be warded off and hollow politeness dominated the picture. But even at this period, and before it, there had been indications of some extreme cruelty and sadism, as yet appearing only in a projected form and highly persecuting. For example, you may remember that I described one type of fetish phantasy in which figures in rubber would start to menace and almost destroy him. Or the sadism appeared in occasional dreams. For example, soon after the first Christmas holidays, there was a dream *in which B. was looking at a film about Hitler, then he was in the film, in a room like a clinic, bodies were being brought in for extermination. A woman in a Bath chair was being pushed backwards by a male attendant in a white coat. The attendant pushed his protruding teeth, which were like a proboscis, into the roof of the woman's mouth through into her brains, and was helped in this by other people. The patient was so terrified that he fled, he nearly blanked out, but he knew that he must listen or he would disappear into nothingness.*

In this dream I think one can clearly see attacks on my brains being done with the teeth, suggesting that my brain and analytic work are equated with a breast. The violence is projected into a male figure, probably connecting with the father's violent outbursts. I reconstructed a link with possible childhood behaviour of thumb-sucking, with the thumb pushed up against the roof of his mouth, which becomes internally the mother's breast. I linked the proboscis with the sensations and accompanying phantasies when he cut his teeth as a baby; he had by now been in analysis a few months; and I reminded him of his current nail-biting. B. was considerably moved by these interpretations, and he recalled that after the dream he had woken with anxieties about choking and with a phantasy of two discs with holes in.[2]

I felt that prognostically this dream was important. He nearly blanked out, but he knew that he must listen.

It was, however, only when we could start to locate this split-off cruelty in the transference that we could begin to see its link with B.'s missing sexuality and get some clues about the connection between the cruelty and the perversion. I want now to try to follow some of B.'s material to illustrate the stages in the development of our understanding. I shall first bring material from the end of the third year of analysis, focusing on his reaction to the summer holidays.

It was the first session after the holidays. B. described how he and his girl friend, Pat, had finally got married. He had not particularly wanted to. They went to the registry office — rather an anticlimax; it reminded him of registering his father's death. He spoke of their having had quite an amount of sexuality and then spoke of the actual sexual difficulties, his difficulties in penetrating, as if he had to be very gentle and had not enough lubricating liquid on his penis. Anyway, Pat had some bleeding and would have to go to hospital for an internal examination. A bit of an anticlimax, he added, why did he wait so long to marry? The fetish, he said, was still around, a bit in the background, and seemed ever more ridiculous now that he was married.

It looked, therefore, to me as if the marriage at that moment was to some extent a flight from the holiday separation from analysis, and in this sense a bit of a flight into the fetish, preferable to a real awareness of a relationship with an absent person. B. then told a dream which he had had just before the last weekend of the holiday and which he felt he could not get rid of.

The dream took place in France, like the French Revolution. There was an avenue of trees going down a hill, and a gap as if a broken-away part. There was an old man who was to be executed, hanged, or rather garrotted. B. had to sign a paper in some way agreeing to it and he could not do anything about it. The man stood on a brick with a wire noose round his neck, which slowly tightened and his head began swelling in a horrible way. It was inevitable; nothing could be done about it. B. felt as if he knew exactly what the man was feeling; it was a nightmare. The paper he signed was something in connection with the idea of the man having had something bad sexually to do with an aunt.

The associations to the aunt were that he had not got an important aunt; the only one who came to his mind was a great-aunt, Barbara, a rather masculine woman, very keen on horticulture; she used to do their garden at home. Mother said that he and the brother next to him were horrid to her, though he thought he had liked her. France related clearly to the holidays.

I showed B. that the anxieties about coming back to analysis were like the anxieties about getting married. The paper he signs condoning the man's death is his father's death certificate and his own marriage certificate, and the fears expressed are the fears of sexual intercourse and analytic intercourse connected with death. Great-aunt Barbara, who did something bad sexually with a man, is myself, keen on horticulture – my garden is very visible. She is rather masculine – related here, I think and shall discuss later, to the idea of strength or toughness in the woman. The anxiety on returning is of being trapped in my inside, as with Pat in the marriage. This arises largely from B.'s attempts to project himself into Pat, the marriage, as a substitute for myself, to avoid relating to and experiencing separation from the analysis in the holidays, as I described earlier with the marriage being used as the fetish, as something which he could get into to avoid some other human relationship. He also projects the infantile dependent parts into the woman to rid himself of them; it was felt to be Pat who wanted to marry him. It is particularly this massive use of projective identification, exacerbated by the holidays, that leads to the fear of being trapped and garrotted on his return. We can now understand why B. had spoken of the difficulties, we could add dangers, of penetration and erection, experienced as the swelling of the head, the penis, and can see what a trap marriage, sexual intercourse, and the return to analysis is. So, while the identification with the dead father out of Oedipal guilt seemed to play a part in his sexual anxieties, the use of his marriage as a fetish seemed more dynamic.

I linked the avenue of trees and the gap with his wife's pubic hair. B. added that the last point reminded him of a further sexual difficulty — as if he felt that Pat's pubic hair was like a coconut mat which he had to get through and felt it to be hard and hurting. And now he thought it was all too late; Pat was near the menopause, her sex was drying up and he was angry he had left it so long, and he felt he had missed so much. I showed B. the confusion between the pubic hair, the vagina, and sexuality that dries up on him and goes hard and dry, and an analyst who takes a holiday, leaving him feeling that the breast internally has dried up and abandoned him, and it is all too late! We can see here the interlinking of oral and genital anxieties and external and internal reality (Gillespie 1964).

B. went on to discuss how he could not tell people he had got married and was frightened about telling me, as if I would feel angry and left out, as if he ought not to have put the marriage before the analysis; almost as if he ought to have married the analyst. It becomes clear how much he has projected his own left-out infantile feelings about the holidays into me, and feels me to be watching, left out, and demanding.

I have brought this material to show, first, the emergence in a split-off, and projected form of B.'s infantile sadistic impulses, particularly oral ones aroused by the holiday, and how, in so far as they are projected into his objects, the object is felt as trapping and garrotting and hard, and that the projection leads to confusion between oral and genital sexuality; a kind of vagina dentata. Second, the woman's body, and the marriage as such, is used as something into which he can project himself to avoid separation and dependence; this also increases the fear of being trapped, and is related to the use of the fetish. Third, I have indicated how his internal objects, particularly here the dried-up and destroyed breast, are projected into the woman, who is then felt to be non-functioning and past repair, menopausal. (Pat was actually about thirty-eight.) This session brought relief, but, as was constant then with B., the relief and sense of being understood unconsciously stimulated feelings of envy, and as he could not allow the goodness to remain, he responded by becoming antagonistic and withdrawn the following day, accompanied by the return of an old oral symptom, nail-biting.

At this stage of the analysis, there was a central element in the dream that we could not clarify. You will recall that, in the dream, the whole execution was focused on the idea of the man having done something bad sexually to the aunt — who was associated to a masculine woman gardener, clearly associated to myself. It looked like some kind of primitive combined figure that had masculine qualities of strength and could sow seeds, and yet was a woman, but what he had done to her sexually we did not understand. I subsequently began to believe that it referred to the question of damaging by the projection of sexuality, but this is a point that I want to investigate further as it emerged, because I believe it to be central to B.'s main problems.

I shall start by looking at B.'s behaviour in the analysis in more detail, and the way in which generally speaking he brought his communications particularly at this period. But, first, a further point. Following the marriage and the summer holidays, that is, after three years of analysis, B. and his wife more or less ceased to have sexual intercourse. I have spoken about B.'s extreme passivity in the sessions; I want to describe this more fully. Usually, after what might be seen by myself as a helpful interpretation, he would go into a very heavy silence, often with deep breathing, then frequently he would slowly emerge from it, making rather trite wordy remarks, so that the whole feeling was flat and verbose; or the silence would go on as if I had to make the next move. Associated to this was a marked negative therapeutic reaction. A good session would usually be followed by a rather silent, empty session or series of sessions, giving the impression that no progress had been made or nothing remained from the good session. The patient was not aware that he had actually done anything to the session. It was clear that in this way my work was kept sterile, the conceptions and connections between sessions being lost, as with his wife, who was very anxious to have babies, but there was no possibility of conceiving as long as there was no sexuality; and when the session, my work, and its contact with the infantile parts of the patient were obliterated, my baby, analytic feeding breast, and creativity were obliterated too. This clearly arose from his envy of the qualities momentarily experienced in myself; they were obliterated and his envy was warded off again (Klein 1957). As I sat through these silent or wordy sessions, I could feel also how another more active process was going on. It was as if B. was intruding into the session the couch, representing myself, as a deadening object paralysing and destroying all life and movement. As we clarified this slowly, there began to be moments when my patient could sometimes feel some vague flickerings of cruel satisfaction as the deadening silence went on.

This then enabled me to make more contact with the destructiveness masked as passivity. Now I want to show how more active sado-masochism also began to emerge, also hidden behind and yet expressed by the passivity. I shall bring a fragment of material, though it is not necessarily convincing, unless I can adequately convey the tone of the transference.

59

On a Monday B. had told an important dream, in which he seemed concerned about his sexual difficulties, or rather sexual passivity and apathy. On the following session, Tuesday, he started with a lot of intellectualization about the previous day, talking around, and I felt we were not in contact. He went on to speak about his difficulties with Pat, how he had been thinking about their sexual difficulties, how he felt they were due to fear, and so on. Last night he was lying by her, stroking her, she said, 'If you go on like that, I shall want to make love', but that was all that happened, he stopped. I showed him that this apparent passivity was going on in the sessions. It seemed to be assumed that I wanted him to get on in the analysis, to use that session to get on with understanding and with his sexuality, as if he were verbally stroking me as he stroked Pat, thus trying to stimulate and frustrate me, to make me want something and to withhold it from me, and that this was all part of his sexual excitement and was going on on the couch. For a moment he seemed to see this, then he was quiet, and started again to intellectualize. He also linked his sexual feelings with trying to prise open a wood-louse, which seemed to me an excellent description of the difficulties I was having in getting anything into him, though I was being very careful not to prise anything open actively at all. I could then show him that we, in the quietest possible manner, were locked in a sado-masochistic relationship, in which I was to be excited and tormented, and that it was far more difficult for him to give up this gratification and have a real relationship with his analytic material and me as a woman and an analyst than to retreat into his heavy silence, his words, and his theories, which I believe are actually being used as the rubber fetish into which he can withdraw from contact.

This type of behaviour became extremely repetitive and we worked through it again and again and could see how the attempt to excite and frustrate, done in a very silent way, this perverse sexualization of the relationship with me, was aimed at destroying understanding, poise, and strength. I began to unravel its history — I knew that B. had felt his father to be disturbed and to have wild outbursts of temper, which I had assumed to be in some way gratifying as well as alarming, which was how he consciously had felt them. But I soon began to feel that it was not only the father's strength that was being undermined, the father as a partner to the mother, but on a part-object level, the strength in the woman, which was in some way being destroyed by being sexualized, instead of being allowed to function quietly and firmly.

I want now to demonstrate this point by bringing some material from the period in which we were working through the problem of B.'s hidden sado-masochism and his attempts at perverting the transference by sexualizing it.

60

B. seemed to be gaining insight, but there was a constant regression into sado-masochistic behaviour or into passivity of a silently provocative type. Thus one day shortly before Christmas, after about three and a half years of analysis, he had been able, as he described it, to 'climb down a bit', in relation to acknowledging understanding, and had reported the following session that subsequently he had felt rather awful, but that he had been able to work better and had felt less tense. I could show him in some detail his actual passivity as an attempt to stimulate me, so as to project into me feelings not only of excitement but that I should want to rouse him into activity, beat him, or be cruel to him (like prising open the wood-louse). This, I by now knew, was the kind of behaviour that in the fetish phantasies and to some extent in the actual acting out of them before he came to analysis, he wanted from prostitutes; for example, to be dressed in rubber, tied, beaten, attacked, and excited in various ways. B. went off again into a general broad talk, roughly appropriate, but, as it were, off at the side of our discussion. I then showed him how he seemed to be attempting to drive me into a state of despair, hopelessness, and madness, as I believe he must have felt he had done with his father, with his terribly violent temper. I reminded him that his usual picture of his boyhood was of his brother being openly rebellious, getting into trouble, and being eaten up with guilt, while B. looked on. Then B. described, in a way he had never done so clearly before, how he and his brother used to mock at the father, making him lose his temper, provoking him until he would storm out of the room. He then described a particular situation, as he put it, 'a very childish thing': he kept playing the same tune on the piano over and over again, until his father was beside himself with rage. I could show him how this was precisely what was going on in the transference. He keeps playing the same tune, repeating old or intellectualized phrases or going off verbally in the same way, in the hope that I shall eventually get terribly worked up and disturbed about it, in the hope that I shall lose my whole paternal strength and poise and therefore collapse. 'A very childish thing!'

The patient went on to describe that after this he and his brother went up into the attic and the father was overcome by a choking attack and looked awful, and the boys laughed and laughed until they were nearly hysterical. I connected up all these points, stressing the gratification and intense sexual excitement in driving the father almost to the brink, and how this was really the situation he was aiming at in the analysis. B. became very uneasy, saying, 'I don't like you saying these things, and now I've got an erection.' This I think is important, because it indicates how this patient was getting not only quiet glee but intense sadistic and masochistic satisfaction and triumph now overtly erotic from this

61

particular type of holding up the analysis. There was, as it were, a perverted negative therapeutic reaction.

But, as I have indicated, I think that behind this destruction of the father's strength by erotization is an attack on the parents as a primitive combined figure — on the strength of the woman, at base on the nipple, as a firm object in the breast. Here I want to remind you first of the very early Hitler dream, with the biting attack on the woman's brains, as an analytic breast, done by the attendant with the proboscis-like object; and, second, to return to the dream of the man being garrotted for having done something bad sexually with the aunt; a masculine type of woman. With hindsight I think that this bad sexual behaviour with the aunt is precisely the destruction of the strength in the woman, her masculine qualities, by the projection of sexual excitement into her, at depth into the woman's feeding quality, the breast.

To clarify this, I shall now go on to the session immediately following the one about driving the father to despair. In this session, B. came with a brief dream.

DREAM

B. was in the kitchen of their old home. He was kissing Pat excitedly, knowing that his mother was outside, and he barred the door with a table, so that she could not come in. There was some additional feeling that if his mother came in she might get involved in the excitement or sexuality.

So here we can clarify the situation. What B. is trying to do is to interpose his sexuality and excitement between himself and a feeding relation to the kitchen-mother; in the transference, myself. By trying, through the way he brings his material, to excite and disturb me, he is misusing the kitchen, breast, and trying to prevent myself from being a quiet, poised, feeding mother; and he knows, in the dream, if the mother comes in, she may get involved in the excitement. I suggested to B. that perhaps yesterday, when he felt so excited and actually had an erection in the session, he felt that I was involved, too, as if I were enjoying interpreting, which was experienced by him as beating him. In all this period I was particularly careful with B. to interpret slowly and undisturbedly and to avoid anything that could be experienced as forcing, hurrying, or trying to get at material. B. replied that what he had particularly got from the whole week was a feeling of my consistency. Be that as it may on a conscious level, as the analysis went on in the next period, the anxieties about involving me or Pat in fetishistic activities became at times very strong.

62

The fear that mother or I might really be involved in his excitement, or Pat in his fetish activities, may in fact be linked with some quality in the mother. It could be that she was actually sexually attracted by him; he has certainly for a long time retained what seemed to him to be an isolated memory from roughly prepuberty of the mother actually touching or holding his penis. If she was sexually stirred by him, it would of course be felt as reinforcing his own phantasies. Certainly one day in the very early part of the analysis, when I agreed to a change in the time of his session, as he had to be away from London on business, and I gave him an evening session, he arrived in a state of quiet high excitement. I was able shortly to sort out that he had more or less consciously believed that I gave him that time because I was actually sexually interested in him, and wanted some kind of non-analytic contact. When the session turned out to be an ordinary session, it was felt by him as a terrible anticlimax; at that moment, therefore, the projection of sexual excitement into me had led the patient into a state of almost delusional conviction.

Returning to the dream in which B. excites one woman, Pat, thus keeping the real mother out of the kitchen, expecting her to become excited, the question arises, how does he in phantasy achieve this in the transference? Here I think it is clearly achieved by the use or misuse of  verbal communication, of words or non-words, silence, as a source of excitement. I have had ample material to show him that words are seen as an extension of his tongue, which he feels he excitedly rubs against the analysis as the breast, hoping to excite it, me, rather than use the interpretations, nipple, and take in their contents. You will recall the first dream that I spoke about, the dream of the duck with its splendid brightly coloured tongue. I visualize an infant who is excitedly rubbing his tongue against his mouth, omnipotently creating the illusion that the tongue is really the nipple, his words are really interpretations, and that this masturbatory excitement is also projected into his objects. In this situation, therefore, he splits the nipple: one part is identified with his tongue, the other is left outside in me — and frustrated. I am not left without a nipple, but with one which he tries to excite and frustrate, which is expressed in the picture of the mother outside the kitchen, or the cruel, excited, phallic woman of the fetish-beating phantasies.

I have discussed here the use of words and silence to excite, sexualize, and thus destroy the strength of the analytic experience, without open active aggression, but as part of, and disguised behind, his passivity. As this was clarified in the analysis and the splitting and projective identification lessened and the aggression and sadism began to be more integrated, guilt and concern started to emerge. The guilt now became attached particularly to B.'s current attacks on the actual analytic work and on insight itself. This meant attacks not only on my good qualities, but on his own mind and its sincerity, and the sexualization process could be seen to be perverting his internal world, his superego, and thus his capacity to experience guilt. I shall try to illustrate the process and how B. attempted again to involve me in it, by bringing a piece of material belonging to roughly the same period.

This session is one where again a great deal seems to hinge on the way in which B. brings his material. It was Monday; he started by describing the weekend: how, because Pat did not have to work, they could stay in bed late, but as there was a phone call from the painter, they could not have sex, just as if he had organized it, and so on.

This kind of remark contains a sort of pseudo-insight, B. half knowing that he had in fact not just organized no sex, but was in the process of organizing me to make a repetitive kind of interpretation or statement about no-sex. I said nothing; he produced a dream.

DREAM

B. was looking at his mother, who was with a man and a monkey or an ape, in a kind of chamber of air, this chamber being on the end of an arm, like the kind of thing you see at a fair. B. must have been on the same level, because he seemed to be looking at them as if through the glass.

I think this pseudo-insight organizing me to make a phoney interpretation is in fact an aping of bringing material to me; that he is this monkey, this ape, who apes the role of bringing himself and me, the mother and the man, together, but he does it for amusement and amuses himself at this fun-fair; it is an analysis for entertainment, and one in which I can get nowhere apparently. On and off in this session he understood this, got into contact and withdrew again, and then told me that he had been to see a play the previous week that had disturbed him immensely. He described that in it there was a policeman questioning a prisoner, the policeman started to kick the prisoner, the prisoner clutched at his knees, and the policeman kicked him away. The prisoner looked up at him and for a second there was a look of horrible complicity in the face of the prisoner. I think that there is no doubt that this is what the patient is becoming aware that he is trying to do with me. There is no question about his complicity, about the intense masochistic gratification that he is trying to gain if he can only feel that I am kicking him around, and his behaviour in the session, contact and withdrawal, is aimed at rousing me in this way. But the notion of policeman and prisoner takes us a step further — namely into his internal world and the relationship between an

64

internal strict analyst—parent and a guilty parent—child, between an aspect of his superego and his ego — and this internal relationship is identical with the relationship that he is still acting out externally. It leads to a type of moral masochism, in which very powerful persecuting guilt is kept at bay by the relationship with his superego and the objects into whom he then projects it, being erotized into a sado-masochistic relationship and beating and excitement thus taking the place of inner guilt (Freud 1924).

But, in addition, this material illustrates another aspect that is connected with splitting and perversion; that is the way in which B. splits off a part of himself and observes what is going on in the session between one part of himself and me. But the observation through glass is a kind of voyeurism, done in order to pervert, ape, and mock. This my patient was starting to know about. At this period he was often able to spot himself in the silence starting to ridicule things that I said, and I began to realize that one of the reasons why he could not bear to notice things about me or my home was his fear of his intense sadistic criticism or ridicule, the fun-fair.

Indeed, one of the ways in which, from one angle, he protects me from his voyeuristic destructive ridicule is to keep my interpretations, and thus his ridicule, at bay, by this wordy talking, so that the talking comes between himself and me, defensively, as a piece of rubber. But it also prevents any real contact and warmth and mutual understanding.

There is another defensive aspect of the fetish which is sometimes brought into the transference and which I should like briefly to illustrate before summarizing. Early in a session a little later in the analysis, B. had been silent. I had the impression again that some unconscious pressure was being exerted silently on me to talk more actively and to bring pressure on B. to speak. This I showed to him and he agreed, adding that he now had feelings of excitement and tickling all over his skin, particularly his legs and round his penis. Then he said he had a powerful phantasy of pulling some rubber garment over his legs and body. Here I could show him what was being acted out: the pseudo-words or silences were being used provocatively to stimulate me into what would be felt as exciting sadistic interpretations; the rubber fetish then enters the session to protect B. from being concretely penetrated by my words.

Summary

I have attempted to make some contribution to the treatment of perversions by bringing material from the analysis of a patient with a rubber fetish. I have tried to show how, behind apparently passive behaviour,

65

it was possible to discover the acting out of sado–masochistic behaviour and a hidden erotization of the transference, and from this to establish some important aspects of the patient's psychopathology. I have stressed especially the splitting and projective identification of sexual excitement, aimed not only to rid the patient of excitement which was too much fused with sadism, but particularly aimed at the destruction of calm and strength in his object, as an analytic feeding breast. This was associated with extreme passivity in his personality and relative impotence in his sexual life. His perversion affected his relationships with his external and internal objects, as well as his sense of truth and guilt, and could only begin to be satisfactorily helped when its main aspects could be located in the transference.

Notes

1 I can, in this paper, only hint briefly at some of the connections between his particular form of projective identification of excitement and certain aspects of the fetish; for example, the defensive use of the fetish as an inanimate object, yet connected with life, into which the patient could project himself totally as a flight from relating to a real and valued human being; or the use of the fetish as an object, into which B. could project his sexual excitement and then have a vivid, controlled, passive sexual experience and thus bypass the terror of relating to an active sexual woman; or the role of the fetish as something with which his object or he himself protected themselves from sadistic attacks.

2 This dream almost certainly also refers to his experiences of the ear operation during latency. These experiences, I believe, would be felt to confirm his phantasies of earlier oral sadism currently being relived in the transference.

4

On passivity and aggression: their interrelationship

This paper was given at the 27th Congress of the International Psychoanalytical Association, Vienna, July 1971, and is here published for the first time.

In this chapter I want to discuss some aspects of aggression in a group of patients whose behaviour in the analysis appears to be strikingly un-aggressive, so that they seem passive and inert — the analyst apparently being expected to carry all responsibility for interest or progress in the analysis. I shall suggest that, in these patients, loss of conscious contact with their aggression is associated with a failure in discovering their own identity, and that their sense of identity and lively activity can only be established if their powerful and self-destructive impulses can be uncovered in the transference, making it possible for them to integrate their aggressivity with the rest of their personality.

In this group there are, of course, variations in type of patient and details of psychopathology. My aim in this brief chapter is to bring forward a few ideas, which I shall illustrate with fragments of material from one, probably fairly typical patient, and then make links with similar problems in different types of passive patients — particularly the very passive perverts and the more schizoid and withdrawn patients, whose passivity is associated with fragmentation of the self.

Patients of the type that I am discussing frequently come to analysis with vague complaints that they are unable to clarify, uncertain about their potentialities and not knowing what to do with their lives or careers. The kind of behaviour one sees in the analysis can be illustrated roughly by my patient A. The patient seems to experience a great need for analysis and attends regularly, yet appears to have little reason for being there. Sessions start with remarks that are diffuse and descriptive, but rarely suggesting that she wants help about any specific difficulty, and almost never is there any reference to previous work done. The material seems superficial, limited, and lacking in free associations. It is often gathered under a closed heading, such as 'I knew it was because I felt jealous' — and the statement comes to a full stop. Sessions are punctuated by long silences in which the analyst may appear to be expected to push, question, or stir the patient into activity. The patient's response to interpretations is usually a long, heavy pause, as if the interpretation had been dropped into a dead silence. She later speaks again, but either to go on to some other topic, giving the impression that in the silence all responses or associations have disappeared, or she speaks quite soon, having picked up the interpretation but on a level at which it was clearly not intended. For example, if the interpretation gathered up facts to show their meaning, the response would be on a factual level, the meaning thus being bypassed. These responses are apparently quiet and unaggressive, and any overt anger or criticism seems absent. This behaviour becomes extremely repetitive, and there appears to be no drive to do anything about it.

A. has been in analysis for just over five years. She is in her early thirties and came into treatment after the breakdown of a disastrous early marriage from which she could not properly free herself. Her confusion about how to deal with this relationship extended into her life generally. She was unable to form satisfactory relationships or join into things wholeheartedly. She felt unsuccessful and inferior to her contemporaries in her achievements. She also mentioned feelings of strain and tension which could be accompanied by physical symptoms such as headaches or difficulty in breathing.

A. is the third of four children, having two older sisters and a younger brother. She always believed that her parents preferred her siblings as being more attractive and interesting, though she was well aware that her brother had considerable difficulties, for which he finally sought analysis. The father, described as a tall, strikingly handsome and intelligent man, runs a successful business in the industrial Midlands. My patient speaks of the mother in a condemning way as dull, complaining, and sad, having little life of her own, living for her family and a drag on her lively and intelligent husband — altogether rather a failure. As the analysis proceeded, the picture of A.'s relationships to her parents began to fill out. She described how her mother could not deal with the children's questions; if she or her brother asked the mother for information the questions would be referred to the father, who always had the answers and seemed to enjoy the situation. According to my patient he did not take his wife's ideas very seriously, or really listen to what she was saying. A. thought that in this and similar ways her father seemed to crush her mother and behave as though he were father and mother. She did not quite like it. It was very distressing to A., early in the analysis, to see how clearly her description of her much-criticized mother could be seen to be also a description of her own self and life. But, however realistic this picture of her external mother, it was certainly a picture of an internal mother, which was constantly projected into myself, now seen as dull, drab, lifeless, living for my work and not only without a husband but without real interests and nothing like as gifted as the male analyst with whom her brother had recently started treatment.

At this point our task seemed to be to sort out A.'s apparent identification with her mother, now emerging as somewhat inactive, unaggressive, probably depressed, rather masochistic and crushed. I am going to show how this identification is the end result of a complex series of checks and balances, silently active aggressions and defences against aggression, that can be seen to be going on in the transference in what emerges as inertia and passivity. I think that the core of the situation is that patients of this type, and A. in particular, cannot tolerate contact with life, equated with activity, in her parents as a couple or in her mother, unconsciously aware that it will arouse grim destructive envy against which she defends herself by a variety of methods, apparently passively. Insight into the problem and guilt about it have been kept at bay by the strength of the identification.

In my patient's behaviour I have described how she seemed to bypass the meaning of interpretations; how she became silent for long periods in a session, and so on. From this it was possible to show her an apparent preference for an analysis that did not succeed and achieved nothing, and how, as interpretations made contact and there was some shift, they would be disregarded or lost, as if any move towards progress would be silently resisted. At the same time I was given so little and such carefully organized material that I too was kept inactive and repetitive — so that A. was projecting her non-aggressive, non-active self into me and thus keeping me paralysed. At this point it became hard to distinguish between a silent passive defence against destroying the analysis and a silently active destructiveness — the balance is very fine and there is a comparable interlocking and balance in the relationship between patient and analyst, reflecting that between infant and mother. A. is unconsciously willing to sacrifice life and development so long as her object, analyst or mother, remains lifeless.

It is only when this identification and the preference for lifelessness or near-death can be demonstrated to the patient that one can begin to discover certain parts of the patient's personality which are more manifestly involved in active aggression, still hidden under the guise of passivity. I could begin to show A. a constant splitting between a part of the self, with which she was more consciously identified, which wanted analysis and health but seemed unable to do anything to achieve it, and another part, which acted as observer, watching and listening to the relation between analyst and the more healthy receptive part of the patient and destroying it silently but actively. It is this observer part which removed the meanings from interpretations, by-passed them, and so on, defeating the analyst and thus depriving the more healthy part. As this was clarified, there were moments when A. began to feel quiet satisfaction, triumph, a fleeting smile, or actual sadistic pleasure momentarily in the analysis, so that her observing could be seen as a kind of sadistic voyeurism. This type of sadistic voyeurism is, I find, of great importance in the analysis of passive perverts, where one is constantly aware that one part of the patient is split off from the rest of the self, watching or listening and mocking at whatever the analyst has said, or is assumed to be going to say, trying to trap the analyst into making useless interpretations and generally sneering at and controlling the relationship between analyst and the potentially more receptive part of the self — thus sadistically blocking any movement in the treatment. In A. this part of the self appears to be acting in identification with the father, listening to the mother with one ear while continuing with his activities and silently mocking at and despising her chatter — my interpretations. The father's 'cleverness' was felt by A. as omnipotent and destructive, and giving no strength or support to the mother, but crushing her.

The type of splitting I have just been describing is supported by a further process. Consciously A. feels that she has come to analysis to get well, but the active wanting, needing part that could grasp for life and progress seems to be missing. This part I believe she in phantasy projects into her objects so that it is the analyst who is unconsciously intended to want to bring pressure on her to get on with things, push her into activity, achieve something, or feel anger, excitement, and frustration. In her environment, friends and relations constantly suggest what she should do and get things going for her. This projection of need and activity into her objects appears to be connected partly with maintaining her own omnipotence and partly with a fear of aggression and excitement associated with activity. But a more detailed understanding of this will, I hope, emerge as the treatment progresses.

At this stage in the analysis, therefore, it would appear that A.'s passivity and inertia were based on specific types of identifications with both parents, most noticeably first with a crushed and masochistic mother. Her unconscious, silent aggressivity was based on a kind of collusive identification with a quietly crushing, omnipotent father. The possibility that he is, in reality, rather crushing also makes it easier for A. to project her destructiveness into him and to lose contact with it. Her

70

passivity is also supported by the projection of her active needs into her objects, and guilt is evaded by her introjecting the crushed mother and living out a failed and depressing life herself.

The situation that I am describing seems to express A.'s method of dealing with her Oedipal jealousy, but she is left not quite admiring and desiring her father. Indeed, because of the use that A. is making of the father, both to carry her own projected destructiveness and silently to collude with his own destructive attitude towards the mother, she largely despises him. In so far as she despises him she mocks at the mother's internal penis that should give strength and support to the mother. Behind this Oedipal situation, however, is an earlier situation that has gone wrong. It seems from her paralysing of me in the transference and her refusal to allow me strength and life that there is a deep, envious hatred of the mother and her potentially good, strong maternal qualities, which is evaded by keeping everything static and preventing any creative, dependent, or enjoyable analytic feeding relationship being established between us externally or internally. Earlier I spoke of the observer part depriving the more healthy and receptive part of the patient of proper analysis. I am suggesting, and hope to show in later material, that this more receptive part is really an infantile aspect of the patient that is being deprived of proper care and feeding in the transference.

When the analysis had proceeded far enough to lessen the paralysis and diminish the splitting and projective identification, life began to creep into the patient's feelings and contact in the transference, and then we could start to see something of the nature and intensity of the anxieties that were ordinarily being kept at bay. For example, in one session when she had been in analysis for about two and a half years, A. began to reminisce about a time when she was sharing a flat with a girl friend, who had her boy friend with her, and how she listened to what was going on, it was awful! In the context of the session it was possible to demonstrate that she was not just talking about triangular Oedipal jealousy of the external and internal parents, but, also, behind this, about one part of herself that was increasingly becoming aware of listening to an analytic intercourse going on between another part of herself and me, and resenting and trying to silence it. She ended the session with some rather trite intellectual pseudo-interpretations.

The following day, Friday, she arrived in a state of considerable anxiety, after an awful, sleepless night. She had had a feeling of terrible panic accompanied by a difficulty in getting her breath; she was in a panic about dying, or wanted to die in the night. She had had a dream, *in which she went to the office, where she was currently doing market research, but it was about Irish independence. She had to interview an Irishwoman who was*

71

carrying a baby in her arms, but as she saw them they exploded. She woke with great anxiety.

A. gave few associations but did refer to the previous session and to her research. The dream was about the time of the bombing and riots in Ireland. I reminded her that in the previous session we had been discussing the voyeuristic part that cannot bear to look on and see a part of herself having some kind of intercourse on any level with myself. This insight had enabled her to see me more as an independent mother concerned with and carrying her baby self, and independent as a woman with a weekend and holidays approaching. It also meant my being independent in the sense of not being dependent on her intellectualizations for my interpretations — on her as a clever little penis, like the intellectual father. But when she could no longer avoid being in contact with this independent analyst something exploded in her, and wiped out this picture and the contact with myself and herself as the baby.

A. started to describe the experience of the panic — that she felt blocked as if unable to breathe and almost wanting to die, but the inability to breathe itself seemed to make a block inside her chest. I suggested that she was describing two separate aspects of the blocking; the one is a renewed attempt to block this internal mother and baby, so that it is locked and imprisoned inside and not independent, but when, thanks to the analytic work and her own progress, the imprisoning and blocking lessens and she begins to see me as independent, she explodes and fragments me. The experience of the explosion and fragmentation is reflected in the breathing difficulty; but her attempt to contain and collect up the fragmentation is again experienced as a blocking, so that no to-and-fro breathing is possible. When she explodes, she explodes her own self and her experiences and perceptions but then she panics, feeling that she is falling to bits and going mad. These interpretations gave her relief, and she felt understood when we were able to link the panic and the feeling of madness with the fragmentation of the self and her wish for and yet fear of death.

I am stressing here the attack on the object, when it is seen as independent, and also the attack on the self so that the self that sees and experiences is fragmented, as Bion describes, and the patient is therefore rendered almost completely passive because fragmented. In addition, this fragmentation of self-observation must be linked with her fear of its sadistic qualities, as I indicated in the discussion on her sadistic voyeurism, and thus her capacity for normal self-observation is constantly interfered with. The importance of this aspect could be seen during the next two sessions when dreams and associations concerned a man, clearly representing herself, who did not want to give information and who was blind; and herself waking in a dream in a panic when a door seemed to open and let in light. It seems that it is of paramount importance to A. that she should remain silent, blind, and in the dark, rather than see, know, and experience her own self and her own alive, internal and external world.

In the period immediately after these sessions we could sort out more about the activities of the critical and destructive part of her personality, which began to emerge in dreams, associations, and behaviour as destroying, as 'cock-teasing' and as perversely exciting itself anally by holding back faeces, nearly letting them go and drawing them back again. This was her actual lavatory behaviour as well as her perverse verbal behaviour in the transference, half-mentioning topics, leaving them, avoiding giving me full material, but rather, little hard fragments of words and quasi-interpretations. This perverse anal quality is also very similar to the behaviour of the passive pervert who attempts silently to turn the transference into a teasing, holding back, anal, sadistic torment. But subsequently A. also began sometimes to be more aware of and more identified with a part of herself that valued warmth, understanding, and help, and she felt temporarily more alive.

I have brought this material to show A.'s passivity in the analysis, seemingly based on an identification with a passively suffering, crushed mother, where at first the identification seemed impenetrable. On further analysis, it could be seen that a paralysed, deadened relationship was the only one the patient felt able to tolerate. Then we could clarify some of the splitting that was going on in the analytic situation and the nature of her projective identifications, and see that the destruction and deadening was really going on actively though silently in the session. When the patient came up against jealousy and envy aroused by experiencing life and progress, she turned on herself and fragmented herself along with her object, thus destroying the experience and her experiencing self, even though this behaviour bore the stamp of psychosis.

The type of fragmentation which I have described in A., done under considerable stress and destroying the experiencing part of the self, is, I find, of very great importance in keeping up a deadened type of passivity in a group of very schizoid, withdrawn, apathetic patients. These patients constantly explode or dissipate in various ways interpretations, emotions, and ideas, thus keeping the whole analysis empty and flat and preserving a chronic state of passivity and inertia.

Summary

I have described a patient belonging to a group of patients whose behaviour in the analysis seems passive and inert, whose lives and personalities seem empty. I have suggested that these patients' passivity is in fact not only defensive but very destructive, and that only if their aggression can be rediscovered, in its various silent manifestations in the transference, can it be worked through and re-integrated with the rest of the personality to give them the possibility of some real sense of activity and identity. In addition, I have briefly tried to link the passivity of this type with two other types of markedly passive patients, in one of which passivity is predominantly associated with perversion and in the other, of a more psychotic type, with constant fragmentation of the self.

5

The patient who is difficult to reach

This paper was first published in P. L. Giovacchini (ed.) *Tactics and Techniques in Psychoanalytic Therapy*, vol. 2, *Countertransference*, New York: Jason Aronson (1975): 205–16; and appears in E. Bott Spillius (ed.) *Melanie Klein Today*, vol. 2, *Mainly Practice*, London: Routledge (1988), 48–60.

In this chapter I intend to concentrate on some problems of technique, focusing on a particular group of patients, very diverse in their psychopathology, but presenting in analysis one main point in common. It is very difficult to reach them with interpretations and therefore to give them real emotional understanding. My aim is to discuss some manifestations of the problem and some technical issues that arise in handling this type of case. I shall not attempt to make a study of the psychopathology of these patients.

In the treatment of such cases I believe we can observe a splitting within the personality, so that one part of the ego is kept at a distance from the analyst and the analytic work. Sometimes this is difficult to see since the patient may appear to be working and co-operating with the analyst, but the part of the personality that is available is actually keeping another more needy or potentially responsive and receptive part split off. Sometimes the split takes the form of one part of the ego standing aside as if observing all that is going on between the analyst and the other part of the patient and destructively preventing real contact being made, using various methods of avoidance and evasion. Sometimes large parts of the ego temporarily seem to disappear in the analysis with resultant apathy or extreme passivity — often associated with the powerful use of projective identification.

It follows from what I am discussing that for long periods in the treatment of these patients the main aim of the analysis is to find a way of getting into touch with the patient's needs and anxiety in such a way as to make more of the personality available and eventually to bring about a greater integration of the ego. I find that with these rather unreachable

75

patients it is often more important to focus one's attention on the patient's method of communication, the actual way in which he speaks and the way in which he reacts to the analyst's interpretations rather than to concentrate primarily on the content of what he says. In other words, I am going to suggest that we have to recognize that these patients, even when they are quite verbal, are in fact doing a great deal of acting, sometimes in speech itself, and our technique has constantly to take account of this.

I want first to examine this problem of the unreachable patient by considering the nature of the splitting in those patients who seem apparently highly co-operative and adult — but in whom this co-operation is a pseudo-cooperation aimed at keeping the analyst away from the really unknown and more needy infantile parts of the self. In the literature this problem has been discussed by such people as Deutsch (1942) with the as-if personality, Winnicott (1960) with the false self, Meltzer (1966) with his work on pseudo-maturity, and Rosenfeld (1964) with the splitting off of the dependent parts of the self in narcissistic patients.

In psychoanalytic discussions on technique, stress has frequently been laid on the importance of a working or therapeutic alliance between analyst and patient. What impresses one early in the treatment of this group of unreachable patients is that what looks like a therapeutic alliance turns out to be inimical to a real alliance, and that what is termed understanding is actually anti-understanding. Many of these patients tend to respond quickly to interpretations or to discuss in a very sensible way previous interpretations, using such expressions as 'do you mean', referring to previous dreams and the like and seeming eminently co-operative and helpful. One finds oneself in a situation that looks exactly like an on-going analysis with understanding, apparent contact, appreciation, and even reported improvement. And yet, one has a feeling of hollowness. If one considers one's countertransference it may seem all a bit too easy, pleasant, and unconflicted, or signs of conflict emerge but are somehow quickly dissipated.

One may find oneself presented with specific problems that a patient wishes to consider: Why did he respond in such and such a way to such and such a situation? The patient makes suggestions, but free associations are conspicuously absent. The analyst finds him or herself working very hard intellectually to understand what is being asked of him, and may begin to feel he is involved in some kind of analytic guessing game. Here we can see one of the types of splitting of the ego I am discussing. The patient talks in an adult way, but relates to the analyst only as an equal, or a near-equal disciple. Sometimes he relates more as a slightly superior ally who tries to help the analyst in his work, with suggestions or minor corrections or references to personal history. If one observes carefully one begins to feel that one is talking to this ally *about* a patient — but never talking *to* the patient. The 'patient' part of the patient seems to remain split off, and it is this part which seems more immediately to need help, to be more infantlike, more dependent and vulnerable. One can talk about this part but the problem is to reach it. I believe that in some of our analyses, which appear repetitive and interminable, we have to examine whether we are not being drawn into colluding with the pseudo-adult or pseudo-cooperative part of the patient.

This type of split can be found in different kinds of patients and may be maintained for different reasons, connected, for example, with unconscious anxiety about infantile feelings, or feelings of dependence, intense, but usually warded-off, rivalry and envy of parental figures, difficulties concerning separateness, and so on. As I have mentioned, I do not want to discuss this aspect of the work, since my principal aim is to look at the technical side.

I shall start with brief material from a patient with a rigid, controlled, and anxious personality, who consciously wants help, but unconsciously struggled against getting it by the use of the kind of splitting I am describing, and whose communications could, in part, be viewed as acting out in the transference. It is, of course, extremely difficult in reporting fragments of case material to convey this acting out, which after all one mainly intuits from the effect that the patient's words produce on oneself and the atmosphere that is created.

This patient, whom I shall call A., was a young teacher. He came into analysis when he was in his early twenties. He was married and had a young baby. He had already read a certain amount of analytic literature. When he had been in analysis over three and a half years and when we had done considerable work on his manic controlling, he started a session saying that he wanted to talk about his problems about clearing out his cupboards. He was spending so much time on them. He described how he had got to clearing things out and how he did not seem to want to stop. This was put forward as if it were a problem with which he needed help. He added that, in fact, he really did not want to go to visit friends in the evening because he wanted to go on with his clearing out.

He paused as if he expected something from me. I had the strong impression that I was expected to say something about his clearing out his mind or something rather pat, so I waited. He added that, anyway, he did not really like going to these people in the evening, because the last time they went the husband was rude. He had turned to watch the TV while my patient and his wife were there and subsequently made dictatorial statements about children's school difficulties. I suggested to him that I got the impression that he had been waiting for me to make some pseudo-Kleinian interpretations about the clearing out of his mind and inner world, and when I did not, I became the rude husband who watched my own TV and was somewhat dictatorial in my views as to what his difficulties were, that is to say, I did not refer to his preconceived remarks. In other words, I considered his preoccupation with cupboards a type of acting out designed to keep our work sterile and to avoid new understanding. At first he was angry and upset, but later in the session he was able to gain some understanding about his touchiness. He also got further insight momentarily into his competitive controlling.

The following day he said that he felt much better and had had a dream. *He dreamed that he and his wife were in a holiday cottage. They were about to leave and were packing things in the car but for some reason he was packing the car farther down the lane, as if he were too modest to bring it to the front door or the lane was too muddy and narrow. This was unclear. Then he was in a market getting food to take home, which was odd: Why should he take food if he were going home? He was choosing some carrots – either he could take Dutch ones which were twisted or some better French ones which were young and straight, possibly slightly more expensive. He chose the Dutch twisted ones and his wife queried why he did so.*

His associations led to plans for the holidays at a house they were thinking of taking, and to his preference for France over Holland. Carrots led to his memory of the advertisements during the war of carrots as good cheap food and a help against night blindness.

Briefly I suggested that his pseudo-modesty about bringing the car to the door was really linked with the fact that he was not too keen that I should see what he packed inside, following the feeling of having been helped the day before. But now we could see that his attempts on the previous day to force me to interpret in a particular way, as well as the understanding he had gained about it, had become linked with attempts to pack my interpretations inside himself, not to use for himself but for other purposes, as, for example, to use for a lecture which he was actually giving that evening. This then becomes food which he himself buys to take home, not food he gets from home-analysis. He chooses carrots which should help his night blindness, which should give him insight, but what he actually selects are the twisted ones. This would suggest that part of him has insight into his tendency to twist and misuse material — the false interpretations he tried to get from me — and avoid the clear, direct contact with firm, straight, fresh, and new carrots — that is, non-text-book interpretations. This insight is not yet felt but is projected into his wife, who queries why he has to do things in this wrong way.

The patient tries to manipulate me into making false and useless interpretations which could then keep me away from contacting anything new and unknown and thus from contacting the part that wants real understanding. The pseudo-cooperative part of the patient therefore clearly works against real emotional understanding. When I did not collude, his anger is described in terms of the anger towards the man who watched TV. Then the dream shows partial insight into the work of the day before. It clarifies the way in which he packs the interpretations into himself secretly, the car up the lane, rather than uses them to help the needy part of himself. This needy part is kept at bay, and from the carrot material we can see it needs feeding.

In this type of situation I like to be certain that each step is clarified with the patient in relation to the immediate material and not left at a symbolic or quasi-symbolic level. Here we clarified the nature of the twist, that is, the falsification of interpretations, the link between interpretations and insight — night blindness. The interpretations are clearly felt as potentially good food, but food that can be used, taken in wrongly, and then emerge twisted. One might then postulate that the twisted carrots stand for the nipples taken in in a twisted way but I would not wish to take that step until the intermediary material has been worked through.

In considering this type of problem I am stressing how often the pseudo-cooperative part of the patient prevents the really needy part from getting into contact with the analyst, and that if we are taken in by this we cannot effect a change in our patients because we do not make contact with the part that needs *the experience of being understood, as opposed to 'getting' understanding*. The transference situation gives us the opportunity to see these different conflicting parts of the personality in action.

I have been stressing, with the unreachable patient, the importance of locating the splitting in the ego and clarifying the activities of the different parts. In many of these patients one part seems to stand aside from the rest of the personality, observing minutely what is going on between the analyst and the rest of the patient, listening to the tone of the voice of the analyst and sensitive to changes real or assumed. The patient is sensitive, for example, to any indication in the analyst of anxiety, pleasure at achievement, frustration at non-progress, and so on.

Thus, it becomes very important to sort out and make contact with these listening and watching parts of the patient; they contain potentially important ego functions of observation, sensitivity, and criticism, but so long as they are being used to ward off the analyst and keep other parts of the self at bay they cannot be healthily available to the patient. The patient may have felt that he observed something in the analyst and may have, to some extent, exploited it. Thus a patient may think that he spotted anxiety in the analyst's voice, and may become excited and triumphant, using the resultant criticism of the analyst to avoid understanding interpretations. In such situations I find it imperative for the analyst to wait, work slowly, carry the patient's criticism, and to avoid any interpretations suggesting that the trouble lies in projections of the patient's anxiety. It is important to show, primarily, the use the patient has made of what he believed to be going on in the analyst's mind. Sometimes we can see the listening or observing part of the patient emerging clearly as a perverse part, which uses interpretive work for purposes of perverse excitement. These patients provocatively 'misunderstand' interpretations, take words out of context, and attempt to disturb or arouse the analyst.

I think that in all these apparently perverse situations there is some degree of splitting going on and that we have both to be aware of the intense acting out in the transference to which we are supposed to respond by acting out towards our patients, and to be aware that somewhere, split off, there is a part of the patient in need. This part may for a long time be beyond reach in the analysis, but if the analyst is aware that it exists, as well as being aware of the violent acting out of the perverse part, his capacity for tolerating without acting out in response is likely to be very much increased. I now wish to discuss further this split–off, observing part and the nature of its activities by bringing material from an apparently different type of patient. But I want to show how here, too, one part of the patient acts as an observer, keeps an eye on the relationship between the rest of the patient and the analyst, and uses evasive techniques.

I have in mind a young woman, whom I shall call B., who was particularly impervious to interpretations. She was touchy, angry, and miserable, constantly blamed the world, and felt hopeless about herself. Consciously, she felt very inferior. She seemed hardly able to take in anything I said and frequently became excessively sleepy after I had spoken.

If she retained what I said it seemed to consist of isolated words with little meaning to her. Often she seemed actually to misunderstand or to become confused. Usually she talked with a quiet shout in her voice. It became increasingly clear that it was futile for me to try to interpret the *content* of what she told me. I assumed that fragmentation occurred whenever anxiety was beginning to be felt. I also had the impression that a part of her was *actively* breaking up interpretations and preventing contact with a more sanely receptive part of herself.

Then I began to notice many references to her boy friend and how she would watch him speaking with interest to another girl. Then she would become consumed with rage. This type of situation began to emerge in dreams. For example, she had dreams of having a row with her boy friend because of his interest in another girl. I commented that the dream situation was being lived out in the analysis.

If something really got through in a session and she felt I was able in a lively and alert way to talk to a part of herself that was interested and in contact, another part of herself immediately felt left out, not really jealous but terribly envious that I did the talking and part of her had actually been listening. The onlooker part became wild and reacted with fury. I believe it was this latter part that enviously could not bear me to make contact with her. It defensively shouted and kept me at bay and then felt attacked. One day, she brought *a dream in which she was watching her mother bathing a baby, but the mother could not cope. The baby kept slipping out of her hands like a slippery fish. Then it was lying face up under the water, almost drowning. My patient then tried to give the mother some help.* It was difficult to convey exactly the way the dream was told — but it stressed the mother's stupidity and ineptness and her need for my patient's help.

I interpreted her self-destructive slipperiness and how the infant in her kept, like a slippery fish, evading being firmly held and explosively shouted so as to make it impossible to hold an interpretation or a bit of understanding. I pointed out that she wanted to make me a poor, inferior, inadequate mother. As I interpreted her further slipperiness bit by bit she stressed that there was a part of herself that was perfectly capable of helping her mother—analyst to hold her and to hold interpretations in herself. This shift was very important, since the problem with the unreachable patient is that one ordinarily has no proper ally. It also interests me as a point of technique that, as a patient gains understanding, aspects of a dream may emerge, a dream which seems to have become part of the current session. If this happens, I believe it is an indication of movement within the session — that is to say, a readjustment between different parts of the personality in a more integrated and constructive way.

Although B. is in almost every respect different from the young teacher A., from the point of view of the difficulty of reaching him there are important similarities. Thus the observing part in B., which we could see in the dreams of jealousy of the boy friend, becomes slippery and evasive. In A. there is a different type of evasiveness, pseudo-co-operation. However, the slippery fish is not so different from the twisted carrot. In both patients one can sometimes find a part capable of responsiveness and contact. In A. this contact can often be quickly established, whereas in B. the enviously watchful aspect of the personality prohibits meaningful communication. It is striking how this watchfulness can confuse and disrupt the patient so that B. almost seems dull and stupid, which I very much doubt. The watching part shows itself to be very quick and terribly destructive and self-destructive. It has a perverse quality.

I want now to consider another method of achieving unreachability, where again the part of the ego that we need to work with us gets split off, and in addition becomes particularly unavailable because of being projected into objects. This type of projective identification was, of course, described as long ago as 1946 by Melanie Klein in 'Notes on some schizoid mechanisms'. In some cases, when real progress has been made, insight has been gained, and, for example, omnipotence has lessened and more warmth and contact have been established, one finds all further progress blocked by a markedly increased, apparently intractable passivity. The patient seems to become apathetic, to lose contact, interest, and any involvement in the work which we may believe to be going on. He does not appear to be actively uncooperative, just helplessly passive. One often gets the impression following an interpretation that everything has gone dead and flat and at the same time that nothing will happen unless one does say something. This is often true. The patient remains quiet or subsequently comes up with a very superficial remark. Then slowly one has the sensation of mounting tension, as if the analyst ought to do or say something, or nothing will ever be achieved. It then feels as though one ought to bring pressure to bear on the patient to talk or respond.

These situations I find extremely instructive. If one does talk because of this kind of silent pressure, without realizing what is going on, nearly always the session gets going but becomes superficial or repetitive or acquires a kind of superego flavour. If one then examines the experience one can often find that the patient appears to have *projected the active, interested, or concerned part of the self into the analyst, who is then supposed to act out, feeling the pressure, the need to be active and the desire to get something achieved.* Technically I think that the first step is for the analyst to be aware of the projective identification taking place and to be willing to carry it long enough to experience the missing part of the patient. *Then it may become possible to interpret without a sense of pressure, about the process being acted out, rather than about the content of whatever may have been under discussion before.*

I have frequently watched this kind of process going on in a very passive patient with a rubber fetish, whom I shall call C. In him I began to see the continual retreat to a kind of balance that he established, in which a weakly pseudo-cooperative self talked to me, but the emotional part remained unavailable. Repeatedly we experienced a sequence in which within one session he made progress, became deeply involved and moved by what was going on, but the following day it was a mere flat memory. Then I would find him talking in a bland way, very superficially: 'Yes, I remember the session, it is fully in my mind,' then nothing, or perhaps a remark of a slightly provocative type, such as that despite the session things were not going too well with his wife. I then felt as though I really ought to spur him into activity and understanding, and that if I would do so he would be perfectly willing to think and remember and get going again. I believe that he had split off his capacity for activity, concern, and active distress about his condition and projected this into me. As a result of his projection, I felt that he would be able to move and to make contact and use his insight if only I would take the initiative.

However, this is exactly the major part of his problem — that is, his hatred of really making contact with the loving, concerned, and very needy part of the self and bringing it into relation to anyone enough to move physically or emotionally towards them from inside himself. If I push him — however analytically discreetly — he has won, and lost. By my pushing I would confirm that no object is good or desirable enough to attract him sufficiently for him to seek it out and involve himself with it, and therefore that part of the self that can take initiative remains unreachable. Next, I want to look at another aspect of this patient's passivity, also based on splitting and projective identification, of a different type, which manifested itself unobtrusively in a type of acting out in the transference and thus threw light on the way he kept part of himself out of contact.

C. was at this time feeling insecure about the progress of the treatment, being very much aware of its length and feeling rather hopeless and impotent. This type of depression and open anxiety was unusual. During a session he was able to understand a point that I had been making. Then he realized that although the understanding seemed helpful to him, he had become quiet. I commented on the feeling of his having made a sudden shift to passivity. C. then started to speak, and explained that he felt 'pulled inside' and as if I would now expect him to speak, to 'perform', and he felt he could not. I was then able to show him that he had felt understood, but this experience of being understood was concretely experienced as if he were being drawn into the understanding, as into my inside, and then frightened that I was going to expect him to pull outside and to talk, 'to perform'.

Subsequently he added that he felt as if he were in a box lying on his side looking outwards, but into the darkness. The box was closed round him. After a few minutes he started to talk about 'something else'. At a dinner party the other night he had met a woman colleague. She was wearing a very lovely dress; he had congratulated her on it; it had three, horizontal eye-shaped slits near the top — if only he had had three eyes and could have looked out of all three at once. It was almost the end of the session, and I commented that what he wanted now was to get completely inside me through the slits with his eyes, with his whole self, totally inside me and remain there, as in the box. I also added that from the way he spoke he was conveying a very urgent need to make me aware of the importance of his desire to be shut away inside.

When he arrived the following day he commented that the end of the previous session had touched him deeply, but afterwards he had felt as though I had caught him in some guilty secret. I suggested that he had experienced my interpretation of his intense desire to be inside via the slits in the dress, as actually encouraging him to project himself into my inside, and that 'understanding' had then been experienced as my doing something exciting and illicit with him. He had therefore been unable to integrate this understanding. It had a concrete quality and had become comparable to his rubber fetish — he could get inside the fetish, nowadays in phantasy only, in such a way as to pull away from relating to me and from maintaining real understanding and communicating with a real person. So one could follow the movement of the session from real understanding and direct contact between analyst and the more responsive parts of the patient to a flight into a concretely experienced inanimate object, which again rendered him passive and withdrawn and largely unable to be reached.

These examples from C. illustrate the living out in the transference of some mechanisms which he used to achieve unreachability. They have certain similarities with those used by the other patients I have discussed. They are based on a splitting off of the responsive part of the patient, but are more clearly associated with projective identification. In the first example, the actively alert, needy, and contacting part is projected into me so that I should bring pressure on him; in the other, the responsive part, which came very much to the fore in the session, was concretely projected into me or my 'understanding' and there became unavailable. Then the situation became sexualized; this made real understanding unavailable.

As a final example of a similar but slightly different mechanism of achieving unreachability and non-understanding, I want to bring material to show a type of splitting and projective identification going on in the session which enabled the patient to get absorbed into — that is to say, project part of himself into — his own thought processes and phantasies, leaving me in contact with only a pseudo-understanding part of the self and therefore unable to give him real understanding. I want to illustrate the technical importance of looking not only at the content but also at the way in which the material emerges. The patient's behaviour and the movement of the material in the session may reveal which parts of the ego have disappeared and where we might look for them.

This fragment of material comes from patient A., whom I described first in this chapter. He had always tended to become absorbed in day-dreams. He came one Monday with *a dream about people being stuck in quicksand in a cave. There was some urgency about rescuing them, but while the patient was fussing around looking for long boards, another man came and quickly helped.* A. then went on to talk about having been absorbed in sexual phantasies over the weekend, but nevertheless feeling more in contact with what had been going on in the analysis. I interpreted that the phantasies seemed to be quicksand in which he tended to get stuck. He told about a phantasy of his childhood, of which he had spoken before, of looking at a cow or horse from behind, watching the anus and thinking of getting inside with only his head sticking out. He also spoke about some excitement in watching animals defecate. I, probably mistakenly (I shall come back to this), discussed how getting into his phantasies was like getting into the animal's body, and I linked this with his mother's body and with his putting his fingers up his own anus. He then had many phantasies about babies being born. I could show him that he was proliferating phantasies in this session and getting absorbed into them, and this became his stuck state, like quicksand, so that instead of trying to understand and examine what had happened he was getting more and more absorbed and trying to pull me in with him. This he understood.

Next, he talked about the summer holidays. He and his wife were exchanging houses with some people from abroad. The other people had sent photos, but he had no photos of his house taken from the outside. I interpreted that as he gets absorbed in his phantasies, like the quicksand, they enable him not to have to see the outside, not to recognize separateness from me or an actual relationship with me, not to have to visualize me as really existing as an analyst in the room or away over the weekend. As I discussed this he became increasingly uncomfortable, suggesting that interpretations which brought him into contact with the analyst and the outside world were disturbing.

I think that it is probable that I made a technical error in interpreting the cow phantasy too fully, or rather prematurely, in terms of the mother's body, and that this encouraged my patient unconsciously to feel that he was actually succeeding in pulling me into his exciting phantasy world and thus encouraged him to proliferate his phantasies about babies being born. It might have been better to have kept more on the preconscious level until he was really in contact with me and my understanding, and only later to have linked the phantasy about cows and the dream about caves with the pull towards the inside of the mother's body.

It is also interesting to compare this material of A. with the previous material quoted about C., since in both the projection of part of the self into an object can be seen: in C., the projection into 'understanding' concretely experienced, and in B., the absorption into phantasies felt as quicksand. In both patients, contact with the external world or with internal reality, and the experience of separateness and relationship with an object, are largely avoided and the patients become temporarily unavailable to interpretive work or real understanding. I have brought this material not only to show this aspect of unreachability but to highlight the importance of considering the way the material is presented as opposed to concentrating primarily on its content or symbolism.

Before concluding, I should like to expand a few of the technical points that I have touched upon in this chapter. The first concerns the nature of the transference situation. I have been stressing the importance of the way in which the material comes into the session and how this enables us to understand the subtle nature of the patient's acting out in the transference and thus to tease out different parts of the ego and their interaction. Throughout the history of psychoanalysis the need for an uncontaminated transference has been stressed. This is, I believe, of particular importance if we are trying to understand the rather unobtrusive type of acting out that I am describing. I have given examples of a patient unconsciously trying to manipulate me into pressing him into action, or a patient trying to convince me to join him in a pseudo-analytic discussion. *If we allow ourselves to be manipulated in this way, the transference situation becomes blurred, and then we are cut off from parts of the ego with which we need to make contact.*

We also then make it extremely difficult to see the shifts and movements of the patient's defences and parts of the personality as they emerge, alter, or disappear in our consulting room. In a sense, our ability to remain constant and unaltered in the face of these movements has been much emphasized recently, particularly following the work on projective identification of Melanie Klein (1946), and then of Bion (1962), Rosenfeld (1964), and others concerning the need of the analyst to be able to contain the patient's projections. The kind of acting out and the projective identification of parts of the ego that I am discussing can very easily pass unnoticed and bring a very subtle type of *pressure on the analyst to live out a part of the patient's self instead of analysing it.*

Associated with this type of acting out in the transference another technical issue arises — this is, the need for the analyst to keep interpretations in constant contact with what is going on in the session, since we are trying, with these unreachable patients, to observe whether our interpretations are really able to make contact or whether they are being held up or in some way evaded. I think we shall only succeed if our interpretations are *immediate* and direct. Except very near a reasonably successful termination, if I find myself giving an interpretation based on events other than those occurring at the moment during the session, I usually assume that I am not in proper contact with the part of the patient that needs to be understood, or that I am talking more to myself than to the patient.

Useful understanding usually comes from an interpretation of events that are immediate. If it is too far from the actual experience going on in the room, it leads only to verbal understanding of theory. Patients capable of considerable ego integration and of good, whole object relationships may at times be able to integrate interpretations based on putting together previous material. But the kind of patients I am concerned with in this chapter are using much more schizoid mechanisms and are communicating much more concretely by acting out in the transference — even though with apparent verbal sophistication. We must pay constant attention to this in considering our technique.

6

Towards the experiencing of psychic pain

This paper was first read to a conference of English-speaking analysts of European societies in London in October 1976, and was first published in 1981 in J. S. Grotstein (ed.) *Do I Dare Disturb the Universe? A Memorial to Wilfred R. Bion*, Beverly Hills, CA: Caesura Press, 92–102.

'People exist who are so intolerant of pain or frustration (or in whom pain or frustration is so intolerable) that they feel the pain but will not suffer it and so cannot be said to discover it ... the patient who will not suffer pain fails to "suffer" pleasure' (Bion, 1970, p. 9). This description of Bion's is central to my thinking in this chapter. I want to describe a type of movement and a type of pain that I think is experienced at periods of transition between feeling pain and suffering it — a borderline situation. Some of our patients describe to us a certain type of pain which is, from their point of view, indefinable. The quality or nature of the pain is not comprehensible to them and they often feel that they cannot convey the experience to the analyst. It may appear to be almost physical, it may be connected with a sense of loss, but it is not what we would define as depression: it may contain feelings of anxiety, but it cannot just be seen as a sense of anxiety. It is, as our patients point out to us, 'pain'. It is this apparently indefinable phenomenon that I want to discuss here.

I am thus trying to describe a type of pain that emerges, I think, at moments when there is an important shift in the balance maintained by the personality — a shift and alteration of the state of mind, which can in some cases even be the precipitating factor that finally brings the patient into analysis. In others this shift is part of the analytic process, and if it can be resolved, can be a very positive step in terms of progress and integration. It is interesting to see how frequently it is felt to be almost physical, the patient locating it often in the lower part of the chest, and yet he or she knows clearly that he is not describing a physical condition; it is not hypochondriacal or psychosomatic, it is known to be

88

mental. It is experienced as on the border between mental and physical. This type of psychic pain is, I believe, in many ways a borderline phenomenon, as I shall discuss again later.

Since the type of pain I am discussing is associated with a loss of a particular state of mind and psychological balance, I first want to consider the nature of this state. I have suggested that the pain is not just anxiety, not just depression. I shall indicate that it is linked with a greater awareness of the self and of the reality of other people, thus that it is linked with a sense of separateness, but it is not just these concepts that I am talking about — I want to explore the experience and the qualities involved. I think that it emerges in patients who, though in many ways living apparently satisfactory lives, have important areas of psychotic anxieties and whose defences have been operating comparatively successfully. They have to some extent achieved peace and freedom from conflict by the use of particular types of relationships with objects, which protect them from realistic emotional experiences. Basically I am describing an aspect of what Melanie Klein subsumes under the heading of 'projective identification'. When this type of pathological tie breaks down, what they experience is new and unknown and is what they, and I here, are calling 'pain'. In the earlier stages of the analysis of such patients, anxiety and persecutory feelings are strong when these defences are felt to be threatened; as they are further analysed and progress is made, then I think the experience changes from anxiety to 'pain'. This movement I shall refer to again later.

According to my experience, this kind of pain can arise, however, not only during analysis, as part of the analytic process, when we would expect it to be a gradual and slowly integrated process, but it can also arise outside analysis, and, indeed, as I have suggested, can be the thing that may finally bring a patient into treatment — when, for example, a particular type of relationship with an object alters and disturbs a previously held balance, then it is usually felt to be much more traumatic and violent.

The methods which such patients have been using to maintain their balance show considerable variety — but they have in common the employment of their important objects to contain parts of the self. This is sometimes achieved in a fairly total way, as with perverts who project themselves mentally or bodily into fetish objects like a rubber suit or a woman's body and thus keep free from anxiety and relating: it is sometimes achieved in a powerful but more limited way as when large parts of the self are projected into other people and not experienced as belonging to the self. Sometimes the process becomes more obvious to the analyst, as the patient having built up a whole delusional system involving specific areas of his life. For example, a patient will project parts of the self into the analyst in such a way that he perceives the analyst as being almost the same as himself in life or in personality, the patient's own difficulties usually being ascribed to the analyst with little or no insight, and the analyst being seen as living a life which is very similar to his own — as, for example, isolated, friendless, or liking the same kind of things. This may carry a conviction of a very close or intimate relationship with the analyst in the present or in the future. It means that there is no real relating, no differentiation.

In such patients, in the early period of the analysis, holidays and gaps can be non-experienced up to a point, because such patients retreat into their world and keep up a type of internal euphoric relationship with the analyst, which is quite different from an internal relationship based on the introjection of an object who has been experienced as physically real and valued, loved, or hated. And we have to distinguish between the two. They do not 'act out' or miss the analyst in the holidays because they seem able to maintain this euphoric idealized relationship, living in a kind of continual presence which does not permit of any distance. The slow breakdown of this type of internal relationship leads to very profound feelings of pain in gaps.

Because of the very concrete nature of this type of projective identification, the coming out of this state of mind is experienced equally concretely. One patient coming out of a partial delusional state of mind used the word 'emerging', which was accompanied by great pain; another talked about being 'pulled out'. Some seem to see the experience in analysis as actually linked with operation scars. One such patient in a session felt an old operation scar pain being reactivated, others dream of scars huge and ugly. I am interested in the link between the experience of such patients as being cut out from, forced out, or pulled out, and the whole idea of actual birth. This I shall discuss further later.

In order to look at the problem of this psychic pain in more detail, I want first to bring an example from one of the patients I spoke about earlier, where the breakdown of a rather specific type of relating helps to precipitate the individual into analysis. This example comes from a young woman who was in the latter part of her university career when she was considering analysis, and difficulties in her relationship with a rather older man finally helped to bring her into treatment. Her man friend, who came from a rather eminent scientific background, had at first been felt to be very interesting and desirable by my patient, but soon there was a shift and she found that she was taking him for granted and he became more and more devoted to her, fitting in with her wishes and demands, putting up with considerable criticism, and even attacks as she found fault with him or his intelligence and so on.

At the same time, the relationship which had seemed to her very safe, as if they were very well matched and in love, became increasingly precarious, and she found she could hardly tolerate being away from him, could hardly let him go when they parted, and could not tolerate the ending of endless telephone calls, and so on. Then came a week when he, temporarily, gave up the relationship, and her pain became absolutely intense, and although they soon re-established it and she felt he was devoted to her, she needed constant reassurance of his devotion and continued to be in almost constant pain. She then slowly began to realize that the problem must be deeper because, despite his apparent devotion, she could never find peace.

I noticed that throughout this early period of analysis I hardly existed for her, but served as someone to come to, to pour out her misery, and my role seemed to be an expectation that I should give her 'understanding', which would put things right. She seemed to have little feeling about the analysis or myself as a person and was unaware consciously of any feelings about gaps or changes, but 'understanding' did not help and she obtained very little relief at that time from being in analysis. I think what was happening was that this patient had some real difficulty about carrying a whole area of her feelings connected with being dependent, waiting and wanting, and the anger, I think, associated with this. So long as this man friend was deeply dependent on her, almost clinging to her, she was all right, but the moment this shifted, however slightly, even the ending of a phone call, there was a panicky feeling which went into awful pain when he withdrew. I want to give an example from the very early part of the analysis.

A session would go something like this: the patient would come in, again describe the difficulties with her man friend, why did he leave her? Then she would describe the terrible feeling of misery and pain, why can't she trust him now, and so on. Then she came back with a very pressuring, strong, demanding question. Why did he change? I noticed that when I tried to help her to expand on what was going on, I would be met with a new barrage of questions. Why does it happen? What should she do now? And the questions in response to any interpretations became more imperious, more demanding, and they seemed to dispense with anything I said and to go on nagging at me. Then I could show her that behind the problem with her friend was something associated with what she was doing with me. Whatever I said, she never gave herself time or the quietness to listen, absorb, and digest, but came back with a terribly urgent demand for more, quickly as it were, before the end of the session. Whatever I gave her did not seem adequate or did not come quickly enough, so it seemed to leave a terrible feeling of emptiness and hunger as if she could never get a sense of relief and so went on demanding more. But the way in which she would say, 'Yes, but . . .', and come back to new questions was as if she was positively chewing at me or chewing into me, holding me concretely with her anxiety and demands. I think it is important to see how she experienced verbal understanding, which would presuppose a relationship between us, as of so little use, and only a concrete thing like advice seemed to her likely to be of any help — which, of course, it actually was not.

Now the point that I am making here is not just that her behaviour in the transference was now mirroring her immediate relation with her man friend, invading, chewing, and panicking, but I believe that the anxiety was that she could not manage a deep emotional relationship with anyone for reasons which were completely unknown then. There seemed to be a need for a relationship with her friend in which distance, difference, separations were wiped out as far as possible and he was kept clinging to her so that a whole desperate part was projected into him. When this structure started to collapse, first anxiety and then terrible pain emerged. I suspect that it was the breaking-down of a structured relationship which threatened to bring into the open various aspects of her relationships with the figures of her infancy. The one aspect that I began to know about was something of the controlling, invasive, and chewing-up behaviour and the strange pressure that this brought to bear on me as a recipient, to try to ease her pain concretely with action as quickly as possible.

Now I want to move to the other side of the issue; that is, when the emergence of pain is part of the movement in analysis. The patient who has been living in a kind of delusional world begins tentatively to make contact with more realistic parts of his world and to the relationship with the analyst. These patients, as I have described earlier, tend to assume a kind of closeness, a very special relationship with the analyst, but at depth it seems to involve a phantasied projection of the self into the analyst's mind or body, and the closeness is of this type, not one of relating and contact. Usually such patients do not realize this and believe they are most admiring and positive towards the analyst — which will turn out to be far from the truth.

It is the slow emergence from this state which brings extreme pain of an incomprehensible type, great distress which the patient often attempts to silence concretely with drugs or alcohol, believing there is no other way of dealing with it. The original reaction is often of a profound loss of a state of excitement or even of bliss, and therefore of impoverishment, and it is very important that the nature of the sense of impoverishment is eventually fully sorted out. But in long term such emergence gives to these patients a sense of greater emotional range and richness; or to paraphrase Bion's idea, the patient who now begins to have the possibility of suffering pain will also be able to suffer pleasure. I shall try to discuss this further by bringing a fragment of material from such a patient, B., a young woman writer who had one lively teenage son.

The background to the material is this. B. had unconsciously been living in an unreal, quasi-delusional relationship with me, which appeared to extend into her other relationships — in which we were a very close, idealized unit and very similar to each other. She had hardly been able to visualize me realistically. She had also apparently previously expected little of the analysis except some kind of remaining here; and however hard I worked and however much we achieved, she tended to lose contact day by day with what had been going on in the sessions. In the period that I am concerned with changes were taking place, particularly in a new kind of realization of differences between us, which I would describe as her emerging from a blurred delusional world, and with this a greater appreciation and valuing of the day-to-day work, but also feelings of great pain.

B. started by talking in a rather light, almost laughing way, being slightly humorous, which contrasted strikingly with the pain and difficulties she had been talking about in the previous session. Then she told a dream *which she said had struck her with great horror. It was that she had had a second baby, though by no known father, as if no father was involved. It was as if the baby had been born all right but then a kind of hole had developed around the side of its cheek by the mouth, so that the mouth itself was like a great slit. There was the problem of how it would feed, because the milk would dribble out – it was vaguely, incomprehensibly felt to be my patient's fault. She wrapped the baby up in a blanket and then saw that the slit was beginning to heal a bit, the baby looked somehow prettier.* My patient's associations were to an aunt of hers who had recently had an operation but who had become disturbed immediately afterwards and behaved in such a way as to open up, to tear open, some of the operation stitches, which the surgeon had then had to repair. This aunt had the same first name as my patient.

The dream seems particularly significant in this period when the patient was almost constantly in a state of intense pain, as if it contained some potential insight. First, I think that the baby is an aspect of herself now experienced as being born, emerging physically from a kind of idealized, closed-in relationship with me — her delusional world concretely experienced. But the birth is not a natural one, but associated with being torn out — the operation scar. Now, once she really starts to emerge, all kinds of psychic troubles and possibilities begin to be opened up. One is the possibility of being responsible for herself and her mind and how it works, she feels in the dream vaguely responsible for the child's mouth, as her aunt is responsible for the damage to her operation scar, and the damage to the surgeon's work. Then she becomes incontinent, the milk will dribble out, which is exactly what had been happening between every session. It did not remain in and get digested.

This session had actually started with a kind of verbal incontinence, joking, a bit light, avoiding real issues. But very recently she had begun to get a grip on it, as if the mouth, in a very slight way, started to heal, to get a grip on the nipple, she was getting prettier! But if she really emerges, then a great deal has to be faced, such things as the fact that I have been there all the time working with her, that there has been a whole world of life going on and that her delusional world was a delusional world, and that babies have two parents, that our work needs her active work with me. She has not yet reached this stage of active responsibility for her mind, including its destructive and suicidal aspect that destroys progress in herself and undoes our work; this would involve 'suffering pain'. But she was moving in that direction. Suicidal feelings are very marked in patients emerging from these states of shut-in-ness because life itself is what they want to avoid, since life, living, relating is exactly what stirs up so much pain and a whole gamut of feelings which have up to now been avoided. Destruction of the self and the mind that experiences is most attractive.

What I also want to stress here is the sense of confusion — not only the patient's own sense of confusion about what is happening, but also the apparent confusing and bringing together of many stages and anxieties, birth, oral anxieties — the dribbling mouth: apparently Oedipal aspects — there was no father; fragments of potential concern and reparation — the baby is wrapped up, the mouth heals, there is a sense of vague self-reproach, and so on. It seems that these patients who live so much in an unreal, delusional world of projective identification have in their development ventured out to some extent — they are not actually psychotic — they have moved forward but never been able to hold on to and work through the basic steps of development, but have retreated immediately in the face of difficulties and anxieties back into their unreal world. As they emerge more fully in treatment, there is a breakthrough of a series of different stages and problems, as it were hinted at, touched on, but never really dealt with, which need to be teased out as the analytic work goes on.

This is, I suspect, associated with the unknownness of the nature of the pain, which is unable to be put under headings. The pain is not experienced as guilt in relation to impulses, concern about objects, or the loss of an object; it has not this clarity. At this stage these patients have not achieved sufficient differentiation to reach and work through the depressive position. The nature of the pain is more unknown, more raw, it is more connected with the emerging into a live world. Retreat from it involves not so much the use of manic defences, but the slipping back into the use of more schizoid mechanisms to achieve peace, even though this involves destruction of progress or of the self, or an attempt to return to an undifferentiated state, as if inside the object. To put it another way, the experience of pain is not yet heartache — though felt often to be related to the heart — but it contains the beginnings of the capacity to feel heartache.

I think it is now understandable that these patients often seem to be the ones who have a puerperal breakdown when their own babies — particularly, I think, the first ones — are born. They tend to be comparatively comfortable and free from anxiety when pregnant, but the birth or the period immediately following delivery is frequently traumatic. My impression is that not only do they feel that the baby is being taken away from them, but also they are so deeply identified with the baby, who is felt to be pulled or torn out of the mother's body, that the very early weeks can be most traumatic and precipitate a quite serious breakdown. The patient's own problem of being outside and born has never been adequately worked through.

I want now to return to a point that I indicated earlier; that is, the nature of the movement within an analysis towards the experiencing of this type of psychic pain. At first, when one is analysing the nature of the patient's projective identification into his objects, and there is some shift in the defences, the shifts are accompanied by anxiety and the quick re-use of the projective mechanisms to restore the old balance. It is only as these aspects are more integrated by the patient and there is a strengthening of the ego that a kind of willingness and active interest is felt in what is going on, externally and internally. It is then that, to my mind, psychic pain is experienced as such, and provided that the patient does not retreat from this, his capacity to suffer pain is increased. Bion describes the need for 'the analytic experience to increase the patient's *capacity* for suffering even though the patient and analyst may hope to decrease pain itself' (Bion, 1963, p. 62), and he goes on to describe the relationship between pain and development, adding that this is 'recognized in the commonly used phrase "growing pains",' a point very relevant to my theme.

I want to illustrate this type of movement briefly. A patient, C., who had been very seriously withdrawn all his life and caught up in fetishistic phantasies, had begun to feel alive, with great pain and alarm, but also with a sense of increased emotional richness. For example, for the first time in his conscious life he had felt real attachment to his old mother. But there was also retreat. Shortly before the summer holidays he brought a dream, *in which he was in a private hospital in his dressing-gown; something to do with a heart condition that he was worried about. Looking out of a window he was aware of a part outside, a kind of extension of the hospital, covering part of the street, where something was going on. A friend of his was going outside.* His associations included a reference to his old night fears of his heart stopping and dying. I suggested now a conflict between his remaining emotionally shut away inside and the notion of moving into contact with a world outside in which things were known to be going on, like leaving the analysis for the holidays with his eyes open, emotionally aware of it, and it might really be touching his heart positively. This suggestion rather moved him. He agreed, saying that it was odd that as he came into the session, he had looked at the date on his watch and noticed, most unusually for him, that the holidays would be here in a fortnight. Usually this only emotionally dawns on him a few hours ahead of a gap. By now, in the session, one could feel there was movement.

In the early part of his analysis when we had been able to analyse his profound projections into his objects there would be feelings of intense anxiety as in a dream recurring in his childhood, of dropping out of a globe into dark terrifying nothingness. Now we can distinguish this anxiety from a feeling of pain and worry about unknown feelings in relation to a world in which things are going on externally and internally. It is now the beginnings of pain where previously it was fragmentation, but he also knows that the pain contains something of richness and even, therefore, hope.

I am putting it this way because I feel that this type of pain has a quality of incomprehensibility to the patient and to the analyst. It seems to be a pain connected with people and life, and if we can help our patients through this, then there is the possibility of a sense of responsibility for themselves and their relationships and their understanding and their impulses, and we get a real shift towards the depressive position with concern for people. But it is only part way towards the depressive position. If one assumes knowledge as to its content prematurely, I suspect that one helps a patient to harden up again. There is an additional technical point; that is, I think one cannot help patients to break out of the old methods of operating and emerge to the experiencing of this type of psychic reality and the beginnings of suffering psychic pain and get through it, except by following minute movements of emergence and retreat, experiencing and avoiding within the transference. 'Knowledge' of these things is of no use to the patient. These two latter issues are essentially linked with Bion's own thinking: the one which he discusses frequently from various angles; that is, the importance of being able to stand not knowing — 'negative capability'. The other concerns the value of distinguishing clearly, in our work, between 'knowing about' and 'becoming', between K and O (Bion, 1970).

I have tried to discuss a particular type of psychic pain that I believe belongs to the emergence from schizoid states of mind in which projective identification is strongly used. I have attempted to discuss it as a borderline phenomenon, on the border between mental and physical, between shut-in-ness and emergence, between anxieties felt in terms of fragmentation and persecution and the beginnings of suffering, integration, and concern.

PART 3

Consolidation

Introduction

Michael Feldman and Elizabeth Bott Spillius

In the first chapter of this section, 'Different types of anxiety and their handling in the analytic situation' (1978), Joseph develops some of the themes introduced in the previous four papers. She is again primarily concerned with the factors which promote shifts within a given session back and forth from the use of defences belonging primarily to the paranoid-schizoid position to the experiences of ambivalence and guilt characteristic of the depressive position.

By careful attention to the immediacy of the transference situation rather than the 'meaning' of the patient's material, Joseph believes we can become aware of the current anxieties the patient is defending against and the mechanisms by which defence is achieved. She emphasizes the need to recognize and try to understand the patient's attempts to involve the analyst in a subtle form of acting out, the purpose of which is to avoid anxiety connected with conflict or guilt.

Thus she describes a patient who used projective identification for two different purposes — first, to disavow, for example, his own anger, cruelty, and guilt; and second, to try to draw the analyst into acting out a kind of sado-masochistic beating of him, which is another means of avoiding the experience of conflict, guilt, or depressive pain. Such patients use us to avoid anxiety rather than to understand it. The patient's use of primitive defence mechanisms (primarily projective identification) makes it imperative that the analyst recognize the extent to which he is being unconsciously involved and used in this very active fashion.

Joseph experienced the second patient she describes as bland and remote, successful in his work, but unable to be deeply involved with

101

anyone, especially women. He brought a dream which showed that he thought a woman, a thinly disguised version of his analyst, was grandiose and paranoid. Joseph makes an important technical point in relation to this patient, namely, that it is necessary first to interpret and to stay with the patient's perception of the analyst as, in this case, grandiose about her own work which he felt to be less important than his own. It may be difficult to resist the temptation to interpret the mechanism of projection that leads to this misperception of the analyst, but Joseph thinks that such 'pseudo-deep' or premature interpretation is not productive; it is either felt by the patient to reflect the analyst's disturbance, or will simply be incorporated into the patient's defensive system. It is more helpful for the patient, however uncomfortable for the analyst, if the patient is given a chance to experience the analyst as someone able to tolerate the nature of the object relationship which is created by such projective processes.

Joseph's concern with working in a way which is likely to promote psychic change leads her to raise the question of the 'level' it is appropriate to address at a given moment with a particular patient. Is he defending himself primarily against persecutory anxiety or against depressive anxiety? She suggests that the most valuable guide to this question lies in the assessment of the use the patient is making of the analyst at that moment. One problem with this, which she highlights, is that the most important and relevant of the patient's anxieties are usually bound up with areas of difficulty in the countertransference. The analyst feels an area in the patient's communication that he (the analyst) wishes to avoid; that is the area the analyst needs to focus on.

In the second chapter of this section, 'Defence mechanisms and phantasy in the psycho-analytical process' (1981), Joseph underlines the importance of thinking about our patients in terms of a complex organization of personality and of defensive structures which each individual has evolved. We need, therefore, to try to understand the unconscious phantasies that shape the way the patient perceives his objects, phantasies which are the basis for his anxieties and defences. Joseph approaches the description of the case material in characteristic fashion. She describes what seemed like an 'ordinary good analysis', but then demonstrates the way in which her understanding of the patient's unconscious phantasies was significantly advanced by attending to the 'atmosphere' — some superordinate quality existing within the session. She describes this in various ways: it seemed hollow, without a feeling of contact, without focus. She describes the patient beginning to cry, but neither patient nor analyst understood the reasons. She reiterates how important it is to refrain from making premature interpretations about the content or the reasons for this state of affairs, and the need to tolerate 'not knowing' (cf. Bion 1962, 1963, 1965, 1967, 1970).

Joseph's careful attention to the transference and countertransference enabled her to build up a picture of this particular patient as someone who felt very despairing about ever being understood or cared for, and who felt that all she could do was to fit in with the analyst in a rather meaningless way, as one assumes she had always done as a child.

As in the previous paper, Joseph stresses the importance of orienting oneself to the level at which the patient is functioning. Thus in this case she felt there was almost no part of the patient's ego available for understanding; she was operating in a more primitive way, with her defences being used to struggle against having to face psychic reality. Joseph thus felt that the only thing that would be of real value to the patient was to build up a picture of the kind of person the patient (unconsciously) felt the analyst to be, which was both the result of the operation of her defensive mechanisms and the reason for their invocation.

It is worth noting that this represents a considerable shift from an earlier style of analysis, where it was felt to be useful to address the unconscious phantasies and anxieties immediately and directly without taking particular account of the patient's capacity to make use of such interpretations — this general change in Kleinian technique is further discussed in Bott Spillius (ed.) 1988, vol. 2: 6—11.

Both 'Addiction to near-death' (1982) and 'On understanding and not understanding' (1983) show a significant development in Joseph's exploration of the way in which the patient's whole defensive organization expresses itself in the analysis. The central themes are related both to Rosenfeld's work on destructive narcissism (1971b) and to Bion's theories of thinking (1962, 1963, 1965, 1970).

In 'Addiction to near-death' Joseph is essentially concerned with the pull towards what she calls 'near-death', in her view a form of expression of the death instinct, and certainly a powerful, destructive, self-destructive, and addictive force, in which the patient sees himself as unable to be helped. While it may be possible to sense real anxiety and misery in the patient, she describes how his thinking is often dominated by an addiction to the living out of a repetitive sado-masochistic phantasy in which the patient *uses* his suffering or despair to triumph over aspects of himself more concerned with life, sanity, and positive change. The pull towards despair and death is not, however, simply a longing for peace and freedom from effort. He is engaged, on the contrary, in a very active process in which anything constructive in the patient himself or in the analyst is attacked in an excited, sadistic fashion. The addictive nature of the process derives from the fact that there is a part of the patient which feels 'enthralled' by the more sadistic part, deriving masochistic excitement from the pain or despair which is caused. Conversely, at this time the patient Joseph describes had insufficient healthy ego function to counteract these destructive forces.

Joseph shows in detail how both the sadism and the masochism manifest themselves in the analytic relationship. The patient may appear to seek understanding and help, but actually talks in a way which unconsciously aims to evoke disturbance or despair in the analyst, or tries to provoke the analyst into becoming harsh or critical. If these procedures are successful, they give rise to a sense of triumph in the patient, since the analyst has been defeated in the exercise of proper analytic function.

Joseph stresses the distinction, which it is always important to make with these patients, between the patient's communication, in which the primary aim is to gain understanding and help with his despair, depression, or anxieties, and the other situation where the primary function of such communications is to perpetuate a sado-masochistic environment in which both patient and analyst remain trapped.

When the analyst *is* able to resist the pressure either to fall into despair or to act out in a harsh or sadistic way, and the patient feels understood, the greater integration which follows may be accompanied by the type of acute pain which Joseph described in her earlier paper on psychic pain. This may, in turn, incline the patient to re-deploy his familiar masochistic defences.

Joseph speculates in an extremely interesting — and, for her, unusual — way about the infantile origins of this pathological constellation. She suggests, briefly, that under stress these patients may in infancy have 'withdrawn into a secret world of violence, where part of the self has been turned against another part, parts of the body being identified with parts of the offending object, and that this violence has been highly sexualized, masturbatory in nature, and often physically expressed'.

In 'On understanding and not understanding' (1983) Joseph is concerned with the situation in which the patient appears to seek help, to gain understanding of himself in order to change, but where it becomes evident that unconsciously he is constantly mobilizing complex defences in order to avoid any real understanding which would threaten his equilibrium. Her focus here is not primarily on the patient's aggressive or envious attack on his own or the analyst's understanding, but on the operation of primitive splitting and projective mechanisms which work *against* understanding, since that part of the psychic apparatus needed for understanding is unavailable to the patient. These defences are not just thought; the unconscious phantasies which embody them are lived out in the transference.

Joseph develops her point that unless the analyst begins to understand how the complex defensive organization is lived out in the transference, he is likely to find himself driven to interpret the patient's material 'endlessly and uselessly'. It is not just that the interpretations are likely to be at the wrong level and cannot reach the patient; he may also come to feel persecuted, excited, or quite hopeless about the activity into which he has induced his analyst.

In this chapter Joseph is actually describing two closely related defensive mechanisms. The first is relatively straightforward. Here the patient splits off and projects into the analyst those part of himself which are primarily concerned with understanding and with dependent needs, and which become, in consequence, unavailable to him. The patient thus becomes passive and indifferent, or functions as if he is unable to think properly. She describes a second, more complex process in which the analyst is subjected to subtle but often powerfully invasive projections, the functions of which are not primarily evacuative and are not intended, consciously or unconsciously, to be communicative; these projections place the analyst under an active pressure to respond in certain ways, to enact a certain role with the patient, a role which will confirm his existing pattern of anxieties and defences.

Joseph has described in many earlier papers the need the patient feels to retain his psychic equilibrium. Here she emphasizes the importance of being able to recognize, largely through the countertransference, the nature of the patient's projections, to contain them, and to try to understand his need to split off and project so much that is potentially valuable in his ego. At times this may pose considerable difficulties for the analyst, who may have to tolerate long and painful periods of not understanding what is going on. If this can be borne, with the analyst constantly working towards gaining a better understanding of what is being enacted in the analytic relationship, analytic progress may be facilitated, which will be indicated by a broadening and deepening of the patient's emotions, with evidence of parts of the patient's ego engaging in a new way in the analytic work.

The alternative, as Joseph so vividly describes, is subtle acting out by patient and analyst, which leads to stalemate, and is almost certainly a form of repetition of what has taken place in the patient's past.

7

Different types of anxiety and their handling in the analytic situation

---

This paper was presented as part of a Dialogue on 'Different types of anxiety and their handling in the analytic situation' at the 30th Congress of the International Psychoanalytical Association, Jerusalem, August 1977, and was first published in the *International Journal of Psycho-Analysis* 59 (1978): 223–8.

In this discussion on different types of anxiety and their handling, my approach will be primarily clinical. I want to start by looking at the way in which patients use us — analysts — to help them with anxiety. After all, the reason which brings patients into analysis is fundamentally that they cannot manage anxiety, though it does not, of course, mean that the patient is consciously aware of this. Following Freud's structural approach and his work, *Inhibitions, Symptoms and Anxiety* (Freud 1926) we would now give the notion of anxiety a central position in our psychoanalytic understanding and the search to discover it and to understand its nature, a central role in our day-to-day work. I think that technically we listen to what our patients are telling us in the sessions in terms not of 'what does this mean?' but 'what is the main immediate anxiety here?' And we start from there in the belief that the immediacy of the transference situation will keep us in contact with the most important anxieties and that we can learn about their nature in this way.

If we start from a clinical fragment — patient A. begins a session by telling me that once again he has been extremely nasty with his wife on the previous night and he enumerates a series of apparently unkind, intolerant things that he has done and his wife's responses. It sounds from this that he might be experiencing what we could call superego anxiety — guilt about what he has done and a desire to get the analyst to understand and explain the reasons for his behaviour. Or he might be speaking about his anxiety about his wife and her ruthlessness and the bad state of the marriage; that is, is it depression, sorrow, and guilt that he is talking about, or persecution and hatred? Or is he telling me about

106

the failure of my work, that once again he has had one of these rows? Or is it to be understood as an acting out from the relationship with the analyst? Actually, from my sense of what was going on, from the way in which the patient was talking and the atmosphere that was being created in the session, it seemed to me that the most important aspect was the patient's attempt to involve me in a kind of verbal sado-masochistic beating of himself. I was being invited to join in by being interpretively condemning or critical. I am suggesting therefore that the attempt here is to get the analyst to act out with the patient, to be disturbed, critical, annoyed. Therefore we are dealing with a patient who uses a particular type of defence against anxiety — that of projective iden-tification into the analyst — here, particularly, the projection of anger and cruelty, criticism and upset. I think the strength and harshness of the superego is felt to be too great to be tolerated by the ego; it is being projected and then, as Freud described, re-sexualized and, I would add, perverted, and the excitement perpetuated by the patient. But the harshness of the superego here is not about the allegedly bad treatment of the wife but more to do with a negative and defensive attitude in the analysis, which is not being fully faced. Of course the use of such defences in a major way, unless understood, can lead to further anxieties.

Freud took an important step forward in his understanding of anxiety when, following his formulation of the new instinct theory and the structure of the personality and then his new work on anxiety, he brought together the various types of anxiety, in relation to the impulses and the superego, thus including feelings of guilt as a type of anxiety. In addition, he stressed that the very existence of the life and death instincts and the awareness of them together, in the form of ambivalence, produced, as he described it, 'the fatal inevitability of a sense of guilt'. Melanie Klein's (1948) work is in line with these findings. She stressed how once the individual is aware that the object he loves is also the one against whom he rages and feels anger, then guilt is fatally inevitable, and she stressed the pain and anxiety caused by such guilt and by the reproaches of the objects towards whom guilt is felt, internal and exter-nal, in the depressive position. In her view, before this position is achieved the death instinct gives rise to anxieties which are of a persecutory nature, and she investigated the defences which the individual uses to deal with these anxieties, and the effects on his later development. I want in this paper to show how patients, who are able to some extent to tolerate guilt and ambivalence and to approach or to work through the depressive position, use the analyst in the transference in ways which are different from those whose anxieties and defences are operating on a more primitive level.

Patient A., whom I have just quoted is, I think, somewhere on the borderline. He can feel love, and at moments concern and guilt. At times, however, his behaviour is marked by secret, negative destructiveness in the analysis, usually indicated by a closed-up silence in response to interpretations. This seems destined to undermine my work, but is not recognized by him as such. The internal analyst, who is undermined, becomes both hostile and reproaching, but this is defended against by being perverted into a sado-masochistic relationship which I have described, and then the potential guilt disappears. He tries to use me not to get understanding, but misunderstanding, and to collude with his defences, so that the central anxiety round guilt and responsibility is avoided, and a persecutory situation emerges. This destructive type of retreat is very powerful, as he pulls back into a silent, infantile, withdrawn, shut-off state, which in a sense is how he has spent much of his analysis and his childhood, unwilling to be pulled out of this.

Of course, toleration of ambivalence with its resultant sense of guilt, if properly elaborated, can, and should, lessen anxiety, because the awareness of affection, of love and concern, and the attempt to do something about this will mitigate anger and resentment and thus reduce anxiety. But it is in patients who have not been able to take this step, the step of working through the depressive position, as Melanie Klein describes it, that anxiety is most primitive and most horrific.

All patients come to analysis, as I said at the beginning, because they cannot cope with anxiety and therefore want to understand what it is about, but they have learned to use their particular defences to avoid anxiety of any kind if it becomes too great. Therefore we, as analysts, have to expect that our patients will use us to some extent to avoid anxiety, rather than, as we might ideally wish, to understand it. Indeed, some, as I shall indicate later, use us to stand rather than understand it.

Freud often spoke about the importance of analysing resistances and defences. What I am suggesting is that one of the ways in which psychoanalytic theory and technique has particularly developed since Freud's time is in the understanding of the way in which resistance and defence express themselves in the transference, and can be experienced in the countertransference, as part of the way the patient uses the analyst. The more the patient is using primarily primitive mechanisms and defences against anxiety, the more the analyst is likely to feel that he is being involved and used by the patient unconsciously, and the more the analysis is a scene for action rather than understanding. By primitive defences I mean primitive in terms of ego development. When the immature ego cannot stand anxiety, it uses various methods to deny or split off major parts of the personality, impulses, internal objects, and anxieties and projects them very powerfully into its world. In the analysis we find the various parts of the self being projected into the analyst, leaving the patient emotionally out of contact with himself and distorting his vision of the analyst. These defences belong to what Melanie Klein termed the paranoid–schizoid position. Such patients will actively try to get the analyst to collude with them in the use of these various defences.

I am going to give two brief examples of patients maintaining their balance by employing these primitive defences, to show how in the first case I am used to collude with denials of his anxieties and feelings and as a receptacle for parts of his self which, if recognized, would cause extreme anxiety. In the second case I am being used to contain objects from his internal world, so that, when they are projected into me, not just his state of mind and his emotions but the condition of his objects can be denied and depression warded off. These cases raise important technical issues.

B., as many patients of this type, tries to get the analyst to collude with him in denying that anxiety is important, maintaining that it can be dealt with by intellectual methods — by understanding. These patients may give a very adult impression, but this pseudo-adulthood is achieved only at the cost of splitting off nearly all real emotional contact with themselves. Their emotional life is unconsciously dreaded because it is felt to contain powerful psychotic features. They feel, unconsciously, in danger of severe breakdown and, having got into analysis, use it to reinforce the non-psychotic parts of their personality and to deny any signs of illness. They are reasonable and reasoning about their difficulties long before, and instead of, trying to experience them. B., a man in his middle twenties, was apparently highly successful in his work, intelligent and co-operative but, though he hardly realized it, was unable to attach himself to anyone and in his relationships with women shifted from one girl to another. There was an empty feeling about him. He talked reasonably, but out of touch with his inner world. From time to time he had to miss sessions because of his work. He expressed regret and disappointment, but one could feel no real emotion about it or about the value, or not, of interpretations, although consciously he thought my work good. His whole attitude was bland, as if anxiety, love, and hate had disappeared. The problem here, as with other similar patients, was to find the lost parts of the self and to locate anxiety. In the early period of his analysis he brought a dream. The dream was that *he went into a next-door flat to see what was going on. When he returned, the owner of the two flats came into his flat as if suspicious of him. But he knew that she was paranoid.*

My patient had been talking about a man with whom he was then working, a man of high standing, but rather grandiose. The woman in the dream looked like a woman whom he used to know, called Mrs Hours.

I want to show, now, the indications of different layers of anxiety and how I, the analyst, am used in my patient's defences against it. Consciously, my patient claims that he regrets that he has to miss sessions and had to miss one hour that week. But the person who misses hours (Mrs Hours) is seen as a woman paranoid and linked with someone grandiose. I think, therefore, that the most immediately available anxiety is about missing hours and that the problem and its concomitant emotions is projected into me, as Mrs Hours. I am portrayed as being touchy about his being away or paranoid and grandiose in my estimation of the importance and significance of my work to him. This I interpreted as his picture of me — discussing the part which I felt to be nearest to consciousness — that is, his anxiety about my attitude to my work — whereas he felt his was actually of much more significance. This could not, at that stage, be consciously clarified or sorted out, though he could intellectually see what I meant. Therefore an interpretation of it as a projection of his own attitude, his grandiosity, into me would be premature and not useful. This unconscious projective identification accompanied by blandness and co-operation was, I believe, warding off, first, an intense grandiosity, of which I think we had had signals, and behind this a potentially paranoid type of reaction, which was felt to be associated with real dependent relationships with women. In other words, I think that this young man was warding off deep psychotic anxieties which made him afraid of women and afraid of me. I was being used to carry these parts of his self which were then denied. In this sense patient B. is different from patient A. because B. was not near to taking responsibility for himself and his own feelings, or to recognizing himself or what his relationships were really like, and seemed to have developed defences against psychotic parts of the personality rather than to be in retreat from responsibility, guilt, and depression, as was more the case with patient A.

Such patients as B. seem to come into analysis to get the analyst to collude with them that there is nothing that cannot be understood and managed intellectually. Others experience extreme anxiety consciously, with fears of falling to pieces, and they may use the analyst at such times more to contain this. For example, the patient may talk with great agitation but be unable to let the analyst speak, as if, for the patient, the important thing is the talking of the anxiety into the analyst. Or a very primitive type of defence may be habitual to the patient — that of, in phantasy, living more or less inside the object, as if being outside and differentiated causes so much anxiety that the analyst is used more as a body to get inside. There may be long empty silences, or the patient may simply want the analyst to talk without seeming to do much except be there; the patient may fall asleep or, in less severely shut-in cases, may constantly withdraw and split off any contact with the notion of the analyst as a person. Here I am only attempting to indicate a few of these primitive concrete types of defences which it seems very important to recognize in the transference. And they raise, as I suggested, important technical issues. Thus I indicated in the case of A. how one might have seen his anxiety in terms, for example, of his guilt about his nastiness to his wife; in face of the pressure in the transference, which begged for such an interpretation, this would have been more comfortable for the analyst to interpret, but would, to my mind, have been not only an acting out in the transference on the part of the analyst, but *ipso facto* on the wrong level. Indeed, this is, I suspect, related to what is often discussed under the rubric of 'at what level does one tackle anxiety?'. I think that our understanding of the nature and the level of anxiety is interlinked, and depends, in large part, on our correct assessment of the use that the patient is making of us.

My impression is that frequently the guide in the transference, as to where the most important anxiety is, lies in an awareness that, in some part of oneself, one can feel an area in the patient's communication that one wishes not to attend to — internally in terms of the effect on oneself, externally in terms of what and how one might interpret. I shall give an example of this later, when I discuss case C. I am bringing a fragment from case C. to show, as I said, a patient who also uses the analyst to carry part of the internal world, particularly internal objects whose condition causes extreme anxiety, which can then be denied. I shall also discuss certain differences between the anxieties and defences in C. and B.

C. was a young woman who before her marriage had been working as a general practitioner in a busy practice. At that time in the analysis I was ordinarily kept rather too free from criticism and rather idealized. During the week of analysis that I am considering she had been angry and with-drawn on the first two sessions. I tried to get into contact. I queried whether the anger was associated in some way with the weekend, but I had the impression that I was not making contact and that the anger was now more connected with her feeling misunderstood than existing just in its own right. The third day she came into my study saying that she thought I looked frightened when I came for her in the waiting room. (I had no feeling of being frightened.) She continued that she knew that she had felt deeply angry and did not know if she expected anything useful to come from the present session. I did not then interpret anything about her belief that I was frightened. Then, as if there was nothing better to do, but little to hope from it, she told me a dream. In the dream *she had to visit a patient, a young woman who was living with her mother. My patient realized that the girl was schizophrenic and that she ought to go into hospital, but could not do so because she was supporting her mother, and therefore could not afford to – so she was really being exploited.* Now I began to think that I understood the difficulties of the current week. I think my patient felt that I had been interpreting her anger and distress on the wrong level, that in fact there was something much more ill and more unknown that had been being expressed and that I had missed it. When I did not understand this she felt, unconsciously, that I was too frightened unconsciously to understand her real madness, so she felt driven to hide it for my sake, in a sense; the girl who could not afford to go into hospital because of her need to support her mother. There is no question that in her early childhood her real mother, who was a very delicate woman, did need a healthy, even though falsely, happy daughter. But if the analyst is felt to need this kind of support then the patient is really being exploited and, as in the dream, the patient has to look after her own madness.

I often think when we are following Bion's (1962) description of the patient's need for the analyst to contain anxiety that some of the patient's most acute anxieties emerge first in the session attached to casual or even minute details of doubts and criticisms, as in the example I have just quoted. We can sometimes 'dispense' with them by using quick, pseudo-deep interpretations demonstrating the patient's supposed projections, which is comfortable for the analyst and is used by the patient to help avoid facing his areas of doubt. I suspect that often the really deep underlying anxieties can only be reached if the patient has the experience that the analyst can actually tolerate these apparently more superficial manifestations and work from there. If we work from this angle, our healthier patients will soon be able to tell us if they feel, rightly or wrongly, that an interpretation suggests that we are on the defensive and interpreting accordingly. In our work with anxiety we not only have to maintain that we can stand our patients' projections, we actually have to do so.

Patient C. is in some ways like B., needing to project into me – here her internal objects, and then she can deny their state, which emerges in the dream: the mother who cannot really stand up to the infant's difficulties is too delicate and needing support herself. This patient can be seen to be highly sensitive to the analyst and to what she believes to be the analyst's state of mind. But the pain, anxiety, and despair that this causes forces her to retreat to the strong use of projective identification and to remain out of contact, ordinarily, with what she feels to be her dangerous feelings, her criticisms and aggression. Thus C. retreats from depression and pain. In her we can see elements of the earliest defences still being used and being reinforced by her need to retreat from depression — a stage which B. cannot yet reach, being caught up in the constant use of schizoid mechanisms and denials.

I have so far been discussing patients who are employing mainly primitive schizoid defences against anxiety and I have indicated how in various different ways they use the analyst concretely to help them with their anxieties. But our patients use us rather differently if they are more integrated and the anxieties on the whole more related to others as real people; anxieties which contain a fear of loss, concern, guilt, a desire to put right, and a desire to get themselves right; these patients are therefore nearer to what Klein has called the depressive position. They are better able to use repression rather than splitting as a defence against anxiety. In the transference, therefore, we tend to feel that there is less unconscious manipulation by projection, we feel less invaded, and there is more possibility of introjection and of communication to and about the patient as a whole; there is less pressure on the analyst to act out in the transference. Of course patients whose anxieties are of this type — that is, more focused on their objects and about what they feel they have done internally and externally to them and to their own selves — these patients, too, will use us to get us to help them to avoid anxiety, but the methods are in various ways different. For example, the patient who has reached the stage of trying to protect the analyst or his inner world from pain will try to keep the analyst free from criticism, doubt, or anger, or protectively turn it against other people, or use various means to try to get the analyst to agree with him that there is nothing to criticize. Or similarly, the patient who is trying to ward off depression or a sense of uneasy guilt, by using manic defences, will not only show this in the transference, but unconsciously try to influence the analyst's state of mind by drawing him into it, so that the analyst may find himself being slightly witty or too quick or humorous, and the underlying anxiety disappears from view.

To illustrate this, I shall give a brief example of a patient whom I shall call D., who was starting to use me less defensively with much less splitting and projection and much more able to take in and use what I said, and to convey his difficulties more directly to me and thus to have a better type of communication. We could see the movement towards a capacity to tolerate anxiety better and thus a greater integration of the self. D. had been almost unaware of me as a person for years, withdrawing into shut-away states and activities, but he had begun to emerge with great pain but with emotional contact. He was at this time separated from his wife, and rather involved in a relationship with an apparently disturbed young woman, which he was trying to give up. One Friday he arrived in great anxiety and stress, forty minutes late. He was frighteningly aware of wanting to smash in my house and of being destructively critical of anything I might say — he left extremely frightened. This was an entirely new experience for him (and for me, with him). On the following session, Monday, he arrived in a quite different mood apparently, and described how he had been to see G., his girl friend, on Saturday; they drove to the town where his old family house is. This is the house, he explained, where he had such a panic at night as a child and made his sister go into his parents' room to see whether they were alive. Then, he continued, they returned to his house and G. stayed the night with him, but he felt terribly haunted by his wife, almost as if he were doing something to spite her. Briefly I showed him how he felt a terror over the weekend, after the violent Friday, that I might really not be alive, and that this fear had driven him back to G. But then he felt haunted by the person he was neglecting, his wife; this seems to be an aspect of myself, neglected, abandoned, and near dead. When I linked this up with his emotional state on Friday, he realized that this had already been forgotten. I had been analytically abandoned. He was now looking at the picture at the end of my study and said: 'I didn't know that there was glass in that picture. I've never noticed it before.'

I showed my patient that this is the anxiety we had been finding, that I could not stand his violence and aggression, as he felt about his mother; and that I had put the glass between myself and him, as if protecting myself, like putting him on to a bottle away from the breast. He then told me a dream he had had on Friday: *he had written two angry letters about some cooking utensils that had not arrived and now the suppliers refused to let him have them.* Now I could show him broadly the problem of his anxiety about the danger of his violence, and potential demands; how this is now clearly linked at the weekend with the idea of a mother whom he wants, but who refuses him food, the cooking utensils. This mother who frustrates is felt by him to be abandoned and dead. In his attitude in the sessions he can see his own active abandoning of me and the work and thus take some responsibility for it and for his fears. There is also the beginnings of a realization of how in identification he feels abandoned. There is an important connection here with his anxiety that I, any woman, cannot stand his body close to her body, become cold and glassy and he goes cold. At this stage in the session the patient was well in contact and felt easier. The movement went to and fro during the week, but progress in his dealing with anxiety could be seen clearly by the next Friday, when he was in good contact with me and brought a dream, in which there were clear signs of greater integration and an ability to use and even value his aggression,

This patient had, I think, in the long preceding period of analysis been

114

able to use me to contain and test out his violence, and now he begins to relate to an object who is strong enough to do so and can be introjected in such a way as to strengthen his own ego. Something of the history of this problem could now be sorted out between us, as I have indicated in the sequence of the material.

Summary

I have attempted to discuss how our understanding of the nature of anxiety in analysis is essentially connected with our understand of the way in which the patient is using us. Patients, particularly those using primitive defence mechanisms based on splitting and projective identification, will unconsciously attempt to use us to project anxiety into, to collude with them to deny anxiety, and so on, and thus to act out with them in various ways in the transference. Patients who are to some extent better integrated, though also often using us to collude with manic and other defences and to carry various parts of their internal world, will, in addition, relate to us more as whole objects and as people to whom they can talk and from whom they can gain understanding.

8

Defence mechanisms and phantasy in the psychoanalytical process

This paper was first given at a meeting of the European Psycho-Analytical Federation, Rome, 1981, and first appeared in the *Bulletin of the European Psychoanalytical Federation* 17 (1981): 11—24.

We are asked in this symposium to have a new look at the question of defence mechanisms and phantasy in the analytic process. When one looks into the literature it is clear that this area has been revisited and reviewed a number of times before. I refer, for example, to Dr Van der Leeuw's interesting survey of the literature as recently as 1971, 'On the development of the concept of defence'. I do not intend to go over the historical background again but rather to concentrate on the question of phantasy in relation to defence mechanisms and some clinical aspects of this.

What I have to say is essentially grounded in the classic paper on phantasy by Susan Isaacs, 'The nature and function of phantasy' (1952). Susan Isaacs discusses the central role of phantasy throughout mental life and functioning — in development, normal character formation, and in illness. Basing her work on Melanie Klein's findings she discusses defence mechanisms in relation to mental mechanisms in general, and describes how these are related to particular forms of phantasy — originating in bodily instinctual experience. Such ideas, she shows, were already, in part, inherent in much of Freud's thinking, for example, on the nature of projection and introjection and hallucinatory wish-fulfilment. She describes how the relation between phantasy and wish-fulfilment, for example, had always been emphasized but that, as she puts it, most phantasies 'also serve other purposes as well, e.g. denial, reassurance, omnipotent control, reparation, etc.'. Thus Klein and Isaacs stress the central role of phantasy in the building of object relations, anxiety, and defences against anxiety.

Freud, as is well known, did not just list defences, but saw them as in some way related to each other and related to certain types of illness — his notion of the 'choice of neurosis'. He also described how certain defences were older in developmental terms, appearing earlier than others; this approach led on to the idea of defensive organizations of personality and of defensive structures. We know that when we are analysing defences we are not just dealing with specific single mechanisms but with a complex organization of personality of an individual, who has found unconsciously his own unique method of preserving his balance and stability, and both in our immediate work and in our assessment of his future this question of balance is always in our minds. Indeed, from this angle we could say that our patients come to us for analysis because their own balance, their own unique defensive organization, is in one way or another breaking down or proving unsatisfactory.

Melanie Klein used the term 'position' rather than 'organization', describing two positions — the paranoid-schizoid and the depressive positions. The term 'position' implies an attitude of mind, a constellation of conjoint phantasies and relationships to objects with characteristic anxieties and defences. The notion of positions helps us, as a framework, to orient ourselves in our listening to our patients. We need to get the feeling of the central position in which his mind is currently operating — whether, for example, he is viewing his world, external and internal, more from a depressive stance with a sense of responsibility, pain, and guilt that has to be dealt with or from a more paranoid stance with much splitting off and projection of impulses and parts of the self and much fear, or idealization, of objects, and flight from contact with psychic reality.

To return to our theme — phantasy and defence mechanisms in the analytic process — I think that particularly following the work of Isaacs and Klein we would take for granted that when we are analysing we try to understand the deep unconscious phantasies that go to building up our patient's picture of his objects and that express themselves in the patient's perception of the analyst, that are the basis of his anxieties and the defences that he uses. Further, that the mechanics of the mechanisms of defence and their emotional content are part and parcel of phantasy. In this contribution I want to illustrate this point and particularly to concentrate on the way in which phantasy and defence emerge as acting-in in the transference, continually.

I want first to bring material to describe an aspect of the latter point — a patient's way of living out in the transference a part of her defensive system and the underlying phantasies. This material comes from the early months of her analysis, when I knew very little about her and was trying to build up some understanding in my own mind. This patient, a young woman in her mid-twenties, just established quite successfully in her profession, came to analysis largely because of a very difficult and tormenting relationship with her boy friend in which she felt sure she was playing some part but could not understand what. During the early weeks of treatment, I was impressed by the fact that she talked a lot and what she said seemed to be descriptive of what was going on but in some way hollow — for example, she might move from mentioning a person, then perhaps where she had met him, his brother, the nature of this man's wife, and so on and so on, with less and less feeling of contact or any kind of focus. When I could interpret she would agree, and the following day would be quite likely to refer back to the interpretation saying that she had thought about it, and so on, by which time it all came over to me as quite empty, both what she had said, and indeed, by now, what I had said. Yet this patient did not seem dissatisfied with all this; sometimes she would start to cry and continue to cry, but often neither she nor I could see a conscious reason for this. I began to build up a picture, from my experience in the transference, of a young woman who was conveying the experience of having no hope at all of being understood, who was too anxious to become conscious of this, who made an adjustment by fitting in with me almost all the time, so that both she and I would behave as if an analysis were going on, as if we were in contact with each other, as if I were a good analyst. I thought at depth that she had deeply unconscious despair about ever achieving anything of value and being understood, valued, or cared for. This I tried to convey to her, showing how she projected into me an internal phantasy mother who was felt not to understand, to be apparently incapable of contact; and how she built up a defensive system against recognizing her despair by fitting in, accepting, flattering, and adjusting to me or what she phantasied about me. At this early stage it was impossible to get such an interpretation taken in or understood so far as I could see, and she would make some kind of adjustment to or agreement with my words as if their real meaning was too terrifying to be grasped. I suspected that this was connected with something vital in her history which she had related, that she was the first child, born very soon after her parents' marriage when her mother was quite unprepared for a baby, actively did not want one, and became very disturbed. I gather the mother must have considered, but rejected, the idea of an abortion. I think this patient was conveying in the transference the nature of her adjustment to being or feeling unwanted and expecting no contact or understanding.

During this period this patient, whom I shall call S., came describing an awful difficulty with her boy friend, with whom she was then living, but despite the difficulties she said she did not lose her temper, which she would have done beforehand, but, she added, they 'would get through it somehow'. I thought and showed her, linking it with the despair I have just been describing, that that was about all she expected from life and from analysis — she would 'get through it somehow', but that was all. She went on to describe now with great misery that she had never felt as depressed as on the previous day. When she woke up she felt she couldn't make friends, she was alone, she couldn't take anything in, she was isolated, and so on. But then she went on to talk about going away with her mother once, just she and her mother, when she was small; they went to X—— it was near to Y——, they were on a farm, they were staying there, it was beautiful. She described the colour of the sky, the fields, the buildings, and how she revisited the place later, and so forth, a long, long description, somewhat idyllic in content but quite unmoving to listen to; in sharp contrast to the description of her depressed waking mood.

I believe that we can see here a shift in the session, not just from the depression she was describing on waking — but the sense of friendlessness and isolation that she experienced momentarily in the session if she had to face the despair about the analysis, the phantasied relationship with myself as the mother from whom she expects nothing — but she would just have to get through it. That despair is evaded by splitting it off, and there is flight to an idealized picture of closeness with the mother and the beautiful countryside — probably to be understood as a symbolic extension of the mother and her body — which, however, is so idealized that it carries no conviction to me in the session; my patient herself seemed to be caught up in her talking almost as if the talk-ing were a beautiful experience in itself.

I am describing, therefore, the re-living in the transference of very primitive defences against pain and despair, which we would describe non-technically, for example, as denial, fitting in, placating, reassuring us both that all is well; and when faced for a moment with the experience of depression and isolation, there is the emergence of the clinging to an idealized image of a relationship with myself, the analyst/mother, as if close and warm. This is, I believe, how she is now keeping her balance in the present and is related to an infantile idealization, almost falseness, that she has clung to from infancy and which has helped to preserve her sanity and round which her personality has become organized. In the sessions the preservation of this organization was so powerful at that period that it left no possible place for insight.

Before going on to discuss this latter point — no place for insight — I want to contrast that piece of material with a tiny fragment, which might look similar, from a different patient, N., with a very different defensive organization.

In N. a lot of progress had been achieved, although it was consistently being lost. The session was on a Friday. He came anxious, saying he was afraid of going backwards again, which meant into his cold, rather perverse behaviour. But I had the impression that this remark was not just a statement about anxiety related to the weekend but more of a threat to himself and me to drive himself backwards. This I worked through with him during the next part of the session and slowly he seemed in contact and insightful again, and then, as he put it, something quite different came into his mind. Yesterday evening he planted the sweet pea plants that he had got over the weekend, a friend who was staying at his house came out and helped him — although it was raining a bit it was very pleasant. He laughed lightly, saying of course he knew that his getting the sweet peas was connected with my having sweet peas in my front garden. Also, when he was child, there were sweet peas in a wild part of the garden at home and he loved them, they meant a great deal to him.

Here we have what might look like a similar situation to that of S., an idealization in the transference as a defence. But I do not believe it is so: indeed, the reference to the rain suggests it is not all ideal. I think here that N. feels relief that the interpretations have given him insight and he has been able to halt the threatening, self-destructive, half coldly defensive 'Friday talking' and take in help; the defensiveness has lessened and he has been able to discover a sweet analyst whom he can introject, plant inside himself, and identify with. This could be seen by the change in mood clear to both of us in the session, so that the shift in the defence was actually experienced in the transference, and the contact with me contained humour and gratitude — the reference to the sweet peas. But, in addition, the phantasy of incorporating, the mental mechanism of introjection, was clearly stated, the sweet peas are now planted inside. In addition, a link is made with some memory of a good experience of his parental home, as if, when the cold defensiveness is currently lessened, contact can be experienced with internal goodness from his past, not quite lost.

In the woman patient, S., one could enumerate a number of defences that I described earlier, which can be seen to be operating — for example, denial of the immediate despair in the transference, idealization lived out in the way that she spoke in the session so that she partially became absorbed in it, projection or projective identification, I am suggesting, putting an internal non-understanding mother into me and then cheering me on falsely. Whether or not everyone would agree with the way that I am putting it is not quite the issue; the point that I am making is that we can see or feel these patients' defences not just as isolated defences but as an aspect of an organization which helps us to orient our understanding and therefore our interpretations; which actually helps us to listen, I hope, on a more correct wavelength, and thus to be more sensitive to our patients' pathology. This patient S. had almost no part of her ego available for understanding — she was operating in a more primitive way, her defences being used to struggle against facing psychic reality. I would not therefore feel it to be of value to her, at that point, to do anything other than begin to build up a picture of her unconscious defences and the kind of person that I think she unconsciously experienced me to be.

This is in sharp contrast to the man N., who was relieved when I got hold of his threats, masquerading as worries, and he felt understood, established contact with me as an object, and could progress and use insight. I believe both patients are bringing into analysis something from their history, the types of object relationships and defences of their infancy or childhood: the man, a cold, rejecting, and cruel attitude, which is now, however, capable of melting; the woman, something pre-verbal, still deeply unconscious, and more potentially desperate.

There is another issue here concerning phantasy and defences and current analytic practice. It will be seen from my discussion about the woman patient that I had taken very seriously her belief that she was an unwanted baby — but I am not concerned with her 'suggestion' that this was the fact or that subsequently everything became all right. I believe that her phantasy was of a mother who was never really close, understanding, or deeply affectionate, which may or may not be accurate. That phantasy is conveyed to me by the way she communicates. I also take it that her description of the holiday alone with her mother on the farm may be a more or less accurate description, but that its coming at that moment in the session — when depression was breaking through — suggests that it is fulfilling a phantasy function, a phantasy used as a defence, and that this was indicated by her absorption in her talking, like an infant hallucinating a wish-fulfilling object.

I am saying something similar about the man N. I am not casting doubt on the accuracy of his description of planting sweet peas on the previous evening, but analytically I am interested in the fact that the description arose at that moment, so that the 'fact' is used as food for phantasy, the phantasy that I have become sweet and he has taken me in; a shift has taken place in the session. Technically, I find this important in listening to our patients — that so often communications about so-called ideas or facts reveal to us, not just the real or unconscious symbolic meaning of the words, but the phantasy meaning of what is going on between two people, patient and analyst, shifts in the defences and in the relationship with the patient's self and with the analyst from moment to moment. In the session with N. the phantasy of the analyst at the beginning of the session was as threatened and dragged down; by the end it was good and sweet.

I want now to bring material from the same patient, N., to show the nature of the defensive balance established by him, and the phantasy aspect of the defence mechanisms as expressed in a dream. Further, I want to describe the way in which the shifts in his defensive system, caused by the interpretive work, then set up new anxieties and defences, which in turn were acted out in the transference.

The background of this session was that on the previous day, Wednesday, I had been showing my patient his way of dealing with his difficulties by trying to force despair into me instead of trying to contact his own depression and understand it. In this session, Thursday, he came in saying he was depressed. He told me a dream. The dream was *that he was standing at the corner of a well-known central London street with someone, a woman. They were standing in the gutter, perhaps surrounded by clothes, old clothes to sell. His elder sister went past in the road with some men friends; he called to her; she nodded but went on. There was something about burglary.*

I briefly linked this dream with what we had been speaking about on the previous day; that is, how he tries to force despair into me. Here the defence mechanism of projective identification is in his phantasy seen as forcing part of the self into me which then drags me down into the gutter into a kind of faecal mud. So there is an invasive anal quality. But now, as if there is unconscious insight into this, in the dream, he knows about it, it is an old problem. It is the old clothes which he is trying to sell me, but I am not buying it — I am also the sister, who goes past with her own friends, her own life, and is not dragged down by despair. But I think we can also see that this trying to force despair into me, pushing me into the mud, is really stealing away from me my capacity to help him to get out and progress. It is perhaps a burglary. My patient, as we discussed this, got a real feeling about the pull and masochistic attraction of being himself dragged down. From the point of view of defences I think we can also see here that the phantasy of being caught in the gutter, the anal filth, is also an identification with the analyst—sister or mother whom internally, in the previous session, he had been actively dragging down. This identification serves as a defence against having to face guilt towards a separate object.

After some contact, relief, and understanding had been established about this in the session, my patient remarked that he felt at that moment as if he had got something in his eye; was it just a hair or was it that old scratch that he had ages ago? Did I, the analyst, remember the scratch? I did indeed, and queried with him if he remembered how it had happened. He replied, of course, that it was when he was dancing with a woman friend called Hope and her fingernail scratched his eye so badly. So I could show him that when we could see and feel why he has to be dragged down into the gutter of misery, in identification with me, and in his masochism and he begins to emerge from it again, then there is pain in his eye, his natural vision, the pain that is caused by hope. In other words, hope, encouragement, progress in this patient immediately sets up new problems, disturbs his closed-in masochistic balance, pushes him towards more depressive feelings — experienced as physical but also, deeply, as mental pain.

We can see first, I think, the defence mechanism of identification with the hurt object to avoid guilt, which is strengthened by the masochistic pleasure he gains from it. Then there is a movement towards integration, there is less splitting and more insight into what he is doing in the session which lessens the defensive identification and brings up hope. But hope is still so much linked with much that is yet unknown — called simply pain, more, I suspect, depressive pain. This patient, therefore, unlike the woman S., moves towards the depressive position, towards integration and taking responsibility for his own impulses — but he is likely to retreat in the face of pain. Also, I think, we see a shift in the nature of his object relationships, from using me as an object to push his depression into, with no concern about me, into becoming aware of a different kind of object, one who stands up to this, who nods but goes on with her own life, with her analysing — in other words, one to whom he is attached who gives him hope but also pain. In parenthesis, I suspect that there is more to be understood about the sister in the dream and her rather rejecting behaviour, connected with his splitting processes; but it was not that aspect which I felt to be most important in the session.

I want now to take this discussion one step further. I have been describing how we can see the phantasy nature of mental mechanisms such as, for example, introjection, being enacted in the session; how the patient unconsciously attempts to use the analyst as part of his defensive system, attaching his phantasies to him; and how we can see conflicts and defences shifting in the session as these phantasies are analysed. Indeed, I doubt if we can achieve real change in our patients' defensive organizations, unless both they and we can experience the defences and phantasies as they are being lived in the analytic situation. In addition, I think that it is only if we can gain experience of how we are being used that we can meaningfully reconstruct the history and significance of these defences. These points I want to exemplify with a further fragment of material from a patient whom I shall call C.

A young woman, a sociologist, had had a reasonably satisfactory analysis, and for various reasons we were discussing termination in some months' time. Shortly after a holiday she brought the following dream. *She was in an hotel room trying on a skirt, but as she had lost a lot of weight and it was much too big it slipped right down. She was wearing nothing underneath. She wanted to go into the lounge to look for P., a previous man friend, with whom she had in reality broken up a long time ago, but she found that she was still nude except now for two small nappies that she was holding in front of her as she walked somewhat self-consciously. But then the man P. whom she was looking for changed into another man, R., and he was to stay at the hotel with her – in this part of the dream it felt almost as if she was sleepwalking.* The man R. was one with whom in reality she had had a sexual relationship over quite a long period of time, but no real love or attachment.

The nappies reminded her of the nappies of her young son, now a schoolboy. She used to sleepwalk occasionally as a young girl and once nearly went through a window, but her parents found her in time. The hotel reminded her of a lecture series she attended, and this led to her speaking about some lectures she had been asked to give to a political group about whose attitude and policy she was very doubtful. She said she was afraid that it was almost like prostituting herself — but she urgently needed the money.

From the point of view of defences and phantasies it seemed to me that the essential elements here are that the holidays, and particularly the discussions about stopping the analysis, have reactivated her old infantile anxieties — denoted by the nappies and being too small for the skirt. She is responding by a defensive flight from being alone back into promiscuity — an old problem. She is searching for men, linked, I think, with her relationship with her father when she was toddler, when she felt much closer to him than she thought her mother was and she used to sit with him in his study. It seems that a part of her knows that this type of flight from me and from thinking about ending the analysis is in the nature of prostituting herself, not only by the flight to men but by a prostituting of her mind, her understanding. Her mind and its knowledge is denied — she is just sleepwalking. My patient seemed angry when I spoke. She claimed that she really had to earn; anyway the lectures and the group might be interesting; if things were hard enough one just had to deal with them, one had to earn. I had the impression that my interpretations had been barely heard or had been bypassed. When I again picked up the way of dealing with loss and termination, I felt no contact with her. She was back to talking about her poverty. When I tried to show the loss as making her feel impoverished, empty, and naked, there was no feeling of being heard. My impression here is that the dream does express the defence of flight from loss of the analysis as the mother to a promiscuous relationship with men, and that in her behaviour in the session she also lives this out. The patient re-lives a defensive rejection of the mother whose words, food, are now nothing. The experience has become so concrete that she can only declare her emptiness, smallness, and need to find her own solution, coldly disregarding me.

In other words, we see a patient at that period of her analysis, generally speaking, better able to face depressive pain, now temporarily regressing in the face of anxieties about the past holiday and particularly the planning of terminating the analysis. She regresses to an earlier defensive system, using mechanisms belonging more to the paranoid–schizoid position, splitting, projective identification, and so on. She uses flight and denial. For example, the phantasy contained in the denial is that she is not left behind, she goes off to the men; the left-behind infant shown in the nappy dream is in the session projected into me, and I am not only rejected but treated as a useless infant and my interpretations are disregarded. We see similar splitting mechanisms in relation to her mind; she splits off contact with a sane understanding part of her mind, projects it into me, and rejects me. She prostitutes her own understanding. I want to link this very strong reaction with her infantile history, since I believe that the loss of the analysis still had the meaning of loss through her own damaging impulses. A few sessions before the one I have just quoted she had had a dream *of a broken plate associated with a cup actually broken by her young son – but it then changed as she woke from a broken plate to a broken button.* This patient's loss of analysis, or rather the threat of loss, was again bringing up a sense of guilt, and this was again forcing her to mobilize her old defences. This patient's mother actually tried to go on breast-feeding her as an infant, but with severely damaged, bleeding nipples. On the face of it, the dream of the hotel might look like a comparatively straightforward Oedipal dream, but we can now see that the promiscuous searching for men is in fact a defence against facing loss, when the loss is reviving a situation coloured by phantasies of destruction, pain, and guilt. Indeed, technically it was only when I began to concentrate more fully on the way in which she was dealing with me in the transference with splitting and rejection that we began to get into some kind of communication again.

In this case, I have tried further to bring out a point which I hope has emerged as a technical issue throughout this chapter; that is, the active dynamic play of phantasy in the transference. Freud mapped out and elaborated the notion of defence mechanisms and their relation to illness and character formation. His work was then elaborated and extended by Klein and Isaacs, particularly their understanding of the central role played by unconscious phantasy in the creation of anxieties and the nature of defences against it and in Melanie Klein's formulation of positions, describing specific constellations of object relations, anxieties, and defences. The point that I have tried to elaborate in this chapter is the way in which we are now better able to see phantasy and its working, not only as helping us to understand the nature and development of anxieties and mental mechanisms, but actually in operation in the transference. We can observe phantasies being attached to the analyst, as if forcing him into a particular role, as a constant process going on in the analytic situation; so that anxieties arise, defences are mobilized, the analyst is in the mind of the patient drawn into the process, continually being used as part of his defensive system. Thus we are now, I believe, increasingly aware that acting out, or acting-in, is not an occasional unfortunate occurrence but a constantly shifting part of the transference situation. I think that our increased awareness of the central role of phantasy in psychoanalysis, and the importance of its continual interaction with external reality, is enabling us in this generation to listen more deeply not just to our patients' material but to our patients.

9

Addiction to near-death

This paper was originally presented to a scientific meeting of the
British Psycho-Analytical Society, 20 May 1981, and was first
published in 1982 in the *International Journal of Psycho-Analysis* 63:
449–56; and appears in E. Bott Spillius (ed.) *Melanie Klein Today*,
vol. 1, *Mainly Theory*, London: Routledge (1988), 311–23.

There is a very malignant type of self-destructiveness, which we see in
a small group of our patients, and which is, I think, in the nature of an
addiction — an addiction to near-death. It dominates these patients' lives;
for long periods it dominates the way in which they bring material to
the analysis and the type of relationship they establish with the analyst;
it dominates their internal relationships, their so-called thinking, and the
way in which they communicate with themselves. It is not a drive
towards a Nirvana type of peace or relief from problems, and it has to
be sharply differentiated from this.

The picture that these patients present is, I am sure, a familiar one —
in their external lives these patients get more and more absorbed into
hopelessness and involved in activities that seem destined to destroy them
physically as well as mentally; for example, considerably over-working,
almost no sleep, avoiding eating properly or secretly over-eating if the
need is to lose weight, drinking more and more and perhaps cutting off
from relationships. In other patients this type of addiction is probably
less striking in their actual living but equally important in their relationship with the analyst and the analysis. Indeed, in all these patients the
place where the pull towards near-death is most obvious is in the
transference. As I want to illustrate in this chapter, these patients bring
material to analysis in a very particular way; for example, they may speak
in a way which seems calculated to communicate or create despair and
a sense of hopelessness in themselves and in the analyst, although
apparently wanting understanding. It is not just that they make progress,
forget it, lose it, or take no responsibility for it. They do show a strong
though frequently silent negative therapeutic reaction, but this negative

reaction is only one part of a much broader and more insidious picture. the pull towards despair and death in such patients is not, as I have said, a longing for peace and freedom from effort; indeed, as I sorted out with one such patient, just to die, although attractive, would be no good. There is a felt need to know and to have the satisfaction of seeing oneself being destroyed.

So I am stressing here that a powerful masochism is at work, and these patients will try to create despair in the analyst and then get him to collude with the despair or become actively involved by being harsh, critical, or in some way or another verbally sadistic to the patient. If they succeed in getting themselves hurt or in creating despair, they triumph, since the analyst has lost his analytic balance or his capacity to understand and help, and then both patient and analyst go down into failure. At the same time the analyst will sense that there is real misery and anxiety around and this will have to be sorted out and differentiated from the masochistic use and exploitation of misery.

The other area that I am going to discuss as part of this whole constellation is that of the patient's internal relationships and a particular type of communication with himself — because I believe that in all such patients one will find a type of mental activity consisting of a going over and over again about happenings or anticipations of an accusatory type in which the patient becomes completely absorbed.

I have described in this introduction the pull of the death instincts, the pull towards near-death, a kind of mental or physical brinkmanship in which the seeing of the self in this dilemma, unable to be helped, is an essential aspect. It is, however, important also to consider where the pull towards life and sanity is. I believe that this part of the patient is located in the analyst, which, in part, accounts for the patient's apparent extreme passivity and indifference to progress. This I shall return to later.

It will be seen that much that I have outlined in this introduction has already been described in the analytic literature. For example, Freud (1924) discusses the working of the death instinct in masochism and distinguishes the nature of the inner conflict in a negative therapeutic reaction from that seen in moral masochism. He adds at the end of the paper, 'even the subject's destruction of himself cannot take place without libidinal satisfaction'. In the patients that I am describing it seems to me that the near-destruction of the self takes place with considerable libidinal satisfaction, however much the concomitant pain. The main additional aspects, however, that I want to discuss are: the way in which these problems make themselves felt in the transference, and in the patient's internal relationships and his thinking; and the deeply addictive nature of this type of masochistic constellation and the fascination and hold on them that it has. Later I want to add a note on some possible aspects of the infantile history of these patients. I shall start by getting into the middle of the problem by bringing a dream.

This dream comes from a patient who is typical of this group. He started analysis many years ago, and was then cold, rather cruel, loveless, highly competent, intelligent, articulate, and successful in his work — but basically very unhappy. During the treatment he had become much warmer, was struggling to build real relationships and had become deeply but ambivalently emotionally involved with a gifted but probably disturbed young woman. This was a very important experience for him. He was also now deeply attached to the analysis although he did not speak of it, did not acknowledge it, was often late, and seemed not to notice or be aware of almost anything about me as a human being. He often had sudden feelings of great hatred towards me. I am going to bring a dream from a Wednesday. On the Monday he had consolidated the work we had been doing on a particular type of provocation and cruelty silently achieved. By the end of the session he had seemed relieved and in good contact. But on the Tuesday he phoned just at the time of the end of his session and said that he had only just woken up. He sounded very distressed, but said that he had hardly slept in the night and would be here the following day. When he arrived on Wednesday he spoke about the Monday, how surprised he was that following the better feeling in the session he had felt so terrible and tense physically, in his stomach and in every way on the Monday night. He had felt much warmer towards K., the girl friend, and really wanted to see her, but she was out for the evening. She said she would phone him when she got back, but she didn't, so he must have been lying awake getting into a bad state. He also knew that he very much wanted to get to analysis and he expressed a strong positive feeling that he felt was emerging since the last session. He had found the work we had done during the Monday session very convincing and a real culmination of the work of the last period of analysis. He altogether sounded unusually appreciative and absolutely puzzled about the complete sense of breakdown, sleeplessness, and the missing of the Tuesday session.

When he was describing the pain and misery of the Monday night, he said that he was reminded of the feeling that he had expressed at the beginning of the Monday session, the feeling that perhaps he was too far into this awful state ever to be helped out by me or to get out himself. At the same time, during and immediately after the session there had been feelings of insight and more hope.

He then told a dream: *he was in a long kind of cave, almost a cavern. It was dark and smoky and it was as if he and other people had been taken captive by brigands. There was a feeling of confusion, as if they had been drinking. They, the captives, were lined up along a wall and he was sitting next to a young man. This man was subsequently described as looking gentle, in the mid-twenties, with a small moustache. The man suddenly turned towards him, grabbed at him and at his genitals, as if he were homosexual, and was about to knife my patient, who was completely terrified. He knew that if he tried to resist the man would knife him and there was tremendous pain.*

After telling the dream, he went on to describe some of the happenings of the last two days. He particularly spoke first about K. He then spoke about a meeting he had been to, in which a business acquaintance had said that a colleague told him that he, the colleague, was so frightened of my patient, A., that he positively trembled when on the phone to him. My patient was amazed, but linked this with something that I had shown him on the Monday, when I had commented on a very cold, cruel way in which he dealt with me when I queried a point about another dream. This association was connected with the idea of the man in the dream looking so gentle but acting in this violent way, and so he felt that the man must somehow be connected with himself, but what about the moustache? Then suddenly he had the notion of D. H. Lawrence — he had been reading a new biography of Lawrence and remembered that he was enormously attracted to him in his adolescence and felt identified with him. Lawrence was a bit homosexual and clearly a strange and violent man.

I worked out with him that it seemed therefore that this long, dark cavern stood for the place where he had felt he was too far in to be pulled out by himself or by me; as if it was his mind, but perhaps also part of his body. But the too-far-in seems to be linked with the notion that he was completely captured and captivated, possibly, by the brigands. But the brigands are manifestly associated with himself, the little man linked with Lawrence, who is experienced as part of himself. We can also see that the giving-in to this brigand is absolutely terrifying, it is a complete nightmare, and yet sexually exciting. The man grabs his genitals.

Here I need to interpose — I had been impressed for some time about the pull of despair and self-destructiveness in this man and one or two other patients with similar difficulties, and was driven to conclude that the actual despair, or the describing of it in the session, contained real masochistic excitement, concretely experienced. We can see it in the way these patients go over and over their unhappiness, failures, things they feel they ought to feel guilty about. They talk as if they are attempting unconsciously to pull the analyst into concurring with the misery or with the descriptions, or they unconsciously try to make the analyst give critical or disturbing interpretations. This becomes a very important

pattern in the way that they speak. It is familiar to us and has been well
described in the literature (Meltzer 1973; Rosenfeld 1971b; Steiner 1982)
that such patients feel in thrall to a part of the self that dominates and
imprisons them and will not let them escape, even though they see life
beckoning outside, as expressed in my patient's dream, outside the
cavern. The point I want to add here is that the patient's experience of
sexual gratification in being in such pain, in being dominated, is one of
the major reasons for the grip that the drive towards death has on him.
These patients are literally 'enthralled' by it. In this patient A., for example, no ordinary pleasure, genital, sexual, or other, offered such delight
as this type of terrible and exciting self-annihilation which annihilates
also the object and is basic to his important relationships to a greater or
lesser extent.

So, I think the dream is clearly a response, not just to the girl friend
K. being out on the Monday night and A. lying in bed getting more and
more disturbed about it, of which he was conscious, but to the fact that
he had felt better, knew he had, and could not allow himself to get out
of his misery and self-destruction — the long cavern — or allow me to
help him out. He was forced back by a part of himself, essentially sado-
masochistic, which operated also as a negative therapeutic reaction, and
which used the distress about the girl friend as fuel. I also stressed here,
and shall return to, his triumph over me when our work and the hope
of the last weeks are knocked down and he and I go under.

I am discussing here, therefore, that it is not only that he is dominated
by an aggressive part of himself, which attempts to control and destroy
my work, but that this part is actively sadistic towards another part of
the self which is masochistically caught up in this process, and that this
has become an addiction. This process has always, I believe, an internal
counterpart, and in patients really dedicated to self-destructiveness, this
internal situation has a very strong hold over their thinking and their
quiet moments, their capacity for mulling things over or the lack of it.
The kind of thing that one sees is this. These patients pick up very
readily something that has been going on in their minds or in an external
relationship and start to use it over and over again in some circular type
of mental activity, in which they get completely caught up, so that they
go over and over with very little variation the same actual or anticipated
issue. This mental activity, which I think is best described by the word
'chuntering', is very important. The *Oxford English Dictionary* (1979)
describes chuntering as 'mutter, murmur, grumble, find fault, complain'.
To give an example: A., in the period when I was trying to explore in
him this dedication to masochism, described one day how he had been
upset the previous evening because K. had been going out with
somebody else. He realized that on the previous evening he had, in his

131

mind, been rehearsing what he might say to K. about this. For example, he would talk about how he could not go on like this with her, while she was going around with another man; how he would have to give up the whole relationship; he could not go on like this, and so on. As he went on speaking about what he was planning to say to K., I got the feeling, not only from the ideas, but from his whole tone, that he was not just thinking what he might say to K., but was caught up in some kind of active cruel dialogue with her. Slowly then he clarified the ideas that he had had, and how he had been going over things in his mind. On this occasion and indeed on others, he realized that he would be saying something cruel, for example, and that K. in the phantasy would reply or cry or plead or cling, she would become provocative, he would get cruel back, and so on. In other words, what he then called 'thinking about what he would say' is actually actively being caught up in his mind in a provocative sado-masochistic phantasy, in which he both hurts and is hurt, verbally repeats and is humiliated, until phantasy activity has such a grip on him that it almost has a life of its own and the content becomes secondary. In such cases, unless I could begin to be aware of the problem of their being caught up in these phantasies and start to draw my patients' attention to them, these phantasies would not come into the analysis, although in some way or another they are conscious. Patients who get so caught up in these activities, chuntering, tend to believe that they are thinking at such times, but of course they are living out experiences which becomes the complete antithesis of thought.

Another patient, when we had finally managed to open up very clearly the enormous importance and sadistic grip that such going over and over in his mind had on him, told me that he felt that he probably spent two-thirds of his free time absorbed in such activities; then in the period when he was trying to give them up he felt that he had almost too much free time on his hands, and had a vague feeling of let-down or disillusionment as he began to do without them; the sense of let-down coming from the relinquishing of the exciting pain of this internal dialogue.

My point about the circular mental activities being the antithesis of thought is, of course, important in the analytic situation. I am stressing that the internal dialogue, the chuntering, is lived out in the analytic dialogue as well as in these patients' lives. Such patients use a great deal of analytic time apparently bringing material to be analysed and understood, but actually unconsciously for other purposes. We are all familiar with the kind of patient who talks in such a way as, they hope unconsciously, to provoke the analyst to be disturbed, repetitive, reproachful, or actually critical. This can then be used by the silently watchful masochistic part of the patient to beat himself with, and an external 'difficulty' can be established in the analysis and perpetuated internally, during the session, with the patient silent and apparently hurt; or outside in an internal dialogue. We can then see that it is not 'understanding' that the patient wants, though the words are presented as if it were so. These self-destructive patients appear very often to be passive in their lives, as on one level did A., and a very important step is taken when they can see how active they are, by projective identification — for example, through the kind of provocation that I am describing or in their thinking and phantasy. But there are other ways of expressing this type of self-destructiveness in the analysis. For example, some patients present 'real' situations, but in such a way as silently and extremely convincingly to make the analyst feel quite hopeless and despairing. The patient appears to feel the same. I think we have here a type of projective identification in which despair is so effectively loaded into the analyst that he seems crushed by it and can see no way out. The analyst is then internalized in this form by the patient, who becomes caught up in this internal crushing and crushed situation, and paralysis and deep gratification ensue.

Two issues arise from all this. First, that this type of patient usually finds it very difficult to see and to acknowledge the awful pleasure that is achieved in this way; and, second, I believe it is technically extremely important to be clear as to whether the patient is telling us about and communicating to us real despair, depression, or fear and persecution, which he wants us to understand and to help him with, or whether he is communicating it in such a way as primarily to create a masochistic situation in which he can become caught up. If this distinction is not clearly made in the analysis from moment to moment, one cannot analyse adequately the underlying deep anxieties because of the whole masochistic overlay and the use that is being made of this. Further, I think that one needs to distinguish very clearly between the masochistic use of anxieties that I am discussing and dramatization. I am here describing something much more malignant and much more desperate to the personality than dramatization.

I want now to bring an example to illustrate further this connection between actual anxieties and the exploitation of anxieties for masochistic purposes: and the connection between genuinely persecuted feelings and the building up of a kind of pseudo-paranoia for masochistic purposes. I shall bring material from the patient A. in a period when he was in great distress. It had been indicated to him that he would be likely to be promoted to a very senior position in the firm where he worked, but he got into a bad relationship with a principal man — himself probably a difficult and tormenting person. For a period of about two years things quietly deteriorated until there was a major reorganization in which he was to be demoted. He was deeply disturbed, and decided he would almost certainly have to leave rather than be put in an inferior position. It should, however, be remembered that in his position there would be no likelihood of his having difficulty in finding other high-grade and financially rewarding work.

I bring a session from a Monday at this time. The patient came in most distressed, then remembered he had not brought his cheque, but would bring it the following day; then described the happenings of the weekend and his talk with his principal on Friday and how worried he felt about his job. K., his girl friend, had been helpful and kind, but he felt sexually dead and as if she was wanting sex from him, which became rather horrifying. Then he queried, 'was he trying to be cruel to her?' — already that question has something a bit suspect about it, as if I was supposed to agree that he was trying to be cruel to her and get caught up in some kind of reproaching of him, so that the question became in itself masochistic rather than thoughtful. He then brought a dream. In the dream, *he was in an old-fashioned shop at a counter, but he was small, about the height of the counter. There was someone behind it, a shop assistant. She was by a ledger but was holding his hand. He was asking her, 'was she a witch?' as if wanting a reply, persistently asking, almost as if he wanted to hear from her that she was a witch. He felt she was getting fed up with him and would withdraw her hand. There were rows of people somewhere in the dream and a vague feeling of being blamed for something he had done. In the shop a horse was being shod but with a piece of white plastic-looking material, about the shape and the size of the material one would put on the heel of a man's shoe.*

In his associations he spoke about his anxiety about his relationship with K. at the moment and his sexuality. He was the height of a child in the dream. He had tremendous feelings of panic and anxiety at night. What would he do? Would he really run out of money, and what would happen to his whole position? We spoke about the realities of this a bit more.

He had seen a lot of horses being shod as a child and well remembered the smell of the iron going into the horse's hoof. He spoke about his guilt about the situation that he felt he had helped to create at work and realized that he must actually have acted very arrogantly with his principal and that this had probably really helped to bring the ceiling down on him.

I linked the ledger with the forgotten cheque and his anxiety about finances. He is worried about his lack of sexual interest at the moment, but seems to want me to be nasty about the cheque, and K. about his lack of libido. In the dream he wanted the woman to say that she was a witch and this attitude appears to be an old story, since he is the height of a child. The guilt, I believe, is not just about his faulty handling of his work situation, his arrogance and harsh attitude, which has really led to serious work problems, but this is used both in his mind and actively in the transference in an attempt to draw me into agreement with his despair, to criticize his arrogance in his relationship with K. and shatter him and create utter despair and a sense of uselessness in both of us. This is the masochistic use of anxiety in his mind and in the session. We can then see something about the sexualized excitement, of a very cruel kind, that he gets in this attitude by looking at the associations to the shoeing of the horse. There is the picture of a burning iron being put into the horse's foot and the fascination and horror of this as a child, feeling that it is bound to hurt, though in fact one subsequently knows it doesn't. So, I could then show him the indulgence in a tremendously masochistic attitude that was going on visibly in the dream, currently in the session, as misery, despair, and pseudo-paranoia were being built up. There is almost a fragment of insight in this dream, as when he demands that the woman tells him if she is a witch and vaguely he knows that he hopes that she will agree that she is. As we went over this he began to see it again very clearly and his whole attitude became more thoughtful and quiet, as opposed to desperate and hopeless. He slowly added that, of course, there is the problem that this kind of sexual excitement and horror seems so great that nothing else can be so important and exciting to him. Now, when he said this, at first there was clearly a sense of insight and truth about, but then there began to be a different feeling in the session as if he really meant there was nothing one could do about it. Even the insight began to contain a different message. So I showed him that there was not only insight, not only anxiety and despair about being so much caught up in this kind of masturbatory excitement, but now there was also a triumph and a kind of sadistic jab at me, as if he were digging a burning iron into my heart to make me feel that nothing we were achieving was really worth anything and nothing could be done. Once again he could see this, and so it was possible to link the desperate sexualized masochistic excitement with the triumphant doing down of his object, external and internal.

I have tried to show in this example how this masochistic excitement was covering up at that time deep anxieties stirred up by his work situation, connected with feelings of rejection, being unwanted, failure, and guilt. But it is only possible to get through to them if the masochistic use, exploitation, is first dealt with. If one does not do this then one gets a situation which is so common with these patients that interpretations may appear to be listened to, but some part of the patient's personality will treat the analyst with contempt, with sneering, and with mockery, though the mockery and the contempt will be silent.

But we are still left with a major problem as to why this type of masochistic self-destruction is so self-perpetuating; why it has such a grip on this type of patient. One reason which I have discussed in this chapter — the sheer unequalled sexual delight of the grim masochism — is undeniable, yet it is usually very difficult for a long time for such patients to see that they are suffering from an addiction, that they are 'hooked' to this kind of self-destruction. With A., by the time we reached the dream about the sexual assault in the cavern, we had worked through a lot of this, and he felt consciously that he was in the grip of an addiction from which he believed he would like to be free. But he felt that the part of him that would like to be freed was nothing like as powerful nor were the possible results as attractive as was the pull of his addiction. And this he could not understand.

This problem needs considering from the angle of these patients' passivity that I mentioned at the beginning of the chapter when I described how the pull towards life and sanity seems to be split off and projected into the analyst. One can see this in the transference, in severe cases going on sometimes over years, roughly like this. The patient comes, talks, dreams, and so on, but one gets the impression of very little real active interest in changing, improving, remembering, getting anywhere with the treatment. Slowly the picture builds up. The analyst seems to be the only person in the room who is actively concerned about change, about progress, about development, as if all the active parts of the patient have been projected into the analyst. If the analyst is not aware of this and therefore does not concentrate his interpretations round this process, a collusion can arise in which the analyst carefully, maybe tactfully, pushes, tries to get the patient's interest or to alert him. The patient briefly responds only quietly to withdraw again and leave the next move to the analyst, and a major piece of psychopathology is acted out in the transference. The patient constantly is pulling back towards the silent kind of deadly paralysis and near-complete passivity. When these lively parts of the patient remain so constantly split off it means that his whole capacity for wanting and appreciating, missing, feeling disturbed at losing, and so on, the very stuff that makes for real whole object relating is projected and the patient remains with his addiction and without the psychological means of combating this. To me, therefore, the understanding of the nature of this apparent passivity is technically of primary importance with these patients. Moreover, it means that with such splitting-off of the life instincts and of loving, ambivalence and guilt are largely evaded. As these patients improve and begin to become more integrated and relationships become more real, they begin to feel acute pain sometimes experienced as almost physical — undifferentiated but extremely intense.

I think it is often at these periods of analysis, when concern and pain near to guilt begin to be experienced, that one can see a quick regression to earlier masochistic methods of avoiding pain linked essentially with infantile and childhood behaviour. To give a very brief example: A., following a good analytic experience, had a dream in which *his mother, dead or near dead, was lying on a slab or couch, and he, to his horror, was pulling off bits of sunburnt skin from one side of her face and eating them.* I think that instead of becoming aware of, and guilty about, the spoiling of the good experience, he is showing here how he again becomes identified with his damaged object by eating it up, and it is also important to see the link between the painful, exciting, physical horror and his earlier nail-biting and skin-tearing, familiar to us.

Freud, of course, describes this process of identification in 'Mourning and melancholia' (1917) and he also adds, 'the self tormenting in melancholia ... is without doubt enjoyable.' Despite certain important similarities, the patients that I am describing are not 'melancholic' – their guilt and self-reproach being so much evaded or swallowed up by their masochism.

My impression is that these patients as infants, because of their pathology, have not just turned away from frustrations or jealousies or envies into a withdrawn state, nor have they been able to rage and yell at their objects. I think they have withdrawn into a secret world of violence, where part of the self has been turned against another part, parts of the body being identified with parts of the offending object, and that this violence has been highly sexualized, masturbatory in nature, and often physically expressed. One sees it, for example, in head-banging, digging nails into fists, pulling at one's own hair and twisting and splitting it until it hurts, and this is what we are still seeing in the verbal chuntering that goes on and on. As one gets into this area and these patients are able to recognize, usually at first with great difficulty and resentment, the excitement and pleasure they get from these apparent self-attacks, they can usually show us their own particular personal predilection. One of my young male patients of this group was still pulling at and splitting his hair when he was well into his analysis. Another, an older man, who spoke of the amount of time used up by his chuntering, used, in times of great disturbance, to lie on the floor drinking and putting on his radio as loud as possible, as if caught up in a wild orgy of rhythmical bodily experience. It seems to me that instead of moving forward and using real relationships, contact with people or bodies as infants, they retreated apparently into themselves and lived out their relationships in this sexualized way, in phantasy or phantasy expressed in violent bodily activity. This deeply masochistic state, then, has a hold on the patient that is much stronger than the pull towards human relationships. Sometimes this is to be seen

137

as an aspect of an actual perversion, in others it is part of a character perversion.

It will be seen that in this chapter I have not attempted to discuss the defensive value of the addiction, but there is one aspect of this problem that I would like to mention before ending. It has something to do with torture and survival. None of the patients whom I have in mind as particularly belonging to this addictive group have really very seriously bad childhood histories, though psychologically in a sense they almost certainly have — as, for example, a lack of warm contact and real understanding, and sometimes a very violent parent. Yet in the transference one gets the feeling of being driven up to the edge of things, as I indicated, and both patient and analyst feel tortured. I get the impression from the difficulty these patients experience in waiting and being aware of gaps and aware of even the simplest type of guilt that such potentially depressive experiences have been felt by them in infancy as terrible pain that goes over into torment, and that they have tried to obviate this by taking over the torment, the inflicting of mental pain on to themselves and building it into a world of perverse excitement, and this necessarily militates against any real progress towards the depressive position.

It is very hard for our patients to find it possible to abandon such terrible delights for the uncertain pleasures of real relationships.

Summary

This chapter describes a very malignant type of self-destructiveness seen in a small group of patients. It is active in the way in which they run their lives and it emerges in a deadly way in the transference. This type of self-destructiveness is, I suggest, in the nature of an addiction of a particular sado-masochistic type, which these patients feel unable to resist. It seems to be like a constant pull towards despair and near-death, so that the patient is fascinated and unconsciously excited by the whole process. Examples are given to show how such addictions dominate the way in which the patient communicates with the analyst and internally, with himself, and thus how they affect his thinking processes. It is clearly extremely difficult for such patients to move towards more real and object-related enjoyments, which would mean giving up the all-consuming addictive gratifications.

10

On understanding and not understanding: some technical issues

This paper was first given at a memorial meeting at the Tavistock Clinic in July 1982 to commemorate the birth of Melanie Klein. It was subsequently published in the *International Journal of Psycho-Analysis* 64 (1983): 291–8.

This chapter is about understanding and being understood. It concerns ways and motives our patients have for making themselves understood or not understood, and the problem for the analyst in gaining understanding as well as tolerating not understanding.

We could describe the beginnings of psychoanalysis as the attempt to make the incomprehensible in mental life comprehensible, and the tools used as free association and listening. Freud started by listening to his patients, taking everything that they said extremely seriously, and from this building up the unconscious meaning of their communication, using, of course, not only words but also tone, gesture, and the like. Following Freud's discoveries Melanie Klein explored the very early period of the child's life, of object relationships, anxieties, and defences, and began to make more comprehensible areas which had previously been beyond our understanding. It is about some of the consequences of her findings on our technique that I want to talk today.

I think that we, as analysts, need to approach the question of understanding our patients, in a sense, differently, depending on whether they seem to be operating more within the paranoid-schizoid or in the depressive position. Broadly we can include under the latter patients who are able to relate to themselves as whole people and to feel some responsibility for their own impulses and themselves, as well as relating to the analyst as a whole person. Those who are still caught up in the paranoid-schizoid position are necessarily splitting off and projecting a great deal of themselves and their impulses and are unable to relate at all fully to either themselves or the analyst.

All our patients come to us, we and they hope, to gain understanding, but how they hope to gain it must vary, I am suggesting, according to their position; that is, according to the basic nature of their object relations, anxieties, and defences. The very nature of the defences used in the paranoid-schizoid position in itself militates against understanding; understanding is frequently, but not always, not what these patients want. In fact, many are against understanding despite their protests to the contrary. Of course, there is another aspect of being against understanding; that is, the aspect of attacking, destroying, and undermining the patient's understanding of his analyst's understanding aggressively and enviously, but it is not this aspect that I so much want to discuss, although, with the patients I am going to speak about, there is often a mixture of destructive anti-understanding and the use of primitive splitting defences which are working against understanding. It is, to my mind, very important that we tease out with our patients, and clarify, the difference between these two elements, and also that we constantly attempt to tune in to our patients sufficiently accurately to gauge where they are: basically in the paranoid-schizoid or depressive position. Otherwise I think we shall find that we are, as it were, able to understand the material but not the patient. I shall try to exemplify these points.

First I want to clarify what I mean by understanding in the depressive position. I suspect that it is only those patients who are really well into the depressive position who can use understanding in the sense that we tend to think about the term ordinarily, I mean in the sense of discussing, standing aside from a problem, seeking, but even more, considering explanations. Such mental activities probably involve the capacity to take responsibility for one's impulses and, as I have said, to relate to the analyst as a whole person and to introject freely, and so on. I want, therefore, to leave aside this slightly hypothetical, more mature group of patients, since they do not present us with our real technical problem, and to concentrate on aspects of gaining and giving understanding to patients who are more tied up in the paranoid-schizoid position.

If we consider briefly Melanie Klein's work on the types of object relationships, anxieties, and defences mainly used in the paranoid-schizoid position (Klein 1946), we are thinking of relationships not just with people, but with people or parts of people used as part objects: we are thinking of the kind of anxieties of a very disturbing or persecuting kind that set going and support defences such as maintaining a highly omnipotent and narcissistic attitude, splitting off various parts of the self or internal objects, and the considerable use of projective identification. Taken at the simplest level it can be seen that constantly to split off and project out parts of the self must necessarily be inimical to understanding. But, as I want to go on to discuss, the problem is not so simple, because even such projective identification can be used as a method of unconscious communication between patient and analyst. Our understanding of this aspect of Melanie Klein's work has been considerably augmented by the work of W.R. Bion (1962, 1963), for example on container and contained, communication between infant and mother — in other words, on aspects of the healthy use of projective identification as opposed to the more pathological. I think it is impossible to overestimate the importance of Melanie Klein's concept of projective identification for the development of our sensitivity and our technique in this generation.

I want to start with an example, to indicate both the difficulties and the importance of locating the main position in which the individual is operating. I shall use a fragment of material from the work of Dr Mauro Morra, who was discussing this case with me. This comes from the analysis of a four-year-old boy who had been in treatment for a few months, and as the holidays were approaching the child had been showing behaviour in which he wanted to be near to the analyst, as if inside him, or, as he demonstrated with sticking plaster, stuck to him. Then on the following day he came in, called the analyst a stupid idiot, threw a small container in the analyst's face, tied up his ankles with string, stuck him round with Sellotape, got glue on to his trousers and a bit of chewed chewing gum on to him. He talked about the analyst being tied up and unable to move, and indeed the analyst felt quite immobilized. Here we can see that there is manifestly an attempt to tie the analyst up, control, and hold on to him before the holidays, but I think there is also another communication going on; that the child is projecting into the analyst his own infantile self, with its experience of being desperate and a stupid idiot of an infant, unable to move, immobilized, stuck in his gluey, gummy faecal nappies, wet and dirty, while his parents came and went and left him alone in his distress, and this is called 'holidays'! (Indeed, there is a story of his having cried ceaselessly for eighteen hours when he was aged only a few months, on being left by his parents.) This is the only way that he can as yet convey something of his experiences, which are outside his verbal range. When the child sticks, attaches, and attacks, his behaviour seems direct — a direct, non-verbal communication. But where Melanie Klein's understanding has given us a new technical tool is in the understanding of projective identification — its concreteness in the transference and in the countertransference. The analyst feels immobilized, responding to a projective identification of the child, as I have tried to describe. The awareness of the use of projective identification in this way gives us an additional dimension, it enables the analyst to use his countertransference as a positive tool in his understanding. But the child, by projecting this experiencing part of the self into the analyst, both communicates his distress and temporarily rids himself of it and therefore of his understanding.

If our patients are operating largely with early defence mechanisms, and to some extent every patient is, then we may expect that our technique has to deal with two factors: one, that the patient who believes he comes in order to be understood, actually comes to use the analyst and analytic situation to maintain his current balance in a myriad of complex and unique ways; two, that verbal communication, therefore, has to be listened to, not only or even primarily as to its content, but in terms of what is being acted in the transference. Defences like projective identification, splitting, omnipotent denial are not just thought; they are in phantasy lived in the transference. These two points I want to develop as I go on.

Understanding, as such, belongs, I am suggesting, to the depressive position. The patients I am concerned to discuss have hardly reached, and certainly not worked through, the depressive position, and, as I said, though they believe they come for understanding, immediately other forces in their personality take over, and unconsciously they attempt to engage the analyst in all kinds of activities, drawing the analyst into their defensive structures and so on. These are the things, then, that need to be understood. All of us, I assume, have had the experience at times of listening to our patients, believing we understood the material and its unconscious meaning, its symbolic content, only to find that our subsequent interpretations seem to fall flat, or that we are getting bored in the middle of an interpretation. If I am bored I stop, assuming I am talking about material but not to the patient. This highlights a point, which in a sense is only too obvious, that analysis to be useful must be an experience, in contrast, for example, to the giving of understanding or explaining.

It also helps to clarify an issue often raised in discussion on technique — does one interpret only in the transference, or also about other areas of the patient's life? I don't think it is only/or, but rather whether one can focus one's understanding and therefore interpretations on what is being lived and experienced and then fan out or down or back from there. Out, I mean, into the outer or inner world, down into history or more unconscious phantasy.

I am going to give a brief example of a patient apparently intellectually trying to understand, though actually negating my attempts at understanding, and yet communicating a very significant part of her early relationships. This is the kind of mixture that I feel we need to tease out. A rather new patient, whom I shall call A., a young professional woman, arrived a few minutes late, explaining that she was very tired and had overslept. Her boss was expecting her to do a great deal of the work which should be shared out to other people as well; she was very angry; she was going to discuss it with him. No, no, no, she was not going to do that work. The reason for anger, if genuine, seemed real enough, but the way that she talked was rather like a self-consciously naughty little girl. I made a rather general interpretation linking what she was saying with what we had been seeing in previous sessions about her actual annoyance being that I don't let her do my work, so she digs in her heels and rejects what I have to say. She replied, 'Yes, I always dig in my heels, I can't let people be over me, just as when I was at the university and people tried to bully me. I . . .'

Now that sounds as if my patient is agreeing with my too general remark that she can't let people be over her (but said very, very easily) but if they, I, am over her then apparently I am like her bullying boss — so one would think she would be right to dig in her heels. So she agrees and placates me — because I am said to be right, but in so far as I am bullying one would assume that I must be in the wrong, but she indicates that her behaviour is wrong. So I am quietly placated by her statement of guilt. But this ambiguity and twist takes all the meaning out of our communication and leaves it useless. I show her this. She quickly adds that this must be 'because . . .', so that long before anything has been established between us, any understanding, it is explained away — 'because . . .' So here I think she shows that there is no belief or trust in the reality of what we are doing together in the analysis. It seems as if there is nothing genuine and sincere going on. I tried to show this point, which is linked, I think, with her ambiguity. Immediately she responded that the word that really affected her in what I was saying was about there being 'no trust' — and she started again to explain about the notion of no trust in the abstract 'because . . .'. But again the meaning has gone, there seems to be no feeling about what I was trying to show her but a quick explaining it away 'because . . .'

I have brought this fragment because it raises the particular kind of issue that I am trying to discuss. One could interpret the contents of parts of her material — for example, how I (and the analysis) am experienced in a persecuting way as her bullying boss, or one could explain something about the fragments of her childhood that are brought up after the 'becauses'. But I believe that that would not help us. I think the experience that is going on, the thing being acted out in the session, is an extraordinary ambiguity constantly followed by a kind of placating and agreeing with me: and my patient always having to know what she means or what I am saying. Actually in this way the meaning of what I am saying disappears. I think this quality in the work needs to be linked with another feeling that I have, almost constantly, with this

143

patient and which seems unique to her. I find I listen to but almost do not believe what she is telling me, as if she were confabulating history, inventing boy friends, or details about boy friends, or stories that she tells me that people have told her. Yet I do not think that I think that she is consciously lying, but my countertransference is very uncomfortable. My suspicion is — and only time will or may show whether I am right — that this patient as an infant or young child had no real belief in her world, in her emotional surroundings, as if deep sincerity was lacking between her parents and herself and that there was a lack of belief in, and a phoney idealization of, her parents — whom I suspect at depth she felt she saw through. And this mixture of disbelief and pretence in real relationships is what she is living out with me in the transference. I have already alluded to that in the fragment of material I gave, but these interpretations, too, get absorbed into the defensive system and cannot, or dare not, be taken seriously by her.

It is interesting that the picture of her family that I get is of a very unreal mother, who, although quite unconnected with psychology, so far as I yet know, seemed to talk to her daughter and husband in a quasi-interpretive way, a role that I am clearly being invited to play, as if interpretations took the place of emotions and real living. What is also manifested in the session is the way in which defences are mobilized at the moment of her nearly having to face her psychic reality. Thus, when I interpret her conviction of the emotional falseness and lack of sincerity in her objects, the very words, or some, that I use, like 'trust', will be used defensively to make it meaningless. And she will get power over the meaning of what I say by dislocating the word from its context and then explaining away its non-meaning with the 'because'. Thus her anxiety is evaded and her psychic history distorted.

This whole complex system of object relationships, phantasy, anxiety, and defences against anxiety is brought into the transference and counter-transference, as I feel useless and impotent in the face of the pseudo-lies. The patient is clearly against understanding — though believes she is for it. Understanding, so far as I know at the present, would mean facing the unsatisfactory nature of her early objects and her complaints and doubts, as well as their value and maybe the value of her current object — myself. We can also see this patient's omnipotence and omniscience; she believes that she wants to be understood but she cannot tolerate not knowing. Her aggression is mobilized when this omniscient balance is disturbed by my interpretations; then placating is mobilized to deal with this, as she unconsciously tries to draw me into her defensive organization and keep us in perpetual agreement. It is also only through my attempts to tolerate long periods of not understanding at all what is going on, that I can perhaps begin to clarify a little what it is about.

In cases such as the one I have just quoted, where primitive defence mechanisms and omnipotence are so striking, we can see that aggression apparently arises when interpretations disturb the patient's balance, since the balance aims in one part to obviate envious aggression. Many patients, as we are only too aware, will try to destroy their understanding, will develop a negative therapeutic reaction and annihilate their knowledge, will enviously beat down and devalue what the analyst has just shown them. But as I indicated at the beginning of the paper, it is not these patients who show such manifest and active, or silent but significant, attacks that I am so concerned about here. I am concerned with those who are more split and stuck and unavailable. The particular ones that I am going on to describe are those in whom part of the apparatus that is needed for understanding, part of the ego, seems to be unavailable owing to early splitting and projective mechanisms. If we do not find the missing parts of the apparatus, we talk, we interpret, in vain.

To take an example from B., who came into analysis worried about his relationship with his wife — or, to be more accurate, worried that she was worried that their relationship seemed poor and unsatisfactory to her; he did not see anything particularly wrong with it. He seemed a very decent man, basically honest, immature, and terribly lacking in awareness of himself and his feelings. It soon seemed that he unconsciously wanted an analysis in which things would be explained in relation to the outside world, not experienced in the transference, and usually when I interpreted he would go quiet, blank, unable to remember what I said, and shift off untouched on to another topic. Or he would repeat what he had just said. The impression I got was that he became anxious, broke up his mind, stopped being able to listen or hold together what we were discussing. This began to improve. Slowly I gained the feeling that I was supposed to follow him, almost pursue him with interpretations, but he did not seem interested in trying to understand or actively to use the analysis — it was as if it was I who wanted him to use individual interpretations or the analysis in general, just as it was his wife who apparently wanted him to have the analysis and who was worried about the marriage. So we could see that the active, alert, wanting part of the self was split off and apparently projected into me and he remained passive and inert.

Unless one becomes aware of this and begins to focus on this aspect of the work, one can interpret endlessly and uselessly about what the patient is talking about, and it will not reach him, or he will become harassed, persecuted, or even excited. In such patients I think progress will be indicated not only by a broadening and deepening of emotions but by signs of parts of the ego engaging in a new way in the analytic

145

work. For example, B. was anxious but also rather relieved as he began to feel himself coming more alive sometimes during the sessions. I have not the space here to give details of such a session with a dream, just before a holiday, when B. became very clear about simple feelings of jealousy and anger linked clearly with his early and current family experiences. He was unusually moved by this dream and our work on it, and as the session was coming to an end, said in a happier voice: 'I must tell you about my grandiose idea. I think that car manufacturers should build a front passenger seat so that it can turn round and the passenger join in with and face the children sitting at the back, or a child could sit in the front and turn to the others. I shall write to the head of BL.'

So I showed him, by his tone and the way that he spoke to me, as well as by what he said, the pleasure in the session of getting into touch with his childhood, the experience of being really able to love and feel jealous, that what he had been talking about had brought him into contact with the child in himself, which he was beginning to turn to and face, instead of his usual way of withdrawing, losing contact, and projecting the needing-to-know part of himself into me. Here some part of him wants to have a look at what is going on. Until he can integrate this part more fully and consciously into his personality he will remain passive, which he complains about, and not able to use his mind properly.

Here we are talking about patients who seem to be beyond understanding, because the part that could aim at understanding and making progress is split off and projected into the analyst — in the transference. We see similar interference when sanity and intelligence is projected, and the patient acts and talks as if stupid — unable to hold things together or draw conclusions about what he or she is saying. I am thinking about a particular man whom I shall call S., who described happenings in such a way that the analyst was bound, and must, I think, be known by the patient to be bound, to draw conclusions. For example, he would give a long description of the behaviour of his girl friend, whether accurate or not is not the issue at the moment, but which seemed to convey that any sane person in the room would assume that she, the girl friend, was very sadistic, to the point of being seriously emotionally disturbed.

This raises an interesting technical problem, since the patient would go on talking as if not drawing any conclusion from his own remarks, thus as if the capacity to understand was split off and projected into the analyst. If the analyst does not deal with this aspect of the transference, but instead acts sane and demonstrates that the patient must realize that he is talking about a girl friend who is deeply disturbed, the patient is likely to react as if the analyst were attacking his girl friend and then be upset, hurt, or offended, and the analyst may find himself or herself urging, almost bullying the patient to see her 'point of view' — so a vaguely forcing or near sado–masochistic situation arises, as if the problem has shifted from the home to the consulting room. I think that in this kind of situation one can see both the projection of apparent sanity into the analyst and the appearance in the patient of naïvety bordering on stupidity — which is apparently innocent but, in fact, is splendidly provocative. Real understanding is not the patient's aim at this moment, but nor is the behaviour consciously provocative, though I think it is secondarily often used in this way.

I have been describing patients in whom understanding seems to become unavailable because the part of the ego that might want it is projected into the analyst, and the analyst becomes identified with that part of the self and is then warded off, as with B. I have also indicated with the man patient, S., how the resulting naïvety or stupidity can often be felt in the transference as having something vaguely provocative about it. In such cases the patient seems unconsciously to be trying to involve the analyst in acting out with him. If the analyst does not watch what is going on in the transference most carefully he may be tempted to prod, as if to suggest that the patient ought to work harder, or be tempted to push superego-ishly to get the patient moving. If the analyst does act out the role of the active ego or superego with the patient it will simply encourage the patient's passivity or his masochism and perpetuate the problem. In fact, the analyst is fortunate in being given the opportunity to experience his impotence, his desire for change, his desire for the patient to make progress. If he can really contain this and try to understand why the patient needs to split off and project so much that is potentially valuable in his ego into the analyst, then analysis will go on, as opposed to subtle acting out and moralizing by both patient and analyst: such acting out must lead to a stalemate and most likely to a repetition of what has gone on in the patient's past.

This type of splitting and projective identification of valuable parts of the ego into the analyst is also seen in another group of patients, who are basically very masochistic and more or less perverse in character or behaviour, a group whom I cannot discuss in detail here. In them one gets the impression that there is a profound split in which the patient remains almost dominated and imprisoned by death instincts, emerging as self-destruction and constant despair, while life instincts, hope, sanity, or the desire for progress, are constantly projected into the analyst. In such cases there is little in the patient to balance the pull of the self-destruction, and the patient becomes enthralled and captivated by the exciting self-destructive part of the personality. The patient will unconsciously attempt constantly and actively to undermine the analyst's hope and drag him down into despair. It is very hard for mere understanding to be anything like as important for these patients as their awful and active masochistic pleasures.

When discussing one group of patients, who use projective identification a great deal to be understood and not understood, I spoke about our being fortunate in being given the opportunity to experience what is going on. And yet we know that the experience is by no means an unmixed blessing, and can be very disturbing or pressurizing or invasive. I shall return to this latter point in a moment. But, in any case, there is always a problem as to how to keep the transference uncontaminated — not, or minimally, contaminated by the analyst's acting out verbally, in tone or attitude, and so on. It is clear that we are demanding that the analyst should be able to feel and explore most carefully the whole range of disturbance and yet not act out and not masochistically suffer without verbalizing. To go back to our first example, the case of the child — the analyst knew he felt immobilized and disgusting; it was important not just to interpret as if the child were only trying to tie him up, but also to suffer, and verbalize to the child the child's own unverbalized and, then, unverbalizable suffering.

It is important to explore in detail the nature of the patient's phantasies, ideas, convictions, ourselves, rather than hurriedly to try to interpret them back into the patient as projections or mere history. With one patient it was possible to open up her feelings that I was antagonistic and controlling, that I did not want her to get on in life or in her career. As we looked at her feelings about my motivation it became clear that in her mind I felt threatened by her, and deeply envious of her as a young intelligent person with her life ahead of her. I would then wish to explore most carefully her picture of me, this old, supposedly lonely, rather embittered person, and her quiet conviction of what I was like, and only very slowly and over a long period, hope to explore how much of these ideas might be linked with actual observations of myself or the way I function, how much projected parts of herself, and so on. This is, after all, in a large part what we mean when we talk about 'containing'. To assume that all these ideas were projections from the beginning would almost certainly be inaccurate, would numb one's sensitivity as to what was going on and prevent one from seeing what else was being talked about or why it came up at that moment.

To return, then, to the issue of invasiveness: the types of projective identification that help us to experience and to understand our patients better are often, as I have tried to indicate, quite subtle and fine. But sometimes they are so powerful that the analyst has difficulty in not being drawn into acting out in one way or another. With a certain group of such patients, who are not interested in real understanding but demand understanding on their own terms, one's personality, one's body and mind are being assaulted. These patients are observant in certain directions, but quite blind in others. They are convinced that they know what is going on, and that their theories are correct — as the woman I have just quoted, who was certain of my subtly envious attitude to her and some of the reasons for my attitude.

In these cases there is a very deeply encroaching type of relating, when the patient unconsciously in phantasy projects his mind and his eyes into the analyst and knows everything that is going on, and since he is living so omnipotently he has no awareness of wanting to know, he has no curiosity, all this is avoided and real relating is obviated. 'Knowing' and 'psychoanalytic knowledge' is put in its place. Such patients are often convinced that they should be psychotherapists or analysts and from an external point of view may, or may not, convince people around them that they are very insightful. But in analysis one can see that the insight is based on a subtle getting in and taking over which will sometimes emerge grossly in dreams, then more subtly in their ways of dealing with sessions and actual interpretations.

In many ways this omnipotent balance is similar to what I described in A., the patient who conveyed a sense of tragic falseness. But the very invasive patients bring an additional, potentially disturbing quality into the analysis which one can experience vividly in the countertransference. With one such patient, as I interpreted, either she did not hear — though this was not obvious because she continued to talk apparently relevantly — or she slightly distorted and altered my interpretations and repeated them in a slightly different form already known to her; or the whole thing became text-book or tied up in some old interpretations, so that the newness, freshness, or unexpected part was lost. But what she said sounded nearly, nearly all right and wasn't. This was a young woman who had anorexic difficulties when young and to some extent even as an adult.

I have raised this difficulty because in a sense the omnipotence and the extreme invasiveness and the sense of conviction and knowledge that these patients have make the problem look obvious — but they are difficult to help and to give real understanding because they depend so deeply on their rigidly held omnipotent and omniscient balance. And there is another technical problem; these patients often appear so narcissistic, so arrogant and disturbing that they ask to be badly treated or humiliated, and if they can get it, by a clumsy or unkind interpretation, they can slip into a, to them, very welcome sado-masochistic transference and insight will be further lost. After all, omnipotence is the hallmark of early defences, and one which we can easily underestimate.

Our patients who in phantasy get into our bodies, our houses, and our minds know and are not curious; in phantasy they live in our minds and therefore can talk about missing and gaps and weekends without having the trouble of experiencing them. We as their analysts have to recognize the omnipotence of omnipotence, and not, I believe, try to interpret their material as if these patients wanted it understood.

I have tried, in this chapter, to raise some technical problems presented by patients locked in the paranoid–schizoid position where understanding is difficult to achieve if our attention remains focused on what they are actually saying. I have tried to show how the analyst, in order to understand, has to tune in to the patient's wavelength, which is a wavelength of action rather than words, though words may be used. All these patients are, to a great extent, using projective identification, either as a method of communication to achieve understanding on a deep nonverbal level, or to maintain their balance, in which case they are not interested in, or are inimical to, understanding as we understand it. If we approach such patients with the notion that they want us to give them real insight, we lose touch with the patient as such, and in any case much that these patients are conveying and projecting will still be beyond our understanding. I have attempted, in this chapter, to show something of the value, the richness, and the depth of Melanie Klein's work on these early processes, and how the implications of her work have increased our sensitivity to what is going on both in our patients and ourselves, and thus have helped to make more comprehensible that which was previously relatively incomprehensible.

Summary

This chapter discusses some technical problems arising from the diverse ways our patients have of making themselves understood or not understood. It aims to show how patients who have reached the depressive position are able to use understanding in a way that is very different from those in the paranoid–schizoid position. It describes particular methods that the latter patients have of avoiding understanding by splitting and projection and attempting unconsciously to draw the analyst into a type of acting out in the transference. It stresses the importance for the analyst of listening to the patient in terms of the position from which he is operating, so that contact can be achieved and with it real understanding, as opposed to subtle acting out and pseudo-understanding.

PART 4

Recent Developments

Introduction

Michael Feldman and Elizabeth Bott Spillius

In the five chapters of this section the themes developed in earlier papers are further explored and refined in relation to several areas, particularly transference, projective identification, envy, psychic change, and object relations. All these areas have been touched on in the earlier chapters, but are here discussed more systematically.

In 'Transference: the total situation' (1985 but written in 1983) Joseph develops some of the implications of Klein's notion that it is essential to think in terms of '*total situations* transferred from the past into the present, as well as of emotions, defences, and object-relations' (Klein 1952a). Her fundamental stress is on the transference as a living, changing set of relationships to which the patient brings the patterns of unconscious phantasy, impulse, conflict, and defence which constitute his psychic life. She stresses that it is important to get the patient's underlying assumptions into the open, for he often communicates his problems and lives out his early history in ways which are beyond his individual associations and beyond what he can express in words. 'Interpretations dealing only with the individual associations', she says, 'would touch only the adult part of the personality, while the part that is really needing to be understood is communicated through the pressures brought to bear on the analyst.' We may be able to capture these experiences which are 'beyond words' only through the reactions and feelings the patient unconsciously attempts to arouse in the analyst. Once again, it is clear that Joseph regards the patient's acting out in the session as our richest source of information about his internal world, his object relationships, and his history.

The second chapter of this section, 'Projective identification: some clinical aspects' (1987 but written in 1984) does not introduce new ideas, but gives a particularly lucid description of Klein's concept of projective identification (Klein 1946) and of Joseph's use of the concept in her own work. The chapter is especially important because very few papers by Kleinian analysts had been written at this time specifically about the topic of projective identification in spite of Melanie Klein's having originally formulated the idea (Klein 1946; see also Bion 1959, Rosenfeld 1971a; use of the concept of projective identification by Kleinian analysts is further discussed by Spillius (ed.) 1988, vol. 1: 81–6; vol. 2: 9–10).

Joseph illustrates the use of projective identification by three patients. The first is a child who sought desperately to rid herself of the experience of being abandoned. Although this enabled her to maintain a semblance of balance, it led to an emptiness of her mind and personality. The second is an adult who used a combination of projective and intro-jective identification to maintain a narcissistic organization which warded off anxiety but led to a stuck analysis and an impoverished life. The third is another adult patient who, overall, had made considerable progress towards tolerating the pain of the depressive position. In the particular session Joseph describes, however, a period of insight and understanding in the session was followed by attempts by the patient to project despair into his analyst and to put her under pressure to act in accordance with his projection. When this was interpreted, he was gradually able to take back his projection and recover his former capacity for understanding.

The next chapter, 'Envy in everyday life' (1986), was written for a more general audience then the other papers of this collection. Joseph describes Klein's concept of envy (Klein 1957), and illustrates its opera-tion both in everyday life and in the analytic situation. She links the concept of envy with her own use of the idea of maintaining equilibrium, especially in the case of a patient who used envious devaluation to main-tain his balance, which might have been threatened if he had been able to recognize the full value of his objects.

In 'Psychic change and the psychoanalytic process' (written in 1986 and published here for the first time) Joseph brings together many of the ideas about psychic change which she had touched on in her earlier papers. In particular she states her thesis that lasting psychic change develops from the constant minute shifts in the analytic situation. She also emphasizes and illustrates the importance of avoiding value judgements about whether the patient's changes are positive or negative.

In 'Object relations in clinical practice' (1988) Joseph gives a clear summary of the way in which Klein's expansion and development of Freud's ideas on object relations enabled her to formulate theories of considerable explanatory power and clinical application. As in the earlier chapters, Joseph emphasizes the importance of attending not only to what the patient says but also to the way in which he acts out his internal object relations in the session, and to his putting pressure on the analyst to join him in the acting out. Even more than conscious verbal memories, it tells the analyst what his patient's past experience with his primary objects has been.

This chapter is notable too for its discussion of the mutual interaction of theory with clinical experience and discovery: analytic theory shapes the analyst's clinical perceptiveness and expectations, which leads to richer observations, and these observations in turn enable the analyst to re-discover and enlarge the theory, making it more truly his own.

—————————————— 11 ——————————————

Transference: the total situation

This paper was given as part of a symposium on Transference
held at a Scientific Meeting of the British Psycho-Analytical
Society, 7 December 1983. It was published in the *International
Journal of Psycho-Analysis* 66 (1985): 447—54; and appears in E.
Bott Spillius (ed.) *Melanie Klein Today*, vol. 2, *Mainly Practice*,
London: Routledge (1988), 61—72.

My intention in this chapter is to discuss how we are using the concept
of transference in our clinical work today. My stress will be on the idea
of transference as a framework, in which something is always going on,
where there is always movement and activity.

Freud's ideas developed from seeing transference as an obstacle, to
seeing it as an essential tool of the analytic process, observing how the
patient's relationships to their original objects were transferred, with all
their richness, to the person of the analyst. Strachey (1934), using
Melanie Klein's discoveries on the way in which projection and introjection colour and build up the individual's inner objects, showed that what
is being transferred is not primarily the external objects of the child's
past, but the internal objects, and that the way that these objects are
constructed helps us to understand how the analytic process can produce
change.

Melanie Klein, through her continued work on early object relationships and early mental mechanisms, perhaps particularly projective identification, extended our understanding of the nature of transference and
the process of transferring. In her (1952a) paper 'The origins of transference' she wrote: 'It is my experience that in unravelling the details of
the transference it is essential to think in terms of *total situations* transferred
from the past into the present, as well as emotions, defences and object
relations' (p. 55). She went on to describe how for many years transference had been understood in terms of direct references to the analyst,
and how only later had it been realized that, for example, such things as
reports about everyday life, and so on gave a clue to the unconscious

anxieties stirred up in the transference situation. It seems to me that the notion of total situations is fundamental to our understanding and our use of the transference today, and it is this I want to explore further. By definition it must include everything that the patient brings into the relationship. What he brings in can best be gauged by our focusing our attention on what is going on within the relationship, how he is using the analyst, alongside and beyond what he is saying. Much of our understanding of the transference comes through our understanding of how our patients act on us to feel things for many varied reasons; how they try to draw us into their defensive systems; how they unconsciously act out with us in the transference, trying to get us to act out with them; how they convey aspects of their inner world built up from infancy — elaborated in childhood and adulthood, experiences often beyond the use of words, which we can often only capture through the feelings aroused in us, through our countertransference, used in the broad sense of the word.

Countertransference, the feelings aroused in the analyst, like transference itself, was originally seen as an obstacle to the analytic work, but now, used in this broader sense, we would see it, too, no longer as an obstacle, but as an essential tool of the analytic process. Further, the notion of our being used and of something constantly going on, if only we can become aware of it, opens up many other aspects of transference, which I shall want to discuss later. For example, that movement and change is an essential aspect of transference — so that no interpretation can be seen as a pure interpretation or explanation but must resonate in the patient in a way which is specific to him and his way of functioning; that the level at which a patient is functioning at any given moment and the nature of his anxieties can best be gauged by trying to be aware of how the transference is actively being used; that shifts that become visible in the transference are an essential part of what should eventually lead to real psychic change. Such points emerge more clearly if we are thinking in terms of total situations being transferred.

I want to exemplify this by bringing a short piece of material in which we can see how the patient's immediate anxieties and the nature of her relationship with her internal figures emerge in the whole situation lived out in the transference, although individual associations and references to many people came up in the material as if asking to be interpreted. This material comes from the discussion of a case at a recent postgraduate seminar of mine. The analyst brought material from a patient who seemed very difficult to help adequately: schizoid, angry, an unhappy childhood with probably emotionally unavailable parents. The analyst was dissatisfied with the work of a particular session which she brought, and with its results. The patient had brought details of individual people and situations.

157

The seminar felt that many of the interpretations about this were sensitive and seemed very adequate. Then the seminar started to work very hard to understand more. Different points of view about various aspects were put forward, but no one felt quite happy about their own or other people's ideas. Slowly it dawned on us that probably this was the clue, that our problem in the seminar was reflecting the analyst's problem in the transference, and that what was probably going on in the transference was a projection of the patient's inner world, in which she, the patient, could not understand and, more, could not make sense of what was going on. She was demonstrating what it felt like to have a mother who could not tune into the child and, we suspected, could not make sense of the child's feelings either, but behaved as if she could, as we, the seminar, were doing. So the patient had developed defences in which she argued or put forward apparently logical ideas, which really satisfied no one, but which silenced the experience of incomprensibility and gave her something to hold on to. If the analyst actually struggles in such situations to give detailed interpretations of the meaning of individual associations, then she is living out the patient's own defensive system, making pseudo-sense of the incomprehensible, rather than trying to make contact with the patient's experience of living in an incomprehensible world. The latter can be a very disturbing experience for the analyst, too. It is more comfortable to believe that one understands 'material' than to live out the role of a mother who cannot understand the infant/patient.

I think that the clue to the transference here (assuming that what I am describing is correct) lay in our taking seriously the striking phenomenon in the seminar, of our struggling to understand and our desperate need to understand instead of getting stuck on the individual associations brought up by the patient, which in themselves would appear to make a lot of possible sense. This we got more through our counter-transference of needing to guess, feeling pressurized to understand at all costs, which enabled us, we thought, to sense a projective identification of a part of the patient's inner world and the distress, of which we got a taste in the seminar.

I am assuming that this type of projective identification is deeply unconscious and not verbalized. If we work only with the part that is verbalized, we do not really take into account the object relationships being acted out in the transference; here, for example, the relationship between the uncomprehending mother and the infant who feels unable to be understood, and it is this that forms the bed-rock of her personality. If we do not get through to this, we shall, I suspect, achieve areas of understanding, even apparent shifts in the material, but real psychic change, which can last beyond the treatment, will, I think, not be possible. I suspect that what has happened in such cases is that something has gone seriously wrong in the patient's very early relationships, but that on top of this has been built up a character structure of apparent or pseudo-normality, so that the patient has been able to get into adulthood without actually breaking down and apparently functioning more or less well in many areas of her life. Interpretations dealing only with the individual associations would touch only the more adult part of the personality, whereas the part that is really needing to be understood is communicated through the pressures brought to bear on the analyst. We can sense here the living out in the transference of something of the nature of the patient's early object relationships, her defensive organization, and her method of communicating her whole conflict.

I want now to continue this point by bringing material from a patient of my own, to show first how the transference was being experienced in a partially idealized way conveyed through the atmosphere that he built up, and linked with his own history; then how, when this broke down, primitive aspects of his early object relationships and defences emerged and were lived out in the transference and he attempted to draw the analyst into acting out; then how work on this led to more movement and some temporary change in his internal objects.

This patient, whom I shall call N., had been in analysis many years and had made some very satisfactory progress, which was, however, never adequately consolidated, and one could never quite see the working through of any particular problem, let alone visualize the termination of treatment. I noticed a vaguely comfortable feeling, as if I quite liked this patient's sessions and as if I found them rather gratifying, despite the fact I always had to work very hard with him. When I started to re-think my countertransference and his material, I realized that my rather gratified experience must correspond to an inner conviction on the patient's part that whatever I interpreted he was somehow all right. Whatever difficulties, even tormenting qualities in him, the work might show, there was an inner certainty that he had some very special place, that my interpretations were, as it were, 'only interpretations'. His place was assured and he had no need to change. One could, therefore, have gone on and one making quasi-correct and not unuseful interpretations, exploring and explaining things, but if the deeper unconscious conviction remained unexamined, the whole treatment could have become falsified. This conviction of his special place and no need to change had an additional quality because it included the notion that I, the analyst, had a particular attachment to or love for him, and that for my own sake I would not wish to let him go — which I think was basic to my comfortable countertransference experience.

I want to make a further brief point about this material, concerning the nature of interpretation. If one sees transference and interpretations as basically living, experiencing, and shifting — as movement — then our interpretations have to express this. N.'s insight into his unconscious conviction of his special place, of the vague unreality of much of our work, of my attachment to him and so on, emerged painfully. It would have been more comfortable to link this quickly with his history — the youngest child, the favourite of his mother, who had a very unhappy relationship with his father, a rather cruel man, though the parents remained together throughout their lives. But had I done this, it would have played into my patient's conviction again that interpretations were 'only interpretations' and that I did not really believe what I was saying. To my mind the important thing was first to get the underlying assumptions into the open, so that, however painful, they could be experienced in the transference as his psychic reality, and only later and slowly to link them up with his history. We shall need to return to the issue of linking with history later.

I shall now bring further material from N. from a period soon after the time I have just discussed, to show how when the omnipotent, special place phantasies were no longer dominating the transference, early anxieties and, as I said, the living out of further psychic conflict came into the transference, emerged in a dream, and how the stuff of the dream was lived out in the transference. At this period, N., despite insight, was still liable to get caught up into a kind of passive despairing masochism. On a Monday he brought the following dream. (I am only giving the dream and my understanding of it, not the whole session nor his associations.)

The dream was: *there was a kind of war going on. My patient was attending a meeting in a room at the seaside. People were sitting round a table when they heard a helicopter outside and knew from the sound that there was something wrong with it. My patient and a major left the table where the meeting was going on and went to the window to look out. The helicopter was in trouble and the pilot had baled out in a parachute. There were two planes, as if watching over the helicopter, but so high up that they looked extremely small and unable to do anything to help. The pilot fell into the water, my patient was wondering whether he would have time to inflate his suit, was he already dead, and so on.*

I am not giving the material on which I based my interpretations, but broadly I showed him how we could see the war that is constantly raging between the patient and myself, which is shown by the way in which he tends to turn his back, in the dream, on the meeting going on at the table, on the work going on from session to session here. When he does look out knowing that something is wrong (as with the helicopter) he sees that there is an analyst, myself, the two planes, the two arms, the breasts, watching over to try to help him, but he is absorbed watching the other aspect, that is the part of himself, the pilot, that is in trouble, is falling out, dying — which is the fascinating world of his masochism. Here I mean that he shows his preference for getting absorbed into situations of painful collapse rather than turning to and enjoying help and progress.

At the time, he seemed, as the session went on, to get well into touch with these interpretations, and to feel the importance of this fascination with his masochism. On the following day he came, saying that he had felt disturbed after the session and the work on the dream. He spoke in various ways about the session and his concern about the fight, how he felt awful, that whatever goes on in the analysis he seemed somehow to get caught up in this rejection and fight; he went on to speak about his awareness of the importance of the excitement when he gets involved in this way. And then he talked about various things that had happened during the day. This sounded like insight, almost concern. In a way it was insight, but I had the impression from the tone of his voice, speaking in a flat, almost boring, way, that all that he was saying was now second-hand, almost as if the apparent insight was being used against progress in the session, as if a particular silent kind of war against me was going on, which I showed him. My patient replied in a gloomy voice: 'There seems to be no part of me that really wants to work, to co-operate' and so on . . . . I heard myself starting to show him that this could not be quite true, since he actually comes to analysis — and then realized, of course, that I was acting as a positive part of himself, as if the part that was capable of knowing and working had been projected into me and so I was trapped into either living out this positive part, so that he was not responsible for it, or for the recognition of it, or I had to agree that there was no part of him that really wanted to co-operate. So either way there was no way out.

My patient saw this, said he could do nothing about it, he quite understood, but he felt depressed, he could see what I meant . . . . More and more the session became locked in the notion of his understanding but not being able to do anything about or with it. (This picture is, I think, in part what the previous day's dream was describing when he became fascinated watching the pilot about to drown, and I myself, as the plane high up, was unable to help, and he was now fascinated with his own words like 'I understand, but it cannot help'. The dream is now lived out in the transference.)

I showed him that he was actively trapping me, by this kind of remark — which was in itself a demonstration of the war going on between us. After some more going to and fro about this, my patient remembered for 'no apparent reason', as he put it, a memory about a cigarette box; how when he was at boarding school and very miserable, he would take a tin, or a cardboard box, and cover it extremely carefully with canvas. Then he would dig out the pages of a book and hide his cigarette box inside the cover. He would then go into the countryside alone, sit, for example, behind an elder bush and smoke; this was the beginning of his smoking. He was lonely, it was very vivid. He subsequently added that there seemed to be no real pleasure in the cigarettes.

I showed him that I thought the difficulty lay in his response to my showing him about how he was trapping me with the remarks such as 'there seems to be no part of me that wants to co-operate', and so on. He realized that he felt some kind of excitement in the fight and the trapping, but that what was really significant was that this excitement had very much lessened during the last sessions and indeed the last year; he was much less addicted to it now, but could not give it up, it would mean giving in to the elders, myself (the reference to sitting behind the elder bush), but he was not really getting much pleasure from the smoking, which, however, he silently, secretly, had to do. The problem now, therefore, in the transference, was not so much that he got such pleasure from the excitement; the problem lay in the recognition and the acknowledgement of his improvement, which would also mean his being willing to give up some of the pleasure in defeating me. He was willing to talk about bad things about himself, sadism or excitement, you will remember, at the beginning of the session, but not his improvement, and he was not yet willing to give in on this point and enjoy feeling better (in terms of yesterday's dream to acknowledge and use the helping hands, the planes).

My patient tended to agree with this and then said that things had changed in the last bit of the session, he realized his mood had altered, the locked and blocked sense had gone, now he felt sadness, perhaps resentment, as if I, the analyst, had not given sufficient attention to the actual memory of the cigarette box incident, which seemed to him vivid and important, as if I had gone away from it too quickly. I went back to the cigarette box memory, and had a look at his feelings that I had missed something of its importance; I also reminded him of the stress he had put on his excitement while I felt that a lot of pleasure had really gone out of this now, as in the non-pleasure in the smoking. But I also showed him his resentment at the fact that his feelings had shifted, he had lost the uncomfortable blocked mood.

N. agreed, but said: 'Still I think you have gone too fast.' He could accept that part of the resentment might be connected with the shift that the analysis had enabled him to make — to undo the blocked feeling — but 'too fast' he explained was as if I, the analyst, had become a kind of Pied Piper and he had allowed himself to be pulled along with me.

I pointed out that it sounded as if he felt that I had not really analysed his problem about being stuck, but had pulled and seduced him out of his position. It was my initiative that had pulled him out, as he felt seduced by his mother as a child. (You will remember the earlier material in which he was convinced I and his mother had a special feeling for him.) He quickly, very quickly, added that there was also the other fear at that moment, the fear of getting caught up into excited warm feelings, like the feeling he used to call puppyish.

I now showed my patient that these two anxieties, that of my seducing him out of his previous state of mind and his fear of his own positive, excited, infantile, or puppyish feelings, might both need further consideration — both were old anxieties that had come up before as important — but I thought they were being used at that moment so that he could project them into me in order not to have to contain and experience and express the actual good feelings and particularly the warmth and gratitude which had been emerging in the latter part of the session (and was linked, I believe, with the awareness in the dream of a helpful quality in the planes overhead). At this point, very near the end of the session, my patient agreed with me and went off, clearly rather moved.

I am bringing this apparently rather straightforward material to stress a number of points that I find of interest in the use of transference. First, the way in which a dream can reveal its meaning in a fairly precise way by being lived out in the session, where we can see the patient's specific and willing involvement with misery and problems rather than meeting up with his helpful and lively objects, the planes, which are minimized, small. The analysis, interpretations, breasts are turned away from, when they are recognized as nourishing and helpful. The helpfulness is recognized specifically, but old problems are mobilized against it — called excitement, badness, non-cooperation. Positive aspects of the personality are seen, but his own capacity to move warmly towards an object is quickly distorted and projected into me: it is I who pull and seduce. But the whole thing is cleverly hidden, like the cigarette box in the book (probably bookish old interpretations, now no longer so meaningful). But he really knows that he doesn't get pleasure from the activity. We have here the specific meaning of the symbols and we can locate them in the transference. The patient gets insight, I believe, into what is almost a choice between moving towards a helpful object or indulging in despair — his defences are mobilized and he goes the latter way and tries to draw the analyst into criticizing and reproaching — into his masochistic defensive organization. Then followed further work and we can see that these defences lessen until he can actually acknowledge relief and warmth.

Further, as he can acknowledge a helpful object, he can relate to it and internalize it, which leads to further internal shifts.

I think in addition we can see here how the transference is full of meaning and history — the story of how the patient turns away, and I suspect always has done, from his good feeding objects. We can get an indication of one way in which, by projecting his loving into his mother and twisting it, he has helped to consolidate the picture of her as so seductive, an anxiety which still to some extent persists about women. Of course we can add that she well may have been a seductive woman towards her youngest son, but we can see how this has been used by him. The question of when and whether to interpret these matters is a technical one that I can only touch on here. My stress throughout this contribution has been on the transference as a relationship in which something is all the time going on, but we know that this something is essentially based on the patient's past and the relationship with his internal objects or his belief about them and what they were like.

I think that we need to make links for our patients from the transference to the past in order to help to build a sense of their own continuity and individuality, to achieve some detachment, and thus to help to free them from their earlier and more distorted sense of the past. About these issues many problems arise, theoretical and technical. For example, is a patient capable of discovering in the transference an object with good qualities if he had never experienced this in his infancy? About this I am doubtful; I suspect that, if the patient has met up with no object in his infancy on whom he can place some, however little, love and trust, he will not come to us in analysis. He will pursue a psychotic path alone. But what we can do, by tracing the movement and conflict within the transference, is bring alive again feelings within a relationship that have been deeply defended against or only fleetingly experienced, and we enable them to get firmer roots in the transference. We are not completely new objects, but, I think, greatly strengthened objects, because stronger and deeper emotions have been worked through in the transference. This type of movement I have tried to demonstrate in N., whose warmth and valuing have, over time, apparently come alive, but I am convinced that they were weakly there before, but much warded off. Now, I think, the emotions have been freed and have been strengthened, and the picture of his objects has shifted accordingly.

There is also the issue as to when and how it is useful to interpret the relation to the past, to reconstruct. I feel that it is important not to make these links if the linking disrupts what is going on in the session and leads to a kind of explanatory discussion or exercise, but rather to wait until the heat is no longer on and the patient has sufficient contact with himself and the situation to want to understand and to help to make links.

Even this, of course, can be used in a defensive way. These, however, are technical issues which do not really belong to this contribution.

I want now to return to a point that I mentioned earlier on, when I spoke of the transference as being the place where we can see not only the nature of the defences being used, but the level of psychic organization within which the patient is operating. To demonstrate this, I shall bring a fragment of material from a patient whom I shall call C., who is a somewhat obsessional personality, with severe limitations in his life, the extent of which he had not realized until he started treatment. I began to gain the impression that beneath the obsessional structure, controlling, superior, and rigid, there was a basically phobic organization. I shall try to reduce the piece of material that I am bringing to its bare bones.

C. had asked during the week to come a quarter of an hour earlier on the Friday, my first session in the day, in order to catch a train, as he had to go to Manchester for work. Then he described in great and obsessional detail on the Friday his worries about catching the train, getting through the traffic, and so on, and how he had safeguarded these problems. He also discussed an anxiety about losing his membership in a club because of non-attendance, and spoke about a friend being slightly unfriendly on the phone. Detailed interpretations about his feeling unwanted related to the weekend, feeling shut out, and a need not to go away but rather to remain here or shut inside, did not seem to make real contact or to help him. But in relation to my showing him his need to be inside and safe he started to talk, now in a very different and smooth way, about how similar this problem was to his difficulty in changing jobs, moving his office, getting new clothes, how he stuck to the old ones, although by now he was short of clothes. Then there was the same problem about changing cars . . ..

At this point I think that an interesting thing had occurred. While all that he was saying seemed accurate and important in itself, the thoughts were no longer being thought, they had become words, concrete analytic objects into which he could sink, get drawn in, as if they were the mental concomitant of a physical body into which he was withdrawing in the session. The question of separating off, mentally as physically, could be evaded since our ideas could now be experienced as completely in tune and he had withdrawn into them. When I pointed this out to C., he was shocked, saying: 'When you said that, Manchester came into my mind, it was like sticking a knife into me.' I thought that the knife that goes in was not just my pushing reality back into his mind, but a knife that goes in between himself and me, separating us off and making him aware of being different and outside, and this aroused immediate anxiety.

I bring this material to show how the interpretations about his obsessional control and his reassuring himself and me, then the interpretations about his needing to avoid separation, new things, and so on, and to be inside, were not experienced as helpful explanations, but were used as concrete objects, as parts of myself that he could get inside defensively, warding off psychotic anxieties of a more agoraphobic type associated with separation. Thus the two levels of operating — obsessional defending against phobic — could be seen to be lived out in the transference, and when the deeper layer was tackled, when I showed him the smooth defensive use of my words, my interpretations were felt as knife-like, and the anxieties re-emerged in the transference. In one sense this material is comparable with the case we discussed in the seminar. In such situations, if interpretations and understanding remain on the level of the individual associations, as contrasted with the total situation and the way that the analyst and his words are used, we shall find that we are being drawn into a pseudo-mature or more neurotic organization and missing the more psychotic anxieties and defences, which manifest themselves once we take into account the total situation — which is being acted out in the transference.

In this chapter, I am concentrating on what is being lived in the transference, and in this last example, as at the beginning, I tried to show how interpretations are rarely heard purely as interpretations, except when the patient is near to the depressive position. Then interpretations and the transference itself becomes more realistic and less loaded with phantasy meaning. Patients operating with more primitive defences of splitting and projective identification tend to 'hear' our interpretations or 'use' them differently, and how they 'use' or 'hear' and the difference between these two concepts needs to be distinguished if we are to clarify the transference situation and the state of the patient's ego and the correctness or not of his perceptions. Sometimes our patients hear our interpretations in a more paranoid way — for example, as a criticism or as an attack. C., after getting absorbed in my thoughts, heard my interpretations about Manchester as a knife that cut into him — between us. Sometimes the situation looks similar, the patient seems disturbed by an interpretation, but has, in fact, heard it, understood it, correctly, but unconsciously used it in an active way, thus involving the analyst.

N., I believe, did not hear my interpretations about his dream of the helicopter as cruel or harsh, but he unconsciously used them to reproach, beat, and torment himself masochistically, thus in his phantasy using me as the beater. Or, to return to C. : having heard certain of my interpretations and their meaning correctly, he used the words and thoughts not to think with, but unconsciously to act with, to get into and try to involve me in this activity, spinning words but not really communicating with them. Such activities not only colour but structure the transference situation and have important implications for technique.

Summary

I have tried in this chapter to discuss how I think we are tending to use the concept of transference today. I have stressed the importance of seeing transference as a living relationship in which there is constant movement and change. I have indicated how everything of importance in the patient's psychic organization based on his early and habitual ways of functioning, his phantasies, impulses, defences, and conflicts, will be lived out in some way in the transference. In addition, everything that the analyst is or says is likely to be responded to according to the patient's own psychic make-up, rather than the analyst's intentions and the meaning he gives to his interpretations. I have thus tried to discuss how the way in which our patients communicate their problems to us is frequently beyond their individual associations and beyond their words, and can often only be gauged by means of the countertransference. These are some of the points that I think we need to consider under the rubric of the total situations which are transferred from the past.

12

Projective identification: some clinical aspects

This paper was first given at a conference on Projection, Identification, and Projective Identification held at the Sigmund Freud Centre of the Hebrew University of Jerusalem in May 1984. It was published in J. Sandler (ed.) *Projection, Identification, Projective Identification*, Madison, CT: International Universities Press, 1987: 65—76; and appears in E. Bott Spillius (ed.) *Melanie Klein Today*, vol. 1, *Mainly Theory*, London: Routledge (1988), 138—50.

The concept of projective identification was introduced into analytic thinking by Melanie Klein in 1946. Since then it has been welcomed, argued about, the name disputed, the links with projection pointed out, and so on; but one aspect seems to stand out above the firing line, and that is its considerable clinical value. It is this aspect on which I shall mainly concentrate, and mainly in relation to the more neurotic patient.

Melanie Klein became aware of projective identification when exploring what she called the paranoid-schizoid position, that is, a constellation of a particular type of object relations, anxieties, and defences against them, typical for the earliest period of the individual's life and, in certain disturbed people, continuing throughout life. This particular position she saw dominated by the infant's need to ward off anxieties and impulses by splitting both the object, originally the mother, and the self, and projecting these split-off parts into an object, which will then be felt to be like, or identified with, these split-off parts, so colouring the infant's perception of the object and its subsequent introjection.

She discussed the manifold aims of different types of projective identification, for example, splitting off and getting rid of unwanted parts of the self that cause anxiety or pain; projecting the self or parts of the self into an object to dominate and control it and thus avoid any feelings of being separate; getting into an object to take over its capacities and make them its own; invading in order to damage or destroy the object. Thus the infant, or adult, who goes on using such mechanisms powerfully can avoid any awareness of separateness, dependence, admiration, or its concomitant sense of loss, anger, envy, and so on. But it sets up anxieties of a persecutory type, claustrophobic, panics, and the like.

We could say that, from the point of view of the individual who uses such mechanisms strongly, projective identification is a phantasy and yet it can have a powerful effect on the recipient. It does not always do so, and when it does we cannot always tell how the effect is brought about, but we cannot doubt its importance. We can see, however, that the concept of projective identification, used in this way, is more object-related, more concrete, and covers more aspects than the term 'projection' would ordinarily imply, and it has opened up a whole area of analytic understanding. These various aspects I am going to discuss later, as we see them operating in our clinical work. Here I want only to stress two points: first, the omnipotent power of these mechanisms and phantasies; second, how, in so far as they originate in a particular constellation, deeply interlocked, we cannot in our thinking isolate projective identification from the omnipotence, the splitting, and the resultant anxieties that go along with it. Indeed, we shall see that they are all part of a balance, rigidly or precariously maintained by the individual, in his own individual way.

As the individual develops, either in normal development or through analytic treatment, these projections lessen, he becomes more able to tolerate his ambivalence, his love and hate and dependence on objects — in other words, he moves towards what Melanie Klein described as the depressive position. This process can be helped in infancy if the child has a supportive environment, if the mother is able to tolerate and contain the child's projections, intuitively to understand and stand its feelings. Bion elaborated and extended this aspect of Melanie Klein's work, suggesting the importance of the mother being able to be used as a container by the infant, and linking this with the process of communication in childhood and with the positive use of the countertransference in analysis. Once the child is better integrated and able to recognize its impulses and feelings as its own, there will be a lessening in the pressure to project, accompanied by an increased concern for the object. In its earliest forms projective identification has no concern for the object — indeed, it is often anti-concern, aimed at dominating, irrespective of the cost to the object. As the child moves towards the depressive position, this necessarily alters, and, although projective identification is probably never entirely given up, it will no longer involve the complete splitting off and disowning of parts of the self, but will be less absolute, more temporary, and more able to be drawn back into the individual's personality — and thus be the basis of empathy. In this chapter I want, first, to consider some further implications of the use of projective identification, and then to discuss and illustrate different aspects of projective identification, first in two patients more or less stuck in the paranoid-schizoid position, and then in a patient beginning to move towards the depressive position.

To begin with: some of the implications, clinical and technical, of the massive use of projective identification as we see it in our work. Sometimes it is used so massively that we get the impression that the patient is, in phantasy, projecting his whole self into his object and may feel trapped or claustrophobic. It is, in any case, a very powerful and effective way of ridding the individual of contact with his own mind; at times the mind can be so weakened or so fragmented by splitting processes or so evacuated by projective identification that the individual appears empty or quasi-psychotic. This I shall show with C., the case of a child. It also has important technical implications; for example, bearing in mind that projective identification is only one aspect of an omnipotent balance established by each individual in his own way, any interpretive attempt on the part of the analyst to locate and give back to the patient missing parts of the self must of necessity be resisted by the total personality, since it is felt to threaten the whole balance and lead to more disturbance. I shall discuss this in case T. Projective identification cannot be seen in isolation.

A further clinical implication that I should like to touch on is about communication. Bion demonstrated how projective identification can be used as a method of communication by the individual, putting, as it were, undigested parts of his experience and inner world into the object, originally the mother, now the analyst, as a way of getting them understood and returned in a more manageable form. But we might add to this that projective identification is, by its very nature, a kind of communication, even in cases where this is not its aim nor its intention. By definition projective identification means the putting of parts of the self into an object. If the analyst on the receiving end is really open to what is going on and able to be aware of what he is experiencing, this can be a powerful method of gaining understanding. Indeed, much of our current appreciation of the richness of the notion of countertransference stems from it. I shall later try to indicate some of the problems this raises, in terms of acting-in, in my discussion of the third case, N.

I want now to give a brief example of a case to illustrate the concreteness of projective identification in the analytic situation, its effectiveness as a method of ridding the child of a whole area of experience and thus keeping some kind of balance, and the effect of such massive projective mechanisms on her state of mind. This is a little girl aged four, in analytic treatment with Mrs Rocha Barros, who was discussing the case with me. The child had only very recently begun treatment, a deeply disturbed and neglected child, whom I shall call C.

A few minutes before the end of a Friday session C. said that she was going to make a candle; the analyst explained her wish to take a warm Mrs Barros with her that day at the end of the session and her fear that there would not be enough time, as there were only three minutes left. C. started to scream, saying that she would have some spare candles; she then started to stare through the window with a vacant, lost expression. The analyst interpreted that the child needed to make the analyst realize how awful it was to end the session, as well as expressing a wish to take home some warmth from the analyst's words for the weekend. The child screamed: 'Bastard! Take off your clothes and jump outside.' Again the analyst tried to interpret C.'s feelings about being dropped and sent into the cold. C. replied: 'Stop your talking, take off your clothes. You are cold. I'm not cold.' The feeling in the session was extremely moving. Here the words carry the concrete meaning, to the child, of the separation of the weekend — the awful coldness. This she tries to force into the analyst. 'You are cold, I am not cold.' I think that here it is not just an attempt to rid herself of the experience by projective identification, but also a kind of retaliatory attack.

The moments when C. looked completely lost and vacant, as in this fragment, were very frequent, and were, I think, indicative not only of her serious loss of contact with reality, but of the emptiness, vacancy of her mind and personality when projective identification was operating so powerfully. I think that much of her screaming is also in the nature of her emptying out. The effectiveness of such emptying is striking, as the whole experience of loss and its concomitant emotions is cut out. One can again see here how the term 'projective identification' describes more vividly and fully the processes involved than the more general and frequently used terms, such as 'reversal' or, as I said, 'projection'.

In this example, then, the child's balance is primarily maintained by the projecting out of parts of the self. I want now to give an example of a familiar kind of case to discuss various kinds of projective identification working together to hold a particular narcissistic, omnipotent balance. This kind of balance is very firmly structured, extremely difficult to influence analytically, and leads to striking persecutory anxieties. It also raises some points about different identificatory processes and problems about the term 'projective identification' itself.

A young teacher, whom I shall call T., came into analysis with difficulties in relationships, but actually with the hope of changing careers and becoming an analyst. His daily material consisted very largely of descriptions of work he had done in helping his pupils, how his colleagues had praised his work, asked him to discuss their work with him, and so on. Little else came into the sessions. He frequently described how one or other of his colleagues felt threatened by him, threatened in the sense of feeling minimized or put in an inferior position by his greater insight and understanding. He was, therefore, uneasy that they felt unfriendly to him at any given moment. (Any idea that his personality might actually put people off did not enter his mind.) It was not difficult to show him certain ideas about myself — for example, that when I did not seem to be encouraging him to give up his career and apply for training as an analyst, he felt that I, being old, felt threatened by this intelligent young person coming forward, and, therefore, would not want him in my professional area.

Clearly, simply to suggest, or interpret, that T. was projecting his envy into his objects and then feeling them as identified with this part of himself might be theoretically accurate, but clinically inept and useless — indeed, it would just be absorbed into his psychoanalytic armoury. We can see that the projective identification of the envious parts of the self was, as it were, only the end result of one aspect of a highly complex balance which he was keeping. To clarify something of the nature of this balance, it is important to see how T. was relating to me in the transference. Usually he spoke of me as a very fine analyst and I was flattered in such ways. Actually he could not take in interpretations meaningfully, he appeared not to listen properly; he would, for example, hear the words partially and then re-interpret them unconsciously, according to some previous theoretical psychoanalytical knowledge, then give them to himself with this slightly altered and generalized meaning. Frequently, when I interpreted more firmly, he would respond very quickly and argumentatively, as if there were a minor explosion which seemed destined not only to expel from his mind what I might be going to say, but enter my mind and break up my thinking at that moment.

In this example we have projective identification operating with various different motives and leading to different identificatory processes — but all aimed at maintaining his narcissistic omnipotent balance. First we see the splitting of his objects — I am flattered and kept in his mind as idealized; at such moments the bad or unhelpful aspect of myself is quite split off, even though I don't seem to be achieving much with him; but this latter has to be denied. He projects part of himself into my mind and takes over; he 'knows' what I am going to say and says it himself. At this point, a part of the self is identified with an idealized aspect of myself, which is talking to, interpreting to, an idealized patient part himself; idealized because it listens to the analyst part of him. We can see what this movement achieves in terms of his balance. It cuts out any real relationship between the patient and myself, between analyst and patient, as mother and child, as a feeding couple. It obviates any separate existence, any relating to me as myself; any relationship in which he takes in directly from me. T. was, in fact, earlier in his life slightly anorexic. If I manage for a moment to get through this T. explodes, so that his mental digestive system is fragmented, and by this verbal explosion, as I said, T. unconsciously tries to enter my mind and break up my thinking, my capacity to feed him. It is important here, as always with projective identification, to distinguish this kind of unconscious entering, invading, and breaking up from a conscious aggressive attack. What I am discussing here is how these patients, using projective identification so omnipotently, actually avoid any such feelings as dependence, envy, jealousy, and so on.

Once T. has in phantasy entered my mind and taken over my interpretations, and my role at that moment, I notice that he has 'added to', 'improved on', 'enriched' my interpretations, and I become the onlooker, who should realize that my interpretations of a few moments ago were not as rich as his are now — and surely I should feel threatened by this young man in my room! Thus the two types of projective identification are working in harmony, the invading of my mind and taking over its contents and the projecting of the potentially dependent, threatened, and envious part of the self into me. This is, of course, mirrored in what we hear is going on in his outside world — the fellow students who ask for help and feel threatened by his brilliance — but then he feels persecuted by their potential unfriendliness. So long as the balance holds so effectively, we cannot see what more subtle, sensitive, and important aspects of the personality are being kept split off, or why — we can see that any relationship to a truly separate object is obviated — with all that this may imply.

A great difficulty is, of course, that all insight tends to get drawn into this process. To give a minute example: one Monday, T. really seemed to become aware of exactly how he was subtly taking the meaning out of what I was saying and not letting real understanding develop. For a moment he felt relief and then a brief, deep feeling of hatred to me emerged into consciousness. A second later he added quietly that he was thinking how the way that he had been feeling just then towards me, that is, the hatred, must have been how his fellow students had felt towards him on the previous day when he had been talking and explaining things to them! So, immediately that T. has a real experience of hating me because I have said something useful, he uses the momentary awareness to speak about the students, and distances himself from the emerging envy and hostility, and the direct receptive contact between the two of us is again lost. What looks like insight is no longer insight but has become a complex projective manoeuvre.

At a period when these problems were very much in the forefront of the analysis, T. brought a dream, right at the end of a session. The dream was simply this: *T. was with the analyst or with a woman, J., or it might have been both, he was excitedly pushing his hand up her knickers into her vagina, thinking that if he could get right in there would be no stopping him.* Here, I think under the pressure of the analytic work going on, T.'s great need and great excitement was to get totally inside the object, with all its implications, including, of course, the annihilation of the analytic situation.

To return to the concept of projective identification. With this patient I have indicated three or four different aspects: attacking the analyst's mind; a kind of total invading, as in the dream fragment I have just quoted; a more partial invading and taking over of aspects of capacities of the analyst; and, finally, putting part of the self, particularly inferior parts, into the analyst. The latter two are mutually dependent, but lead to different types of identification. In the one, the patient, in taking over, becomes identified with the analyst's idealized capacities; in the other, it is the analyst who becomes identified with the lost, projected, here inferior or envious parts of the patient. I think it is partly because the term is broad and covers many aspects that there has been some unease about the name itself.

I have so far discussed projective identification in two cases caught up in the paranoid–schizoid position, a borderline child and a man in a rigid omnipotent narcissistic state. Now I want to discuss aspects of projective identification as one sees it in a patient moving towards the depressive position. I shall illustrate some points from the case of a man as he was becoming less rigid, more integrated, better able to tolerate what was previously projected, but constantly also pulling back, returning to the use of the earlier projective mechanisms; then I want to show the effect of this on subsequent identifications and the light that it throws on previous identifications. I also want to attempt to forge a link between the nature of the patient's residual use of projective identification and its early infantile counterpart and the relation of this to phobia formation. I bring this material also to discuss briefly the communicative nature of projective identification.

To start with this latter point, as I said earlier, since projective identification by its very nature means the putting of parts of the self into the object, in the transference we are of necessity on the receiving end of the projections and, therefore, providing we can tune into them, we have an opportunity *par excellence* to understand them and what is going on. In this sense, it acts as a communication, whatever its motivation, and is the basis for the positive use of countertransference. As I want to describe with this patient, N., it is frequently difficult to clarify whether, at any given moment, projective identification is primarily aimed at communicating a state of mind that cannot be verbalized by the patient or whether it is aimed more at entering and controlling or attacking the analyst, or whether all these elements are active and need consideration.

A patient, N., who had been in analysis many years, had recently married and, after a few weeks, was becoming anxious about his sexual interest and his potency, particularly in view of the fact that his wife was considerably younger. He came on a Monday, saying that he felt that 'the thing' was never really going to get right, 'the sexual thing', yes, they did have sex on Sunday, but somehow he had to force himself and he knew it wasn't quite all right, and his wife noticed this and commented. It was an all-right kind of weekend, just about. He spoke about this a bit more and explained that they went to a place outside London, to a party, they had meant to stay the night in an hotel nearby, but couldn't find anywhere nice enough and came home and so were late.

What was being conveyed to me was a quiet, sad discomfort, leading to despair, and I pointed out to N. how he was conveying an awful long-term hopelessness and despair, with no hope for the future. He replied to the effect that he supposed that he was feeling left out, and linked this with what had been a rather helpful and vivid session on the Friday, but now, as he made the remark, it was quite dead and flat. When I tried to look at this with him, he agreed, commenting that he supposed he was starting to attack the analysis, and so on. The feeling in the session now was awful; N. was making a kind of sense and saying analytic things himself, which could have been right — for example, about the Friday — and which one could have picked up, but, since they seemed flat and quite unhelpful to him, what he seemed to me to be doing was putting despair into me, not only about the reality of his marriage and potency, but also about his analysis, as was indicated, for example, by the useless, and by now somewhat irrelevant, comment about being left out. N. denied my interpretation about his despair about the progress of the analysis, but in such a way, it seemed to me, as to be encouraging me to make false interpretations and to pick up his pseudo-interpretations as if I believed in them, while knowing that they and we were getting nowhere. He vaguely talked about this, went quiet, and said: 'I was listening to your voice, the timbre changes in different voices. W. (his wife), being younger, makes more sounds per second, older voices are deeper because they make less sounds per second, etc.'

I showed N. his great fear that I showed with my voice, rather than through my actual words, that I could not stand the extent of his hopelessness and his doubts about myself, about what we could achieve in the analysis and, therefore, in his life, and that I would cheat and in some way try to encourage. I queried whether he had perhaps felt that, in that session, my voice had changed in order to sound more encouraging and encouraged, rather than contain the despair he was expressing. By this part of the session my patient had got into contact and said with some relief that, if I did do this kind of encouraging, the whole bottom would fall out of the analysis.

First, the nature of the communication, which I could understand primarily through my countertransference, through the way in which I was being pushed and pulled to feel and to react. We see here the concrete quality of projective identification structuring the counter-transference. It seems that the way in which N. was speaking was not asking me to try to understand the sexual difficulties or unhappiness, but to invade me with despair, while at the same time unconsciously trying to force me to reassure myself that it was all right, that interpretations, now empty of meaning and hollow, were meaningful, and that the analysis at that moment was going ahead satisfactorily. Thus it was not only the despair that N. was projecting into me, but his defences against it, a false reassurance and denial, which it was intended I should act out with him. I think that this also suggests a projective identification of an internal figure, probably primarily mother, who was felt to be weak, kind, but unable to stand up to emotion. In the transference (to oversimplify the picture) this figure is projected into me, and I find myself pushed to live it out.

We have here the important issue of teasing out the motivation for this projective identification: was it aimed primarily at communicating something to me; was there a depth of despair that we had not previously sufficiently understood; or was the forcing of despair into me motivated by something different? At this stage, at the end of the session, I did not know and left it open.

I have so much condensed the material here that I cannot convey adequately the atmosphere and to-and-fro of the session. But towards the end, as I have tried to show, my patient experienced and expressed relief and appreciation of what had been going on. There was a shift in mood and behaviour as my patient started to accept understanding and face the nature of his forcing into me, and he could then experience me as an object that could stand up to his acting-in, not get caught into it, but contain it. He could then identify temporarily with a stronger object, and he himself became firmer. I also sensed some feeling of concern about what he had been doing to me and my work — it was not openly acknowledged and expressed — but there is some movement towards the depressive position with its real concern and guilt.

In order to clarify the motivation as well as the effect of this kind of projective identification on subsequent introjective identification, we need to go briefly into the beginning of the next session, when N. brought a dream, *in which he was on a boat like a ferry boat, on a grey-green sea surrounded by mist; he did not know where they were going. Then nearby there was another boat which was clearly going down under the water and drowning. He stepped on to this boat as it went down; he did not feel wet or afraid, which was puzzling.* Among his associations we heard of his wife being very gentle and affectionate, but he added that he himself was concerned, was she behind this really making more demands on him? She, knowing his fondness for steak and kidney pudding, had made him one the night before. It was excellent, but the taste was too strong, which he told her!

Now the interesting thing, I think, was that, on the previous day I had felt rather at sea, as I said, not knowing exactly where we were going, but I was clear that the understanding about the hopelessness and the defences against it was right, and, though I had not thought it out in this way, my belief would have been that the mists would clear as we went on. But what does my patient do with this? He gratuitously steps off this boat (this understanding) on to one that is going down, and he is not afraid! In other works, he prefers to drown in despair rather than clarify it, prefers to see affection as demands, and my decent, well-cooked steak and kidney interpretations as too tasty. At this point, as we worked on it, N. could see that the notion of drowning here was actually exciting to him.

Now we can see more about the motivation. It becomes clear that N. was not just trying to communicate and get understood something about his despair, important as this element is, but that he was also attacking me and our work, by trying to drag me down by the despair, when there was actually progress. After a session in which he expressed appreciation about my work and capacity to stand up to him, he dreamed of willingly stepping on to a sinking boat, so that either, internally, I collude and go down with him or am forced to watch him go under and my hope is destroyed and I am kept impotent to help. This activity also leads to an introjective identification with an analyst—parent who is felt to be down, joyless, and impotent, and this identification contributes considerably to his lack of sexual confidence and potency. Following this period of the analysis, there was real improvement in the symptom.

Naturally, these considerations lead one to think about the nature of the patient's internal objects — for example, the weak mother — that I described as being projected into me in the transference. How much is this figure based on N.'s real experience with his mother? How much did he exploit her weaknesses and thus contribute to building in his inner world a mother, weak, inadequate, and on the defensive, as we saw in the transference? In other words, when we talk of an object projected in to the analyst in the transference, we are discussing an internal object that has been structured in part from the child's earlier projective identifications, and the whole process can be seen being revived in the transference.

I want now to digress and look at this material from a slightly different angle, related to the patient's very early history and anxieties. I have shown how N. pulls back and goes into an object, in the dream, into the sinking boat, as in the first session he goes into despair, which is then projected into me, rather than his thinking about it. This going into an object, acted out in the session, is, I believe, linked with a more total type of projective identification that I indicated in the sexual dream of T. and referred to briefly at the beginning of this paper as being connected with phobia formation. At the very primitive end of projective identification is the attempt to get back into an object — to become, as it were, undifferentiated and mindless and thus avoid all pain. Most human beings develop beyond this in early infancy; some of our patients attempt to use projective identification in this way over many years.

N., when he came into analysis, came because he had a fetish, a tremendous pull towards getting inside a rubber object which would totally cover, absorb, and excite him. In his early childhood he had nightmares of falling out of a globe into endless space. In the early period of analysis he would have severe panic states when alone in the house, and would be seriously disturbed or lose contact if he had to be away from London on business. At the same time there are minor indications of anxieties about being trapped in a claustrophobic way; for example, at night he would have to keep blankets on the bed loose or throw them off altogether; in intercourse phantasies emerged of his penis being cut off and lost inside the woman's body. As the analysis went on, the fetishistic activities disappeared and real relationships improved and the projecting of the self into the object could clearly be seen in the transference. He would get absorbed in his own words or ideas or in the sound of my words and my speaking, and the meaning would be unimportant compared with the concrete nature of the experience. This type of absorption into words and sounds with the analyst, as a person, quite disregarded is not unlike the kind of process that one sometimes sees in child patients, who come into the playroom, on to the couch, and fall so deeply asleep that they are unable to be woken by interpretations. It is, therefore, interesting to see in N. how he has always concretely attempted to get into an object, apparently largely in order to escape from being outside, to become absorbed and free from relating and from thought and mental pain. And yet we know that this is only half the story, since the object he mainly got into was a fetish and highly sexualized. And still in the modern dream of getting into the drowning boat there was masochistic excitement that he tried to pull me into and in this sense it needs to be compared with T. I described how, as his constant invading and taking over was being analysed, we could see in T.'s sexual dream in an attempt totally to get inside me with great excitement. I suspect there is much yet to be teased out about the relation between certain types of massive projective identification of the self and erotization.

Now I want to return to the material that I quoted and to the question of projective identification in patients who are becoming more integrated and nearer to the depressive position. We can see in the case of N. — unlike T., who is still imprisoned in his own omnipotent, narcissistic structure — that there is now a movement, in the transference, towards more genuine whole object relations. At times he can really appreciate the strong containing qualities of his object; true, he will then try to draw me in and drag me down again, but there is now potential conflict about this. The object can be valued and loved, at times he can consciously experience hostility about this — and ambivalence is present. As his loving is freed, he is able to introject and identify with a whole valued and potent object, and the effect on his character and potency is striking. This is a very different quality of identification from that based on forcing despairing parts of the self into an object, who then in his phantasy becomes like a despairing part of himself. It is very different from the type of identification we saw in T., where the patient invaded my mind and took over the split and idealized aspects, leaving the object, myself, denuded and inferior. With N., in the example I have just given, he could experience and value me as a whole, different, and properly separate person with my own qualities, and these he could introject and thereby feel strengthened. But we still have a task ahead, to enable N. to be truly outside and able to give up the analysis, aware of its meaning to him and yet secure.

Summary

I have tried in this chapter to discuss projective identification as we see it operating in our clinical work. I have described various types of projective identification, from the more primitive and massive type to the more empathic and mature. I have discussed how we see alterations in its manifestation as progress is made in treatment and the patient moves towards the depressive position, is better integrated and able to use his objects less omnipotently, relate to them as separate objects, and introject them and their qualities more fully and realistically, and thus also to separate from them.

13

Envy in everyday life

This paper was first given at a Tavistock public lecture in November 1985 and was subsequently published in *Psychoanalytic Psychotherapy* 2 (1986): 13–22.

Introduction

It may perhaps seem strange to be writing about envy in everyday life, because, one might say, it is such an everyday emotion, known to everyone. It has always been talked about; we find throughout literature abounding references to and descriptions of envy and its workings. We know about the green-eyed monster from *Othello*:

Iago: O beware, my lord, of jealousy;
It is the green-ey'd monster which doth mock
The meat it feeds on.

Here Shakespeare uses the word 'jealousy', but it is very close to what we would feel to be an essential aspect of envy. I shall come back to the relationship between the two. Yet, in a strange way, psychoanalysis, until about thirty years ago, paid attention to envy but only from a very limited standpoint. Freud talked, almost entirely, about one kind of envy, which he called 'penis envy'. That was the envy of the woman for the man's penis and his masculine attributes, her resentment at not having one, and so on, but broader ideas about the significance of envy and its ubiquity, or the notion that a man might envy a woman's attributes and capacities, really scarcely entered into Freud's writing. It was probably not until the 1950s, particularly 1957, when Melanie Klein published her book *Envy and Gratitude*, that the significance of envy became more fully discussed and understood. Anyone who knows this book will see that what I am going to discuss is essentially derived from Melanie Klein's thinking.

It is interesting to consider why the significance of envy took so long to be recognized, while its near relation, jealousy, had been in the analytic literature and part of general understanding for a very long time. Now I think that our understanding and recognition of jealousy, as compared with our neglect of envy, has very important roots. If one thinks about jealousy, what do we mean? We mean a relationship which involves three people; one is jealous because someone one loves, or to whom one is attached, shows more interest or affection for someone else. But this is considered, broadly speaking, all right. I think this is because the jealousy is based on love of or affection for one person; otherwise one wouldn't feel jealous. So there is a reason for jealousy which makes it, to some extent, tolerable and forgivable. Indeed, we know that certain crimes committed under the pressure of extreme jealousy may be said to have extenuating circumstances, and the verdict and sentence will be mitigated accordingly.

But with envy the picture is different: it involves basically two people; and the envy is about what the other person possesses, or his capacities, achievements, personal qualities, and so on; and it involves to a greater or less extent a spoiling quality or at least hostility towards the good abilities of the other person, though this may not be recognized. The *Oxford English Dictionary* (1979 edition) describes 'The feeling of mortification and ill will occasioned by the contemplation of superior advantages possessed by another'. If one destroys from jealousy, there is some reason for it; but in envy the spoiling is done from hatred and there appear to be no extenuating circumstances. As one of my patients put it, it is so 'meaningless'.

Envy often seems to be connected with greed and yet it is different from greed. The person who is greedy wants to get something, disregarding the cost to the person from whom he wants it, and recognizes there is something good to be obtained; but the envious person is not so much interested in getting something for himself and enjoying it, even greedily; but rather in taking something away from the other person, which he may then make over to himself, so that it becomes part of himself.

What I want to do now is to look at envy as we see it operating in everyday life and then consider some of its implications. The conscious end we all know about, in a sense — feelings of resentment at someone being ahead, doing better, and vague hostility, rivalry, competitiveness — but it is when it is more powerful that the trouble starts; for example, when it leads to a kind of constant carping criticism or snide remarks. Or the other way round, when the envious individual cannot see anything to praise or value in another individual, but always finds doubts, 'well, it was good, but . . .' — and he will find some reason to doubt or knock the other person. And as there really always is some ground for criticism in any of us or in what we do, the envious attitude can easily be missed and the criticisms or doubts can look real.

Another way in which envy can be seen more easily is when it leads openly to a kind of ruthless determination to get what the other person has, so that if X. has a good job or a new cooking pot, his envious friend will not be satisfied until he has a similar or better one. This kind of attitude is, of course, much nearer to an overweening ambition. It is probably less dangerous and troublesome than the more insidious type, which causes the real trouble. The manifestations of envy that concern us more here are those more clearly associated with spoiling — spoiling being probably fundamental to envy. The envious person can spoil literally by mud-slinging, damaging, or hurting another person or his possessions; or he can spoil by psychological mud-slinging, hurting another person's attributes or achievements in his own mind, in his thinking, or externally by criticism, mockery, or provocation. I say 'provocation' because it is a marvellous spoiler, well-known to many people, often very visible, say in adolescence and in psychoanalytic treatment. We can see this kind of thing when the envious person envies the other person's quiet intelligence and peace of mind and sets about to needle and provoke until the other loses his cool. This can be a very clear weapon in analysis.

To put the problem round the other way. What a really envious person cannot bear is to face another's success, enjoyment, pleasure; and the nearer to home one gets, the more difficult this is likely to feel. So the really envious person cannot bear that something good is given to him by another person. He cannot enjoy it; he will begrudge recognizing its goodness, begrudge acknowledging its value; and will be unable to experience and to express gratitude. As one of my patients describes it, faced with the problem of experiencing and expressing gratitude, he just 'cannot get it out' — it sticks in his throat. Now if this is so on a verbal level with a man who has been in analysis some time, who has considerable insight and a great wish to change, we can get a feeling of the depth of the underlying problem.

An excessively envious person, therefore, may find it so hard to tolerate that another person has something to give him that he cannot recognize or use the other person constructively. It may be seen emerging as real inability to take in information or help, actually to understand it. It can be an important element in children who cannot learn at school, as if they simply have to reject any help at all. (This is, of course, only one element in a total situation, but the element we are considering here.) This problem can prevent the individual from reading and using books, scientific papers, and so on, because the feeling is of having to know what is written before he reads it, and, therefore, his mind is not free to follow the argument of the book or paper. It can prevent him or her from using or believing in available professional help or advice. We can see a similar aspect in what I would call 'the deadening of conversations'. A very envious person can hardly bear to listen to what another person has to tell and may find all kinds of ways of stopping the conversation, taking it over, paralysing it, because he or she cannot bear to listen to entertaining things, experiences, interesting thoughts coming from someone else.

Before I go on to look at some further implications of what I am describing, I want to bring a brief example of the workings of destructive envy in a case in analytic treatment. A man who had been in analysis for some time, who originally had considerable sexual difficulties, was cold, detached, and unfeeling in a rather cruel way, but had made a great deal of progress, had married, and now was hoping that, after some initial difficulties in conceiving, his wife might be pregnant. He came in one session and told me the following dream. *My patient and his wife went to X—— by plane and were met by some friends of his, let us call them Andrew and Barbara. He found he couldn't remember Barbara's name, so he couldn't introduce her properly to his wife, who hadn't met her before. The couple took them to another town to a restaurant. They sat at a long table and my patient noticed how Barbara had become small, angular, peaked, and dull. His wife talked a lot, but became clearly out of her depth and a bit silly, but, he said in a kind but slightly patronizing way, it didn't really matter much, it was nothing. She also looked a bit like a young boy. After this, the friends, Andrew and Barbara, took my patient and his wife to the town, where they were to catch their plane back to London.*

My patient gave a number of associations to the dream and spoke about the details, which I cannot attempt to give here. I just want to describe what I think the dream was about and hope my reasoning will be followed. Here is a man who really consciously wants his wife to have a baby and wants the analysis to go well, but we see that the two women, wife and Barbara, become diminished. The wife loses her femininity, goes boyish and silly, but he forgives her. The friend, Barbara, goes dull, small, and angular. Small and angular sounds to me a bit like myself, but he had not been finding the analysis dull or lifeless recently! I think that these two women, who are immediately important in his life, have had their particular qualities removed in the dream, those very qualities which he values in them — my capacity to be alert and alive to what is going on, so I become small and angular, not just in body, but in mind; and his wife's capacity to be intelligent, alert, and feminine and conceiving — all this goes.

After this, the two couples went to the town from which my patient and his wife would get the plane home. This, he explained to me, was odd, because the town where they had been eating also has an airport, and therefore they could in reality have travelled directly from there to London. I think this latter point suggests that once my patient has got his good objects, his wife and myself, in a patronized or devalued condition, then his mental balance is restored and he can return to his usual base, his old habitual way of relating to people, seeing them as inferior and not enviable. This is the way he returns home. This balance had been disturbed by his awareness of his wife's unique position if pregnant and my value as the analysis proceeded, myself seen as analytically pregnant with ideas.

We can see in this material a very important element, that of what this patient used to call the meaninglessness of his spoiling. He does not himself gain from taking away his wife's femininity or my aliveness; on the contrary, from the reality angle, he would lose by it. But, as I suggested, the envious person is actually more interested in spoiling what the other person has than in getting actual good things or experiences for himself. My patient cannot get himself pregnant by attacking his wife's femininity. If I become a dull, stupid analyst I am not much use to him, but his envy is appeased. There is nothing left to envy and his mental balance is restored. Thus we can see in this brief example how the patient's envy 'doth mock the meat it feeds on'.

There are many layers of problems that are revealed in this apparently simple example. On the level of adult relationships, we can see how his envy can lead to a mean spoiling of his wife's femininity; but it could also push into his relationship with the baby: if the wife does become pregnant, for example, his envy could emerge as his resenting his wife's capacity to care for and bring up and feed the baby. This kind of resentment might look more like jealousy of the mother-and-baby relationship, but behind that the envy in this patient would, I think, be the more dangerous element, unless I am able to help him enough. In parenthesis, I would add that I think it is very often the case that situations that look like jealousy or pathological jealousy are really based on this kind of fundamental envy — but that is another issue.

To return to this patient, I have tried to indicate some of the deeper layers behind the current adult problems with his wife: for example, how he becomes unable to get good analytic nourishment from me, unable happily to be on the receiving end. I am trying here to indicate how the early problems of receiving and enjoying in such people are likely to emerge at every step of development and interfere with progress in new relationships and situations.

I want now to look at some further implications of this type of envious attitude. As I have discussed, the really envious person cannot enjoy what comes from somebody else and cannot experience gratitude, which means that his capacity to enjoy and to love is severely interfered with. We know that we build our characters by taking into ourselves — introjecting — our early relationships to our parents and close figures of our infancy and childhood as we experience them, and that we feel about ourselves according to the world we build up inside, our internal world. If envy, for whatever reason, prevents the individual from building good, warm, trusting relationships, his whole inner world, and thus his character, will be influenced, and he is likely to remain correspondingly insecure. This very insecurity or sense of inadequacy will increase the hatred of others who are more comfortable, more confident, and more stable; and so the insecurity increases the envy, and we get a vicious circle.

And there are other problems. The person who is very envious and spoiling in his relationships, even in a hidden way, including hidden from himself, will experience his world as hostile or spoiling towards him and become more paranoid or suspicious in his attitude to people, so that his world becomes unpleasant to him and he becomes more and more on the defensive and less able to enjoy. Indeed, one of the great problems about very envious people, even where it is not conscious, is that they have so little real enjoyment in life. When they do have good experiences and pleasure, there is the nagging feeling that they could get more, or someone else has better; or there is something wrong with it, or, if they get it now, why couldn't they have had it before; it would have been so much better when they were younger. This we see again in the analysis with the patient who, when he does accept that something we have said is helpful, will in the next moment let us know that, in so far as we have shown it to him now, it would have been so much more helpful had be been able to understand it a year ago.

Of course, by this time, it is not only the patient who is deprived of happy experiences, but analytically also the analyst, who is given little chance to enjoy his position as analyst of this patient.

It is, of course, very uncomfortable to be constantly or frequently aware of envious feelings; it is unpleasant and disturbing; and most people, probably all of us to a greater or less extent, try unconsciously to protect themselves with various manoeuvres against it, try to build defences against experiencing envy. These defences can help the individual temporarily to suffer less, but, like all defences, can also cause further trouble, especially if they are strong.

I want now to talk about some of these defences and some of the troubles they cause. There is often a mixture of the actual expression of envy and defences against that envy. It is not always possible to say whether a thing is an envious attack or whether it is a defence against it. Take, for example, the dream of the man with the wife who hoped she was pregnant: if he can keep me in his mind as dull and non-conceiving, he protects himself from being hostile to me for being helpful, and yet, in making me, as I am suggesting he did in the dream, dull and small mentally, this can be seen in itself to be an attack on me. In treatment it can be very important to sort this out.

Let us now look at other types of defences as they emerge in ordinary living, and are reflected in the analytic situation. One way to avoid too much envy is to idealize the person who stirs it up; so to idealize that the other person is seen as so beautiful or having such striking capacities, to have done such an outstanding piece of work, and so on, that the gap between the other person and the self becomes so enormous that apparently no comparison is possible. This keeps the potentially envied person on a pedestal and out of range. In analysis one can often see this happening, when the patient has to keep the analyst as so good, just loved and valued, and the whole relationship kept positive, no criticism allowed in. This can be quite a problem with some very ill patients, who cling to this state of affairs as if terrified of what would happen if envious or critical thoughts emerged, as if the patient simply could not contain them. This can actually be quite hard for the young or inexperienced therapist or analyst to handle, since it is very much nicer and more comfortable to believe one really is a good, intelligent, and lively kind of analyst; it is much pleasanter to hear about stupidity, heavy-handedness, insensitivity, and so forth as being the qualities which other people's therapists or analysts have; and in this way both patient and analyst can keep some real problems nicely split off.

A different, but probably related, kind of splitting can be seen in the kind of defence in which the individual tends to devalue the self, making out that he has nothing to give, that he is so poor and so limited, and in this way he increases the gap between the self and the other person. For example, how could such a poor creature in any way compare himself with X., and so on. This type of defence can be very close to a kind of masochism, placating and flattering. It cannot of course work, because it tends to make the individual either very self-righteous or more depressed, feeling worthless, giving up hope; and often, in fact, starting to wallow in this state, which makes things even worse and more difficult to get out of.

Another type of defence, which I have already just touched on, is more connected with a particular kind of greed, and is very important in some people who have difficulties in learning and absorbing information, including, of course, analytic information, though it may not look like that. Certain patients in analysis may appear highly co-operative and understanding; but, as one looks at the development of the session, one may see that what they are actually doing is not responding to interpretations and to understanding, being able to agree to differ, to chew things over, digest them, and so on; they are doing something else. They listen and, as it were, swallow up and take over the analyst's ideas, very often without actually following through what the analyst or therapist is really saying or meaning, and failing to register anything new or fresh or any subtlety or nuance in what is being said. Thus one gets the impression that the patient has in his phantasy got into the analyst's mind so that he has at that moment become analyst to himself or to the patient on the couch, so to speak, and the analyst proper has become almost redundant, almost non-existent. It may look like insight, but it is very different, and the process can be very subtle. It is clear why I am describing this as a defence against envy. In so far as the patient has taken over in this very quick way, he never has the experience of being given something good and digestible or of knowing that it comes from someone else, here the analyst, who might therefore be helpful, even enviable; so envy this way can be obviated. One can also see how this type of defence can be linked with learning difficulties, as I said before, and also with earlier feeding difficulties, even actual anorexia, and with frigidity, but this is a vast topic on which we cannot embark here.

This type of taking over mentally is probably closely connected with a very familiar kind of behaviour, also based on projection. I say 'also', because the getting into the analyst's mind is really in the nature of a projective identification with the analyst.

But the kind that I want to go on to discuss now is when the envious person, instead of being aware of his envy, tries, usually unconsciously, to stir it up in other people, subtly or not so subtly, making others aware of his or her particular qualities or capacities, in such a way as to provoke envy in the others. It can be a very deep characterological trait. Of course, it creates further problems, because such individuals become preoccupied with other people's competitiveness, hostility, and envy, and feel both in a sense superior, as though they contain all the good qualities, and also very threatened. I am going to give an example from analysis, but I think the picture that emerges will be a familiar one.

This is a young woman, who came from abroad to complete some postgraduate scientific work and then stayed on here to get analytic treatment. She was attractive, lively, and very intelligent. On the one hand, she kept me in her mind, in the way I described previously, as quite idealized. I was consciously seen as a very good analyst — straight, cultured, decent, and so on. But just behind this I began to sense a very different picture of me — of which she was not aware at that point — me seen as an envious old spinster who didn't really want her, the patient, to have a good time and full social life, lots of friends and be admired by young men (all of which she had). The picture of me as an old spinster, that is all right, but what about my spoiling, envious attitude, split off from her consciousness, but beginning to emerge? It could, of course, be true, but it might not be. What I did notice was an enormous concern in my patient to discuss and re-discuss endlessly in her analysis and outside what was going on, which boy friend had telephoned, what he said, what she thought about what he said, and so on, largely focusing on herself and her central role in her world. Any awareness, any evidence as to my being a human being with my own life hardly came alive in her mind. Her girl friends, of her own generation, increasingly emerged in the analysis as a bit 'paranoid', her word, trying to make her feel low, enjoying pointing out unhappy things in her relationships or competitive with her, and so forth. Now I do not doubt that there was some truth in it, but . . .

What I think was really happening was that her balance had been maintained in the past by her holding on to and building up her relationships in which she was largely unaware of success, pleasure, interest in other people's lives, as we see in the analysis, and unconsciously tried to stimulate interest, preoccupation with her relationships, particularly with men, excitement, envy, and competitiveness in her friends, as she tried with me. And I suspect she was very successful. That she did become an object of envy and that the way she talked, dressed, hinted, was aimed at stirring this up, now seems clear. She worked among a very gifted group of young scientists and managed to convey their interests in a way which was, I think, unconsciously intended to fascinate me and yet make me feel, in the kindest possible way, how ignorant I happened to be about her field.

It is, of course, no wonder that this young woman felt herself to be uncomfortably surrounded by envious friends and an envious and begrudging old analyst, and then had to try to put this right. People like this patient try to get rid of, or project, envious and similar feelings. Others seem more actively to stifle, almost kill off, such feelings and emotions. For example, the man, with the wife who hoped to be pregnant, when he came into analysis and still to some extent much later on, would just dry up his feelings and not feel them. People's coming or going, what they did, or analytic holidays or changes, just apparently did not touch him, and therefore all kinds of emotion, and certainly envy, were kept at bay. He then gave the impression of being a very cold person and yet, in fact, this is not so, and only time will show if we can really release the feelings which I am convinced are there and are potentially available.

Of course, restricting contacts, avoiding areas of living that stimulate rivalry and envy is another important way of defending against envy and one that is very familiar. It is almost certainly one important root of male homosexuality: if the male homosexual avoids close emotional and physical contact with women, he does not have to face up to strong awareness of differences that could stir up envy and allied anxieties. But a more massive restricting of life can also be seen, almost characterologically, in certain people, who manage quite effectively as long as the restrictions hold, but can become very disturbed when the restrictions shift.

I remember well a patient of mine, who was successful in his work, married with children. He managed to live such a closed-in life that he and his wife never invited people to their home other than close relatives, and then very rarely, and one or two very lame ducks, so to speak. He somewhat looked down on his wife and was rather contemptuous in a polite way towards his colleagues. He tried to avoid all social occasions, which was sometimes extremely awkward at work. He did not travel. So he almost did not have to talk to people or hear what other people were doing or thinking about, apart from his specific work area. What this very restricted life was achieving, from the angle which we are considering today, was that he was never really challenged. He could almost avoid being put in a position where he would hear anything said that might make him feel inferior or envious or feel in need of help or people. Eventually even these restrictions did not work and he broke down and then came into analysis.

One further point: I feel I neither have the knowledge, nor am I in a position to talk about the broader sociological implications of envy, which I nevertheless think are immense; but on an individual level I am sure that in people who have not sufficiently come to terms with it in themselves, there are bound to be difficulties at every new stage of development and perhaps particularly in ageing. To age, with what one might call proper resignation, means to be able to allow the younger generations to have things, knowledge, gifts, and a future that the ageing generation cannot have; and it means making way for the next generations, being able to identify with and even enjoy their success, and to regret what one has not achieved as well as to enjoy what one has. Excessive envy can make this particular stage of development very difficult and yet everyone has to reach it.

I have been discussing envy as we see it emerging, or even not emerging, in our everyday life. An issue I have not touched on is how we actually do try to deal with it. I have suggested it is ubiquitous, and indicated that we are all born with a potentiality for envy; and that we all have to deal with it in our own lives and have to live with it as part of our personalities. Perhaps all I can say at this stage is that ordinarily we would hope that the individual has sufficient available affection and love, and capacity to feel warmth and gratitude, to be able to counterbalance his rivalry and his envy, and yet be aware of its existence and allow other human beings to be seen as worthy of envy. This is, in a sense, one of the things that we hope to achieve in analysing our patients who have not been able to cope with these problems in their own lives; that is, to bring about insight into the real depths of the envy and to rediscover and release the split-off or stifled love and gratitude, and so help the patient to integrate them. This in itself can lead to considerable relief and help to loosen the awful grip of the envious feelings, and lead to a more benign circle.

I have thus tried to discuss the enormous power and significance of envy, not just in our detailed work as analysts and therapists, but even more in our everyday living.

Summary

This chapter aims to describe and discuss the notion of envy, from its most simple and conscious manifestations, to its deeply destructive and spoiling ones, both conscious and unconscious; to see it as an inevitable part of mental life and everyday living. If envy is too powerful and not sufficiently mitigated by love, it will disturb normal relations with people and the building up of a healthy and comfortable character structure; and will contribute to serious emotional difficulties. The pain of envy leads us to attempt to build various differing defences which are described here. Brief case material is quoted to show envy in operation during analytical treatment, and the aims of therapy are discussed in terms of bringing about greater integration between the various conflicting forces and so lessening the vicious circle that insufficiently mitigated envy tends to perpetuate.

14

Psychic change and the psychoanalytic process

This paper was first given as a public lecture of the British
Psycho-Analytical Society in November 1986, and is here
published for the first time.

There is some ambiguity about our use of the term 'psychic change'. We
sometimes use it to mean any kind of change in the mental state or functioning of our patients; sometimes we use it to mean a more long-term,
durable, and desirable kind of change. In this chapter I want to consider
both uses of the term and their interrelationship.

One of the main points that I want to make here is that psychic change
is not just an end, a final state, but is always going on in treatment and
that we as analysts need to be able to find and follow the moment-to-
moment changes in our patients, without concerning ourselves as to
whether they are positive, or signs of progress or of retreat, but seeing
them as our patient's own individual method of dealing with his anxieties
and relationships in his own unique way. Otherwise we cannot hope to
help our patients to achieve real, long-term, positive psychic change as
a result of treatment. If we get caught up in preoccupations about
whether the shifts show progress or not, looking for evidence to support
this, we may become enthusiastic for what we feel to be progress or
disappointed when there is apparent regression; we shall find that we get
thrown off course and unable to listen fully; or we may well bring
unconscious pressure on our patients to fit in, to comply with our felt
wishes, our needs; or our patients may just feel misunderstood.

Indeed, our capacity to listen fully and stay with our patients must help
them increasingly to be able to observe, tolerate, and understand their
own habitual ways of dealing with anxiety and relationships, and this is
part of the process of changing these habitual ways and becoming what
we could call psychically 'more healthy'. However, although we need, I
am suggesting, to be able to stay with and to follow our patient's own

192

ways of dealing with his problems, we do have in our minds ideas, theories, about desirable long-term psychic change, which I want to discuss in a moment.

First, it is important to look at our patient's attitude to change. Patients come into analysis because they are dissatisfied with the way things are and they want to alter, or want things to alter. There is a desire for change and pressure towards greater integration; without it analysis would fail. And yet there is a dread of change. Unconsciously they know that the change that they ask for involves an internal shifting of forces, a disturbance of an established mental and emotional equilibrium, a balance unconsciously established of feelings, impulses, defences, and internal figures, which is mirrored in their behaviour in the external world. This balance is maintained by very tightly and finely interlocked elements, and a disturbance in one part must reverberate throughout the personality. Our patients unconsciously sense this and tend therefore to feel the whole process of analysis as potentially threatening. This is, of course, essentially linked with Freud's ideas on resistance.

For example, a patient whose balance depends largely on the maintaining of a highly narcissistic structure will be unable to let us help properly or to take in our interpretations, and, for example, will tend to take them over or repeat them intellectually or alter them. When we are able to get through this momentarily we may see a sudden flash of anger, but this anger disturbs the balance and is therefore immediately intolerable to the patient and a new shift takes place and the balance is re-established. Why such anger is so intolerable at this stage we cannot tell. Is it felt to be so cruel, or does it cause so much guilt or humiliation and is this so unbearable, and, if so why? These issues will have to be teased out over time.

Another patient's basic method of keeping his equilibrium may be more obviously phobic, with anxiety defended against by various avoidances, self-limitations, and related defences. With some patients passivity and a kind of inertia in response to movement or change may be more obvious. But what I am stressing here is not just the obvious point that all our patients use different defence mechanisms, but that the interlocking of their defences is so fine that shifts in one area must always cause disturbances in another and that a major part of achieving psychic change lies in our trying to unravel within the analysis the various layers and interlockings so that they may be re-experienced and opened up within the transference. This opening up and re-experiencing within the transference, with all the shifting of balance that this implies, is part of psychic change — this changing is going on all the time within the analytic process; so that moment-to-moment shifts and change is what we are analysing all the time and is the stuff that we hope is

193

eventually going to lead to long-term, positive psychic change. I do not think that the latter long-term psychic change is ever an achieved absolute state but rather a better and more healthy balance of forces within the personality, always to some extent in a state of flux and movement and conflict.

To return now to the issue of what we are hoping to achieve in long-term psychic change: Freud in various places discussed the aims of analysis, which includes, of course, the question of change. I am not attempting to consider his ideas, only to indicate that he put much stress on making the unconscious conscious and on the idea that he expressed succinctly in 'Where id was, there ego shall be', implying not only making impulses conscious, but making them available to be used by, and under the control of, the ego. The notion of greater integration between ego and impulses, love and hate, superego and ego, runs through his work, especially in the middle and later years.

Melanie Klein, following on Freud's thinking, worked out in great detail the problems that the individual meets with in his attempt to achieve greater integration, and her ideas are fundamental to our understanding of psychic change today. She described what she called two positions (by positions she meant a configuration of impulses, defences, anxieties, and relationships to objects which she called the 'paranoid-schizoid' and 'depressive' positions). In the paranoid-schizoid position she saw that the individual, or infant, attempts to deal with anxiety caused by painful or conflicting feelings and disturbing parts of the self by splitting them off and projecting them into other objects, people, and thus relieving himself of them. She stressed how this is a normal mental state in a young infant and that it colours what he feels about his objects, as it does in older children and adults who continue to operate in this way in later life. Thus the individual who splits off, for example, his rage, and unconsciously in phantasy projects it into his nearest object will feel that object as hostile, will tend to withdraw or to fight it. Further, the way in which the infant experiences objects is, of course, fundamental to the way in which he takes them into his inner world, to the building up of his ego and his superego and the way he relates to people. It is only as the infant develops over the early weeks and months and splitting and projection lessen, that he begins to be increasingly aware that his impulses are his own, and he is then able to bear both his love and his hate at the same time and towards the same person. His perception of human beings then becomes more real, more human, and they can be introjected and identified with as such. This step, or rather, minute series of steps, forward and backward, towards integrating love and hate, brings with it momentous changes within the personality. Guilt and concern emerge. Once the individual starts to recognize and take responsibility for his own impulses and for what he has done in fact or in phantasy to his object, then guilt for this is inevitable, but also there opens up the possibility of feeling for and repairing the object. With this there is also relief and a deepening of emotions.

I have naturally described these positions in a somewhat schematic way, but I am trying to convey that the problem that every individual has in his own development, in relating to people as they really are, in coping with his own feelings and phantasies and dealing with the pain of guilt that arises from them, all these problems will necessarily emerge again in the analytic treatment, and the analysis gives the individual the opportunity to rework them in a different way.

But it is more than that. The shifts towards taking more responsibility for one's impulses, or away from it; the emerging of concern and guilt, and the wish to put things right, or going into flight from it; the awareness of part of the personality, the ego, feeling able to look at and struggle with what is going on and face anxiety, or starting to deny it — these movements are the very stuff that is inherent in our understanding of psychic change and will emerge being lived out minutely in the transference, if we are able to follow the shifts. This is, in fact, psychic changing.

As part of this process we see changes in our patients' object relationships — in the way that they see, feel, anticipate, and remember people. If there were not changes in object relationships, both external and internal, there could be no real changes in the ego and vice versa. To give an example, a patient felt he had altered a lot in relation to his parents, things were much better, since his previous therapy, which I am sure was so. Nevertheless, from the beginning of his treatment with me, I felt that there was a lack of real strength and masculinity. In the analysis, he would constantly, unconsciously, take back any doubt or criticism, reassure me that I was right and behave in a way that was over-smooth and vaguely seductive in the broad sense of the word. At first it appeared as if he felt me unconsciously as someone unable to tolerate anger and criticism and needing reassurance — which was not his conscious picture of me. Later we learned that one picture he had of his mother was of a person who was especially fondly attached to him, subtly influencing him to agree with her and with her criticisms of the father. We have, therefore, a number of elements here that need to be teased out in order to achieve real psychic change. There seems to be a projective identification of his own fear of his aggression into the object, myself, so that I am felt to be a timid person — mother, who needs reassurance, and he introjects this object into himself. There seems to be a relationship to mother, who may well have been rather seductive with her son, although we do not know how much this picture is built up from projections, and with whom he is in collusion and has partially identified with. There seems to be a need to control me by agreeing with me, slightly seducing me and becoming at times my favourite patient—child, at times my near equal, in our thinking.

All these elements and many more will need to be teased out as they recur and shift in different forms and with different motives, before he will really be able to relate to me as a more real object and be able to introject and identify with a stronger and firmer object, which should help in the development of a more real masculinity. Thus, when we are talking about psychic change in relation to objects, we are considering the importance of our patients being able to withdraw their projections, take more responsibility for their own impulses, and, alongside this, their being able to face the separateness of their objects, and the state of their objects — in a sense, thus, the reality of their objects, and the reality of their feelings towards them: their own psychic reality.

In order to look further at some of the problems that we have been talking about, change and antagonism to and fear of change, and the process of change, I shall bring some brief examples. I shall bring, first, material to show changes that took place during or between two sessions and how the picture of the analyst and the patient's self shifts, and then discuss something of the mechanisms involved. Then I shall try to discuss changes going on in the transference as a response to analytical interpretive work.

First, I want to discuss a dream from a basically phobic man, whom I shall call C., who came to analysis with a great wish to change but who, as I discussed at the beginning, shows a very deep fear of inner disturbance and very rigid defences. He had recently increasingly been able to become aware of problems going on in people around him, of their difficulties or their illnesses, and had even started to allow himself to enquire a little into them — even to become aware of his triumph over sufferers, so that the analysis seemed to be helping him to open his mind where he would previously have remained shut into his own world and closed off from other people. During the early part of the week with which we are concerned he had told me how disturbed and invaded he had felt by so many people around apparently being in a bad state: a colleague admitted to mental hospital, another man who had become suicidal, somebody else whose marriage was breaking down. Such things would somehow have passed over him before. The following day he came to a session and brought a dream.

In the dream *C. had gone to the doctor with a sore throat. The doctor examined him and said it was due to stones in the bladder. He understood by stones, minute ones like gravel. But the doctor said they could be operated on not by cutting out but by the use of an endoscope which would apparently suck them out of the urethra. The patient asked would it be very painful. The doctor said Yes, if they didn't use an anaesthetic, but an anaesthetic would be used. C. thought he had better get a second opinion. The GP then seemed to go mad. He came round his desk in a menacing way and started digging something into my patient's groin, saying it would hurt as much as that!*

I shall give some associations rather briefly. C. had had a slight sore throat the previous day. About the endoscope, his father when old had prostate trouble and was told that it could be dealt with, without surgery, in some way as in the dream. The father, however, had become very anxious, postponed the operation but died before it actually became necessary. C. then started to link the dream with his son's dental problems; the dentist had said that the boy needed to have two teeth removed for a brace to be fixed. C. thought that this was excessive if it was just for cosmetic purposes and that he himself should go and see the dentist and if necessary get a second opinion. There had been a mention of second opinions the day before concerning the colleague who had been admitted to a mental hospital.

I reminded C. that his son has himself had three operations on his penis for a congenital deformity. (I have always felt that C. has very much denied the importance of this to the boy.) C. was upset to realize that he had failed to connect this with the operation in the dream. What we also knew was that C. had had a better education and gone further in his life than his parents, and his father had been in some ways dependent on him as he grew older. Indeed, when his father lost his job, C. found him some rather lowly work in the firm in which he himself was employed in a comparatively senior capacity.

What I particularly want to show in this material is the change that we can see taking place during or between the two sessions, manifested in the dream; changes both in his way of facing, or not facing, impulses and anxieties, and in the nature of his objects, and how this latter takes place.

In the previous session C. had been better able to open his mind, be curious, and look at what was going on around him (and, I suspect, but am not discussing here, what was going on inside him as his balance shifted). He had been able to think about the various breakdowns, but felt invaded by them; and, as I suggested, had been able to tolerate up to a point feelings of triumph and excitement over the people who were breaking down. This meant that he had been able to put some trust in me — as we see at first in the GP in the dream. Then there is a shift. He begins to think about a second opinion, as if turning with hostility against the trusted object. The GP goes mad, as if he, the GP could not stand the doubts, and we see in this a projection of the patient's own inability to stand self-doubts and feelings of rejection, or stand pain after a certain point. Then there is the nature of the madness — I think that for C. interest and curiosity are so much linked with crazy excitement and triumph that they have to be got rid of. They are projected into me, so that, instead of my remaining a dispassionate, helpful analyst, I become the doctor who does not just examine him, but becomes madly, excitedly invasive, digging hurtfully into his groin. Then there is the issue of how much pain, near-guilt, he can bear. I think C.'s triumph over his suffering colleagues has become linked with his old unconscious triumph over his own father and his current concern about his son. He can tolerate pain up to a point and then it becomes too much. Instead of tolerating it, he introjects his object, here the father—son, and suffers his operation, his pain. C.'s way of dealing with these various anxieties and parts of his mind is to fragment them into bits like gravel and evacuate them. In these various ways mental pain is avoided and he is anaesthetized.

In C.'s case we can see a patient who consciously really wants to change, but is caught up in the paranoid-schizoid position with much splitting and projective identification. He makes brief sorties towards trying to make contact with his own feelings and parts of his self that he usually keeps split off, and then retreats again in the face of anxieties. But for brief moments now, a part of the ego can stand outside and actually help to investigate what is going on inside himself. In terms of psychic change I think it is most important that the analyst should search out the part of the ego that is able from moment to moment to take responsibility for the patient's own insight into his impulses, even though that part may quickly be lost again. For long-term psychic change, and for thinking about the ending of an analysis, the strengthening of this part of the personality is, I am sure, fundamental, and is, I think, based on a healthy and comfortable identification with the analyst and the analytical process. It is quite different from a constant self-conscious self-questioning which may have more masochistic roots, or a constant need to have theoretical analytical ideas about self and others — which may be more associated with narcissistic and omniscient attitudes.

I have discussed something of the nature of psychic change and have given brief examples of change taking place, within and between sessions in C., leading to some regression. Now I would like to look briefly at change taking place within a session from moment to moment. It would, of course, only be possible to consider this convincingly if we could follow the session in much greater detail than is possible in a brief chapter like this. So I intend just to look at a small piece of one session.

I am stressing that changes in a session mirror the changes that are taking place within the patient constantly in his everyday living as anxieties emerge, defences are mobilized, and the picture of the analyst shifts and the inner world shifts accordingly. Interpretations, of course, play a very major part in stimulating this change, partly because they give understanding and insight, but not only this. They frequently stimulate change not in the way we intended, not the way we were thinking. What we say may arouse anxiety, or ease anxiety; our speaking may reassure our patient that we understand or concern ourselves with him; our interpretations may be right but arouse rivalry; or wrong and then reassure him for the wrong reason; our words may cease to have the meaning that they have to us and become like a tune that the patient can lull himself with or a gloomy bog into which he can sink. All this becomes part of the movement that is going on in the session as we are trying to understand our patients.

I am going to bring shortened material from a session of a patient at a time when the ending of the analysis was under discussion. The result of treatment, so far, in view of the nature of the patient, seemed quite encouraging, though far from perfect. He had come as a very schizoid, passive man, who, by now, was happily married, positively enjoying life and much more thoughtful and concerned as a human being. Before actually giving the material, I should add a general point about it. Of course it is deeply influenced by our planning the ending of the treatment, and you will see how this was, almost certainly, in itself bringing up a great need to protest, to go backwards and mobilize old defensive retreats, and so forth. It needs to be kept in mind from this angle, as well as from the detailed movement in the session. But it is on the latter that I particularly want to concentrate here.

The session was a Friday. My patient, N., arrived saying that he felt bad and anxious, as if too much was going on. He and his wife were currently selling their house and there were important changes going on in his work. I clarified that it seemed that the anxiety was more focused round the issue of stopping the analysis. This he agreed but went on to describe in detail his feelings of discomfort as if he was angry and resentful. I thought at that point, and suggested that it was partly that he had not really been able to believe that I could let him go, but that now he was having to face this aspect of stopping. (This patient had for a very long time lived in the belief that he was the very special child of his mother, he was in fact the youngest of the family; and he believed that he was my very special patient, and from this angle alone the idea of stopping treatment had been very difficult to accept.)

My patient responded, however, to my remark by going back to discussing his difficulties, his resentment, his coldness, and so on. I thought, and showed him, that he was sinking into a kind of anger and misery — shown by his settling into and stressing all the difficulties and getting caught up into it, in order to avoid the specific feelings about actually leaving and what it really meant to him at that moment. In other words, I thought that he was sinking into a kind of bog of misery as a defence, so that the anger was part of the bog and was not anger in its own right.

N. became silent — a pause — and then he said he had the thought, 'clever old bag'. He explained he thought I was right and that he was aware when he made that remark that he resented my being right, so he went quiet. Now we could both agree about the misery, being used actively as a kind of masochistic defence, and he himself had clear insight into his resentment about my being right.

N. went on to talk about this and how, when I had first spoken about the defensiveness and he went quiet, he felt he was taking over what I was saying and, as he put it, 'putting it into a box'. I discussed with him the way he had not quite been able to acknowledge that I was right — and that he was grateful and how this very awareness stimulated rivalry and envy. Clearly, by now his mood had changed and he was talking freely. N. went on to say that he had now gone off at a tangent. He was thinking about yesterday. They had been invited to the Xes where the wife is a very poor cook, so his wife had a brilliant idea. She would offer to make a summer pudding, which the patient just adores, and they would take it with them to the supper. He would help his wife by topping and tailing the fruit. This was said in a very positive and warm way.

Here it was clear that N. was describing a movement, that he had now got into contact with a good experience again, with a feeling that there was a good smell and a good taste about, and appreciation of what I had been able to see and what he really deeply knew about the analysis. Also there was awareness that he could help to get hold of these feelings and get the analysis consolidated, as is shown by his telling about helping his wife preparing the fruit.

I shall leave the description of the to-and-fro of the session at this point and only add that towards the end of the session N. talked about a feeling that he had had about analysis, how he thought that not only he, but he believed, I, the analyst, must have some special feelings about his leaving and about our work together. I think that we can see the shift in my patient's feelings during the session. At the beginning he was largely sinking into a bog of mindless misery, by the end he was well in contact with very moving feelings of loss and contact with myself.

We can see here how this patient, though moving towards the ending of analysis, is not in a state of achieved change, but still in a state of psychic changing in which the positive gains and increased flexibility are now very clear. I want to look briefly at some of the shifts as we see them in the session; we can see the movement, after interpretations, out of the bog of verbal misery, so that very soon insight is available. In the old days N. would get caught up for sessions, dragged down by and almost wallowing in masochistic misery. Here with insight appreciation emerges, even though ambivalently so, and I become the 'clever old bag', and he files away what I have said. At this point his envious resentment is obvious, but is limited. It indicates an important piece of integration — since this awareness of naked envy came very late in the analysis and can now be felt by my patient quite clearly and not too strongly. The shift that is indicated by the 'brilliant idea' of the summer pudding, with which he will help, shows not only appreciation again, but a capacity for sensual and emotional enjoyment, strikingly missing throughout much of this patient's analysis and life, also the enjoyment and appreciation is on a symbolical level — the good food with its lovely taste and smell; and the capacity to help make it is there in contrast with his old tendency to retreat into gloomy passivity.

It is also important to see the shift in this patient's notion of being special. Through much of N.'s analysis he had maintained an omnipotent superior picture of himself in relation to his mother, his place in the family, and, clearly, in relation to myself. This slowly altered in the analysis and here we see a picture of myself as a person who must, after this long analysis, have some unique feelings about him and my work with him, as we could assume every healthy mother must have with each of her children. This sense of his being special and unique had a warmth and concern which was completely lacking in the old omnipotent, narcissistic phantasies of being special.

I have brought this material to indicate very briefly the kind of moment-to-moment change that one sees going on in the ordinary analytic session as part of the analytic process. In this way we have the opportunity to see hopes, anxieties, defences, phantasies, and relationships emerging in the transference and shifting according to the patient's own pathology, stimulated by the analytic situation and interpretive work. I think that one of the main aims in our therapy is to work with such shifts, to enable them to happen less blindly and automatically, to make them and their elements more conscious and more manageable to the ego in a more healthy, flexible, and realistic way, and thus to achieve a change in the balance. If we were to believe that we could eliminate them, we should really be encouraging splitting.

I have tried to indicate some of our aims when we are considering long-term psychic change, in terms of movement towards and into the depressive position; in terms of greater integration of the self and a more whole and realistic relation to objects. I have suggested that long-term psychic change is based on, and is a continuation of, the constant minute shifts and movements that we see from moment to moment in the transference, and, like all manifestations of conflict, it can never be ended.

15

Object relations in clinical practice

This paper was written for a special issue of *The Psychoanalytic Quarterly* 57 (October 1988): part iv, devoted to the topic of object relations.

Object relations are at the core of psychoanalytic work — they are the stuff of the transference — and whatever our theory of object relations, it must deeply influence our understanding of the nature of transference. Freud discovered the existence of transference directly from clinical observation, where he saw that the patient inevitably repeated parts of his past relationships with his analyst. Only subsequently did he start to formulate his ideas on object relations. All analysts now hold theories of object relations, basically rooted in Freud's work. I want to start from a theoretical angle, bringing first some theoretical observations, and then some vignettes of clinical material, in order to show object relations as they are lived out in the consulting room. I shall discuss how my understanding of this clinical material derives from my theoretical background, but also how such theory has constantly to be re-discovered in actual clinical work. I think that this re-discovery can best take place by examining object relations as they emerge dynamically in the transference.

Freud, in his work on object relations, described the various stages that the child went through in the course of its development. He assumed that in the earliest stages, there was no emotional relationship to objects, only to the self; this he described as primary narcissism. He thought that only later did the young child begin to relate to people outside himself. From this assumption he described how some individuals continued to build their relationships on the basis of a narcissistic type of object choice. He discussed how, for example, in schizophrenia the patient could be seen to have withdrawn back into an objectless, narcissistic state. Freud (1914) emphasized that clinically what we usually see is what he called

203

'secondary narcissism' — that is, the introjection of the object into the ego, which then becomes identified with it. He first described this process in relation to melancholia (1917), but soon recognized it as a universal process, building up the ego and the internal world of objects, particularly the superego. As Freud explored these ideas, particularly from 1923 onwards, he struggled to understand why the objects taken into, say, the superego were apparently so different from the external, real parents. In this whole discussion he came to see the great significance of the child's feelings and impulses towards the parents, and how these impulses coloured the child's picture, and this influenced the nature of the objects that he introjected. Clinically he did not seem to take this reasoning much further.

Melanie Klein started doing clinical work with children with Freud's theories in her mind, but soon realized from her observations in the playroom that these observations did not entirely tally with Freud's ideas (Klein 1932). The main points of difference concerned the dating of the child's relating to objects, the beginnings of ego formation and, associated with this, the nature of his early defences. As I shall describe later, her discoveries concerned not only the meaning of the transference, but the nature of the processes involved in transferring. Klein found that the infant, far from *not* relating emotionally to an object at the beginning of life, related very powerfully, although at first in a quite unintegrated way. Thus he would relate to the mother, or rather the part of the mother that he was concerned with at that moment, as a good or ideal object, if in a good or contented mood; or would feel her as dangerous and persecuting, if in an angry or frustrated mood. In this early, unintegrated state the child would relate to parts of his objects, and his feelings and anxieties would be correspondingly split and absolute.

Freud, as I have indicated, thought that the child, comparatively late in its development, introjected into its superego objects coloured by its own impulses. This process of the individual's impulses towards the object, helping to form and shape its image of the object, was explored further by Klein and played an important part in her theoretical formulations. She saw it as a normal, inevitable process starting, not late in development, but from the beginning of life — the impulses that the child felt towards his object were projected into the latter, and the object therefore taken in, introjected, as coloured by these projected impulses. Parts of the self — for example, angry, biting, loving — would be projected and the object taken in accordingly. This process of projection and introjection she saw as basic to all relating and to the building up of the inner world of objects and of the ego and superego (1952b). Thus her work in this area continued that of Freud, placed it earlier in life, deepened and extended it. Klein described the phantasy of splitting off and projecting impulses and parts of the self into objects, as projective identification, in so far as the object then becomes identified with the parts of the self that have been projected into it. She discussed how, at the beginning, this normal mechanism of projective identification serves important defensive functions: the infant in the grip of violent feelings splits them off and feels them to be outside himself, in the object, and thus rids himself of disturbance. But this process sets up anxieties about the state of the object and further defences must be resorted to, to protect himself from persecution. She also described in detail various other defensive purposes it serves — as, for example, how the infant's attempt, in phantasy, to enter and control the object aims to avoid any awareness of separateness and its concomitant emotions (Klein 1946).

This understanding of projective identification, operating from the beginning of life, throws light on the whole issue of narcissism and narcissistic object relations, and thus opens up the possibility of analysing these conditions more fully. Klein thought of narcissism not as a stage preceding object relations but a state to which the individual retreats, in which the self or body is felt to contain an idealized object, and it is to this self that withdrawal takes place (1952a). The idea of projective identification also adds a new dimension to our understanding the individual who, as Freud describes it, continues to love 'according to the narcissistic type, what he himself is, was, or would like to be'. In other words, we can now see that he loves the other person because he has, in phantasy, projected parts of his own self into the latter, who is then identified with these parts, and it is this that makes him so attractive to the narcissistic individual.

In this discussion I have temporarily moved on to the later manifestations that we see in individuals who have remained very much tied to the use of these early mechanisms of splitting and projection. Returning now to the question of normal development, we observe increasing integration as the infant or young child progresses. He will split and project less and become more able to remain in contact with his feelings, and become more aware of himself as a whole person, and his object as a whole real person. As he becomes more integrated, able to feel love and hate, ambivalence, towards the same person, we see the beginnings of concern and guilt, and a wish to repair. This links, of course, with what Freud, in discussing ambivalence in relation to the life and death instincts, spoke of as the 'fatal inevitability of the sense of guilt' (1930). Such developments, bringing guilt and a sense of separateness and loss, inevitably bring pain. New defences are then built up, or further splitting and projective identification may be resorted to, but there is now the possibility of a more realistic relation to objects and to the interaction between other objects, the Oedipus complex.

I have here outlined, in a rather oversimplified way, something of Melanie Klein's theory of object relations and have indicated what she described as the two main positions: the early paranoid–schizoid position when the infant operates largely with mechanisms of splitting and projective identification and fragmentation, and his objects and impulses remain separate, or are actively split up and projected; and then the depressive position, when the infant or child begins to relate to a whole, more real object with ambivalence, concern, and guilt.

These ideas are, to my mind, fundamental to our understanding in a dynamic way of what is being lived out in transference. In fact transference itself and the process of transferring are based on projective identification; parts of the self, impulses, and internal objects are projected into the analyst and the patient then behaves towards the analyst as if this were the truth. Melanie Klein's findings in relation to transference were greatly opened up by Bion, who described, in detail, projective identification as a means of communication and the need for the analyst to be able to tune in to the patient, to be aware of his projections and able to contain them. Such projections may exist purely in the patient's phantasy, not emotionally affecting the analyst at all; or the patient may unconsciously attempt to stimulate and provoke the analyst to act them out and to behave according to his unconscious expectations. In these ways the history of the patient's object relations comes alive in the transference.

I think that this process is so powerful and yet so subtle that it makes it essential for the analyst in his work first of all to focus his attention on what is going on in the room, on the nature of what is being lived out, how he is being pushed or pulled emotionally to experience or behave in various ways. What the patient says is in itself of course extremely important, but it has to be seen within the framework of what he does. This, of course, implies that there is always an object relationship in the consulting room and that our first task is to be aware of the active nature of this relationship, an issue vividly described by Bion (1963). This may even be especially important in patients who present themselves as highly narcissistic — for example, as if scarcely aware of the analyst's presence. The meaning of this and its connection with objects, as I have indicated earlier, will need to be understood. Others will reject any transference interpretations as if irrelevant or invasive, or as if self-opinionated on the part of the analyst. The apparent implicit belief of such patients that there can be two people in the room, the existence of one of whom should be considered irrelevant, in itself must tell us something about the nature of the patient's relationships to people. Such issues are interestingly described by Greenberg and Mitchell in their discussion of what they describe as the relational model:

Whatever the analyst does shapes the transference paradigm, whether he responds to the patient or fails to respond. The analyst's participation exerts a pull on the patient . . . .. Similarly, the patient's experience of and behavior towards the analyst exert pulls on the analyst, who can usefully employ his awareness of these pulls in the service of understanding the patient's *relational* patterns.

(Greenberg and Mitchell 1983: 389)

I would add that how the patient uses the analyst, whether to a greater or lesser extent pushing and pulling us emotionally, or whether in a more realistic fashion and able to talk and listen to us, is in itself an indication of the patient's state of maturity or disturbance.

I want now to bring a fragment of material to discuss some of the issues that I have been outlining. I shall first particularly discuss how focusing primarily on the object relationship that the patient lives out in the room can help us to listen analytically and therefore to sort out the nature of his immediate conflicts and his method of dealing with them. As the nature and use of the relationship alters within the session, we can see shifts in the use of defences and thus gain some understanding of his level of functioning, and reconstruct something of its history.

This is a young man who came into analysis knowing that we would have only a limited time for his treatment, as he was in London on a research project which was most likely to end within a very few years — which is in fact what happened. A., as I shall call him, was intelligent and consciously very keen to have analysis but much restricted by his narcissistic omnipotence. He was originally somewhat too concerned about his weight and general appearance. He was deeply interested in psychoanalysis and its applications, and on the day before the session that I wish to discuss, he had attended a general lecture by a well-known analyst. In the session he criticized the speaker strongly, not so much for the content of the lecture, but for his personality, how he handled the discussion, what kind of person he really was, and so on. He assumed, correctly, that I would know this man. He talked on and on, and I had the clear impression that the longer he talked, the more he was expecting me to take up what he was saying, as if I did not like or agree with his viewpoint, and was myself disturbed by his criticism of the lecturer; almost as if he expected me to be caught up in a kind of argument with him, however much it might be concealed by interpretive work.

If, for a moment, we disregard my experience in the transference, and look primarily at the content of what he was saying, we could see it as an attack on an older man, suggesting that he was making a split between myself and the lecturer, perhaps in the role of his father. This might well, on one level, be true and contain elements of classical Oedipal rivalry. But I think that the way that will take us into the heart of the patient's immediate conflicts is to start from my awareness of what was being acted out with me, where I was unconsciously being pushed into having a difference of opinion or a row with my patient. This of course I did not do. I tried to show him what I thought was going on, how he expected me to ally myself with Dr X., the lecturer, and take offence at what he, my patient, was saying, and somehow reveal my disturbance. For a moment he was silent, and then went on to tell me about a piece of work that he himself had just done and how well people had spoken about it and praised him.

Here we can see that he shifted from considering what I had said, that might have been worth thinking about, to telling me about his having done a piece of work that other people had praised. Here I think some introjective identification had taken place. Instead of my patient becoming aware that I had opened up something useful and feeling anything about it, he introjected this useful object—analyst and, using projective identification, forced the listening, valuing part of his own self into me, then split up and projected into the people listening to his work and praising him. I and they hear of his success. On occasions when he did hear my interpretations, there would be a sudden outburst of anger which would immediately disappear. This then was the way in which my patient was operating at that moment. If he could get me, in his mind, to join into some kind of explosive row or difference of opinion with him, then we could both be similar, both caught up in a sado–masochistic relationship, and he would be left with no sense of my being different from him, more poised or containing. Then he would have no need to value or admire me and no envy is stirred up. When it is almost stirred up — for example, after my first interpretation — it is almost immediately dealt with by his swallowing me up, and his becoming the praised and successful person.

I am suggesting that if we listen to our patients first of all from the angle of the object relationship that is alive at the moment, this will enable us to see better the nature of the patient's conflicts and his method of maintaining his psychic balance. The apparent Oedipal material in this example was not, I felt, the live material; the unconscious attempt to get me on to his level of a sado–masochistic row was. His taking over my useful interpreting put him in the enviable position — this was an example of his powerfully operating narcissism. It was a primitive object relationship based on projective and introjective identification, which could be seen to be operating in the movement that I have described in the session. We see hints of another element of his very early object relationships here; when I made a potentially useful partial interpretation, he could not use it, take it in, and digest it, as if he still could not enjoy a warm grateful and loving relationship to the analyst as a feeding person. The way in which the patient operates in the session shows the use of powerful primitive defences of splitting and projective and introjective identification to maintain his psychic equilibrium. His relating appears as highly narcissistic, but this narcissism is not just to himself but to a self containing a desirable part of an object, introjected so quickly that he had neither time to desire nor to be hostile to it. This whole concatenation of object relationships and defences is consistent with a man who is still largely caught up in what Melanie Klein has described as the paranoid-schizoid position; and narcissistically related to part objects.

In this case, theory comes alive as one finds one's real personality being wiped out, one's ideas disregarded, one's patient omnipotently taking over. A background of theory is needed to focus one's listening and make sense of it. With this one can stay steady, not be drawn into some kind of emotional or verbal acting out, but contain, be interested, and explore what is going. Or to put it the other way round: our theory, if reasonably correct and alive, is part of our analytic thinking and will be re-discovered as we work. This I have tried to show in the shifts in this fragment of material. Further, if one can watch the shifting, one's own understanding will become more sensitive to the nuances of the object relations, defences, and phantasies involved.

I want now to bring material to illustrate the type of relationship shown by a patient primarily still using primitive paranoid-schizoid defences, but moving towards moments of concern and unbearable guilt in relation to his objects; a patient who, although he has time on his side, could, I believe, easily follow a very ill line of development.

This is a child of three and a half, whom I will call C., with as yet a rather limited use of language. He came with fears at night, many phobias, about eating, defecating, and was altogether a very anxious, demanding, and passionate little boy. I want briefly to discuss two sessions. In the first, he suddenly flung himself at me, dragged at my hair, and pulled out a very small fistful; he opened his hand, looked at the hairs with horror, got hold of the rug, and covered my head with it, so that I was in a kind of tent. I tried to help him to understand his anxieties about what he might see if he looked at me, and about what he felt he had done. Slowly he came up, peeped under the rug at my head, then pulled away. When I tried to emerge to talk to him more easily, he ran at me with the pillow and covered my head with that.

I again spoke about his anxieties. He then specified things, saying very clearly, 'You'll pull my hair', and retreated further from me. When it came to the last minutes of the session, he ran away from the playroom a minute or two before time.

In this fragment of material I think we can see something of the child's dilemma: could he bear to face what he felt he had done to me? He covered my head but attempted to look under the cover, as if concern and guilt were emerging — but the fear and horror of what he might see, and then the fear of a persecuting, retaliating figure seemed to predominate, and this latter, in the end, drove him away. We can see projective identification operating here, his impulses and internal objects were projected into me; I would pull his hair. Such projections go to form his phantasy of his objects. I became his terrifying internal figures that had always persecuted him. In fact, I did not feel angry or upset about the hair-pulling, but these internal figures carried such conviction that he could not take in interpretations, nor was the reality of a benign me of much immediate help; he ran off prematurely.

This material then disappeared, but a few weeks later C. came to a session very wild and apparently disturbed. There were a number of references to me, the analyst as being a 'naughty boy', and one to my being 'a nuisance'. I thought that he was in this way showing me, in this session, great anxieties about himself being bad and a trouble and nuisance to his parents, particularly as his mother had been unwell. As the session went on he became calmer, and standing at the table holding things together with rubber bands, he said quietly, as if out of the blue, 'I pulled your hair, remember?' I simply commented on his worry and guilt about what he felt he had done to me, and he added, 'I kissed, remember?' This is of course, from one angle, clearly a denial, he did not kiss, he fled. But I think there is something more dynamic to be understood here. C. was able to bring into the session a memory showing the burden of guilt and anxiety that he was carrying around inside himself — but also, now, affection. It suggests that within this second session there was relief at his being able to tell, and my being able to accept, the memory of his 'bad' actions, and this may have, in part, prompted the idea of the kiss. In addition I think that he was here able, even if only in re-structuring his past, in phantasy, to move towards another solution; that is, the repairing of the object with the kiss.

In these fragments from two sessions, we see in the transference a shift in the nature of his relation to objects. In the first, the child gets caught up in guilt that becomes so persecuting that he has to project the impulses and go into flight. In the second, the burden of guilt is clearly too great and projection still operates, and throughout the early part of the session I am 'the naughty boy' or the 'nuisance', but it is soon taken back into himself in a manageable form and in phantasy he moves towards repairing his object. The problem that is being enacted in the playroom is one that we hope the analysis is going to be able to help him with; that is, the lessening of the power of his internal figures and the strengthening of his ego and his belief in his capacity to love, think, control, and repair.

I want now to compare elements of this case, C., with that of an adult, also showing a mixture of persecutory and depressive anxieties and a complex structure of internal figures. In this latter case, whom I will call D., we can start to reconstruct something of the history of his relationships.

I am particularly concerned here with the issue of reconstruction, since I believe that we can only reconstruct history convincingly if it emerges dynamically, as an actual experience in the here and now, not just, or primarily, talked about as historical facts or handed on as history. By reconstruction I mean not only the broad lost or forgotten elements of the patient's life, but also the reconstruction of the way in which our patients have dealt with their anxieties, the defences used, the conflicts involved.

I am bringing material from a young man who was in his late twenties when he came into analysis, a treatment that, unfortunately, had to be terminated very prematurely, when his work took him abroad. I shall start by looking at the emergence of a powerful unconscious denial, a defence against any awareness of the significance of an approaching summer holiday. It came into the session in this way.

D. talked at some length about his despair about the relationship with his current girl friend, and how, since they lived separately, but very near each other, he did not feel free to bring another girl home to his flat and have sex with her. The relationship with the current girl friend had slowly deteriorated very seriously. The stress, as he went on talking, became more and more focused on two points, the immediate importance of sex with the new girl, and his anger that he had put so much into the relationship with the old girl friend, and now realized that it was impossible to go on with it, and so was desperate to get into bed with the new one. Interpretations about his having put so much into the relationship with me and the analysis, now abandoning him for the holidays, and his need at once to turn to someone else (as he had done after a previous long relationship had broken down, and he had become quite promiscuous), seemed correct but of limited value to him; therefore, probably on the wrong level, or addressed to the wrong part of the personality. The more concrete issue of putting himself, via his penis, right into the new girl's body to avoid all separateness and mental, almost physical pain, seemed to help me to focus on the reality of his problem better. However, I did not feel that I was able to get through to him at any real depth in the session.

The following session he spoke of feeling calmer, and the session seemed rather empty. Then, three minutes before the end he brought a dream — which at that stage we could to little with. The dream was as follows. *The patient was watching a well-known actor being slowly bled to death. It was as if someone had cut a vein in his hand, perhaps because he had done something wrong. D. stayed watching, then went off to his ex-girl friend, called Elizabeth.* (He knows that my name is Betty.) *They returned with Elizabeth's daughter and continued to watch the bleeding, but the daughter was not allowed in. The man then died. D. was then on a train telling the other passengers what he had just seen; they asked what was the matter with the man – my patient said psoriasis; they asked did he mean cirrhosis, like cirrhosis of the liver? He said No, indicating it was a skin disease – it all seemed incomprehensible to him.*

As I said, it was too late to get associations to and work on the dream, and it is in itself interesting that the dream was brought so late. It is I think, in part, an acting out of the dream in the session, before the dream was told, letting the life-blood of the session leak away, while I, unknowingly, stood looking on, unable to help, kept incompetent by my patient's withholding, and he then, without knowing why, became the guilty one.

The dream itself suggests that the last few sessions before the beginning of the holidays were unconsciously experienced as his slowly bleeding to death, so that it would be easier emotionally, less painful, once the term was over and the holidays started. I think that the bleeding–to–death self contained and was largely identified with an object, myself, felt at the end of the term to be wasted, worn out, and almost dying. (I have indicated how he actually leaked away the session and thus wasted me.) Following the previous session he knew that he *ought* to look at what was going on, behind the denials, in the session, but the part of the self more directly related to his infantile feelings, Elizabeth's child in the dream, could not be allowed in. My rather adult interpretations, linking his associations to his previous promiscuity, were probably on the wrong level and could not get through to the child or infant in him. Is this story told again in a different version in the second half of the dream? There he maintains, or part of him does, that the problem is only skin deep, the psoriasis; but another part, called the passengers, maintain it is a more serious issue, the cirrhosis. So the argument in the train was an argument between two parts of the self, one putting forward a view that was more reassuring, only skin-deep, the other about facing a more worrying, deeper situation. But I think that he must have unconsciously registered that my interpretations were on

212

too mature a level, so that the part of the self that says 'superficial is better' is in part an identification with what he felt my interpretations showed about my attitude. By this attitude I showed my weakness and became a worn-out object, and as I shall show, one I think to be despised.

In addition we can see that the defence against facing that separation matters is connected in some way with guilt; in the dream the man has done something wrong. Further, although the patient's defences against looking and going into things deeply suggest an identification with myself from the day before, this object is also a split one, suggesting internal conflict over this issue. In the dream, one figure, Elizabeth, does go with him to look at the man thought to be guilty and dying, as of course, I had consciously attempted to do in the previous session.

I had the impression from what I had seen and learned of D. that his picture of his mother was of a person who, in fact, did not stand emotional pain or anxiety well. If so, this identification with the analyst as someone who helps to deny and avoid experiencing emotions is also an identification with an internal mother, as if this mother was projected into me and I by my rather adult interpretations became a good recipient for the projections and became easily identified with her. But D.'s unconscious picture of me and of his mother, and his reactions to this are also more complex and can only really be reconstructed from the object relationship lived out in the transference, as I want to show.

From the early months of the analysis a particular type of behaviour frequently emerged. He would have an angry reaction against some specific interpretation, it would go on for some time, then he would appear to shift ground, 'give in', become benign and 'forgiving', and start to smooth things over. Or without there being any conflict between us, he would adopt a very smooth, bland, and 'understanding' attitude, in a way which kept any movement, change, or new insight, out. It seemed as though the unconscious expectation was that I should join in, agree, feel satisfied with the work going on at that moment and peace would reign; or I should feel assured that, after the anger, we were once more at one. From his behaviour, therefore, it would seem as if D. had a picture of me as someone who could not stand criticism or difficulties; who needed comforting and reassuring about my value, and who only felt secure in a benign, smooth atmosphere. When I showed my patient this, it in no way corresponded to his conscious picture of me, but it continued and it clearly left him with a sense of superiority to me, as I indicated in relation to the dream.

As we worked on this kind of behaviour D. told me that his mother had been ill through much of his childhood, seriously so in his first few years, and again in his early adolescence, when he would come home from school and cook supper for his father, a busy general practitioner, and sister. This verbal account of history helps us, but it contains little of the richness and fixity that is lived out in the object relationship that emerges in the transference, where I am treated as someone physically and emotionally fragile, and somewhat inferior.

I am not attempting here to elucidate the various elements that go to make up the complex picture of the mother that I can sense through my countertransference, as I am reassured and carefully handled. The kind of elements that I refer to are the actual illnesses and personality of the mother, surely contributed to by the patient—child's projections of his own fear of his anxiety into her; his identification with her, as a person unable to contain much anxiety; his terror of the strength and danger of his own impulses — as seen in the quick withdrawal of anger and criticism; his terror at guilt, dealt with by premature and false reparation, as in the speedy reassuring and comforting. This is frequently followed by a sense of superiority and self-righteousness, a striking part of his character. Many of these elements can be seen in action in this patient's living out of his expectations about me, and then with his dealing with this me, as he unconsciously believes me to be. In this way elements of his history unfold, to some extent come together and can in part be reconstructed.

In C. and in D. we can see certain apparent similarities in the manifestation of their object relationships. Both show a marked difficulty in facing a damaged or dying object; the child glances under the rug at my head, and runs; D.'s internal objects say 'don't look'. Both patients mobilize manic defences, D. in the near-total denial of the significance of the holidays; C. in his 'wild' behaviour and frequent shouting and yelling so that my words could not be heard. In both patients the difference between the internal and external object is striking. I described how C., the child, reacted as if I were really hurt and hostile, and although only three and a half, his behaviour can be seen at present to be somewhat fixed. D., despite much work on this aspect, returns again and again to treating me as if I needed comfort and reassurance, though he stoutly maintained that this is not his vision of me. But despite these apparent similarities it is clear that the differences in the nature of their object relations and character structure are very great.

I am suggesting that in our analytic work our focus needs to be first of all on the nature of the object relation being lived out in the room, however hidden this may be; the nature of this relationship will show us something of the nature of the patient's pathology, his conflicts, and his ways of dealing with them. I think that if we do concentrate primarily on what is actually being experienced in the transference, something of the patient's life history, and the nature and movement of his phantasies and defences will be enabled to unfold, rather than have to be explained theoretically. But for the immediacy of the analytic experience to have meaning, we need to have a relevant theory of object relations at the back of our minds, which we have constantly to rediscover as we work. I have tried to illustrate in this chapter how Melanie Klein's theory of object relations can inform our thinking and give meaning to our clinical work.

References

Alexander, F. (1930) 'The neurotic character', *International Journal of Psycho-Analysis* 11: 292—311.

Bibring, E. (1943) 'The conception of the repetition compulsion', *The Psychoanalytic Quarterly* 12: 486—519.

Bion, W.R. (1959) 'Attacks on linking', *International Journal of Psycho-Analysis*, 40: 308—15; also in *Second Thoughts*, London: Heinemann (1967); reprinted in paperback, London: Maresfield Reprints, H. Karnac Books (1984), 93—109.

—— (1962) *Learning From Experience*, London: Heinemann; reprinted in paperback, London: Maresfield Reprints, H. Karnac Books (1984).

—— (1963) *Elements of Psycho-Analysis*, London: Heinemann; reprinted in paperback, London: Maresfield Reprints, H. Karnac Books (1984).

—— (1965) *Transformations*, London: Heinemann; reprinted in paperback, London: Maresfield Reprints, H. Karnac Books (1984).

—— (1967) 'Notes on memory and desire', *The Psychoanalytic Forum* 2: 272—3 and 279—80; and in E. Bott Spillius (ed.) *Melanie Klein Today*, vol. 2, *Mainly Practice*, London: Routledge (1988), 17—21.

—— (1970) *Attention and Interpretation*, London: Tavistock Publications; reprinted in paperback, London: Maresfield Reprints, H. Karnac Books (1984).

Bromberg, W. (1948) 'Dynamic aspects of the psychopathic personality', *The Psychoanalytic Quarterly* 17: 58—70.

Deutsch, H. (1955) 'The impostor', *The Psychoanalytic Quarterly*, 24: 483—505.

—— (1942) 'Some forms of emotional disturbance and their relationship to schizophrenia', in *Neuroses and Character Types*, London:

Hogarth Press (1965), 262—81.

Fenichel, O. (1945) *The Psychoanalytic Theory of Neurosis*, New York: Norton.

Freud, S. (1914) 'On narcissism: an introduction', in the Standard Edition (SE) of the *Complete Psychological Works of Sigmund Freud*, London: Hogarth Press (1950—1974), 14: 69—102.

—— (1917) 'Mourning and melancholia', SE 14: 237—60.

—— (1920) *Beyond the Pleasure Principle*, SE 18: 3—64.

—— (1923) *The Ego and the Id*, SE 19: 3—66.

—— (1924) 'The economic problem of masochism', SE 19: 157—70.

—— (1926) *Inhibitions, Symptoms and Anxiety*, SE 20: 77—175.

—— (1930) *Civilization and its Discontents*, SE 21: 59—145.

Gillespie, W.H. (1964) 'The psychoanalytic theory of sexual deviation with specific reference to fetishism', in I. Rosen (ed.) *The Pathology and Treatment of Sexual Deviation*, London: Oxford University Press, 123—45.

Greenacre, P. (1945) 'Conscience in the psychopath', *American Journal of Orthopsychiatry* 15: 495—509.

Greenberg, J.R. and Mitchell, S.A. (1983) *Object Relations in Psychoanalytic Theory*, Cambridge, MA: Cambridge University Press.

Heimann, P. (1950) 'On counter-transference', *International Journal of Psycho-Analysis* 31: 81—4.

—— (1956) 'Dynamics of transference interpretations', *International Journal of Psycho-Analysis* 37: 303—10.

Hendrick, I. (1947) 'Instinct and ego during infancy', *The Psychoanalytic Quarterly* 11: 33—58.

Hinshelwood, R. (1989) *Dictionary of Kleinian Thought*, London: Free Association Books.

Isaacs, S. (1952) 'The nature and function of phantasy', in M. Klein, P. Heimann, S. Isaacs, and J. Riviere, *Developments in Psycho-Analysis*, London: Hogarth Press, 67—121.

King, P. (1973) 'The therapist—patient relationship', *Journal of Analytical Psychology* 18: 1—8.

—— (1978) 'Affective response of the analyst to the patient's communication', *International Journal of Psycho-Analysis* 59: 329—34.

Klein, M. (1932) *The Psycho-Analysis of Children*, vol. 2 of *The Writings of Melanie Klein*, London: Hogarth Press; paperback, New York: Dell Publishing Co. (1977).

—— (1935) 'A contribution to the psychogenesis of manic-depressive states', in *The Writings of Melanie Klein*, vol. 1, *Love, Guilt and Reparation*, London: Hogarth Press (1975), 262—89; paperback, New York: Dell Publishing Co. (1977); and London: Virago Press (1988).

—— (1940) 'Mourning and its relation to manic-depressive states', in

217

The Writings of Melanie Klein, vol. 1, *Love, Guilt and Reparation*, London: Hogarth Press (1975), 344—69.

—————— (1946) 'Notes on some schizoid mechanisms', in *The Writings of Melanie Klein*, vol. 3, *Envy and Gratitude and Other Works*, London: Hogarth Press (1975), 1—24; paperback, New York: Dell Publishing Co. (1977); and London: Virago Press (1988).

—————— (1948) 'On the theory of anxiety and guilt', in *The Writings of Melanie Klein*, vol. 3, *Envy and Gratitude and Other Works*, London: Hogarth Press (1975), 25—42; paperback, New York: Dell Publishing Co. (1977); and London: Virago Press (1988).

—————— (1952a) 'The origins of transference', in *The Writings of Melanie Klein*, vol. 3, *Envy and Gratitude and Other Works*, London: Hogarth Press (1975), 48—56; paperback, New York: Dell Publishing Co. (1977); and London: Virago Press (1988).

—————— (1952b) 'Some theoretical conclusions regarding the emotional life of the infant', in *The Writings of Melanie Klein*, vol. 3, *Envy and Gratitude and Other Works*, London: Hogarth Press (1975), 61—93; paperback, New York: Dell Publishing Co. (1977); and London: Virago Press (1988).

—————— (1957) *Envy and Gratitude*, in *The Writings of Melanie Klein*, vol. 3, *Envy and Gratitude and Other Works*, London: Hogarth Press (1975), 176—235; paperback, New York: Dell Publishing Co. (1977); and London: Virago Press (1988).

Kubie, L.S. (1939) 'A critical analysis of the concept of repetition compulsion', *International Journal of Psycho-Analysis* 20: 390—407.

Meltzer, D. (1966) 'The relation of anal masturbation to projective identification', *International Journal of Psycho-Analysis* 47: 335—42; also in E. Bott Spillius (ed.) *Melanie Klein Today*, vol. 1, *Mainly Theory*, London: Routledge (1988), 102—16.

—————— (1973) *Sexual States of Mind*, Strath Tay, Perthshire: Clunie Press.

Money-Kyrle, R. (1956) 'Normal countertransference and some of its deviations', *International Journal of Psycho-Analysis* 37: 360—6. Reprinted in *The Collected Papers of Roger Money-Kyrle*, D. Meltzer (ed.) with the assistance of E. O'Shaughnessy, Strath Tay, Perthshire: Clunie Press (1978), 330—42; and in E. Bott Spillius (ed.) *Melanie Klein Today*, vol. 2, *Mainly Practice*, London: Routledge (1988), 22—33.

Oxford English Dictionary (1979) *Compact Edition*, London: Oxford University Press.

Payne, S. (1947) 'Notes on developments in the theory and practice of psychoanalytical technique', *Yearbook of Psycho-Analysis* 3: 159—73.

Pick, I. Brenman (1985) 'Working through in the countertransference', *International Journal of Psycho-Analysis* 66: 157—66; also, in a revised form, in E. Bott Spillius (ed.) *Melanie Klein Today*, vol. 2, *Mainly*

Practice, London: Routledge (1988) 34—47.

Reich, W. (1925) *Der Triebhafte Charakter*, Leipzig: Int. Psychoanal. Verlag.

Rosenfeld, H. (1964) 'On the psychopathology of narcissism: a clinical approach', *International Journal of Psycho-Analysis* 45: 332—7; also in *Psychotic States: a Psychoanalytical Approach*, London: Hogarth Press (1965), 169—79; also published in New York: International Universities Press (1966); reprinted in paperback, London: Maresfield Reprints, H. Karnac Books (1982).

—————— (1971a) 'Contribution to the psychopathology of psychotic states: the importance of projective identification in the ego structure and the object relations of the psychotic patient', in P. Doucet and C. Laurin (eds) *Problems of Psychosis*, The Hague: Excerpta Medica, 115—28; also reprinted in E. Bott Spillius (ed.) *Melanie Klein Today*, vol. 1, *Mainly Theory*, London: Routledge (1988), 117—37.

—————— (1971b) 'A clinical approach to the psychoanalytic theory of the life and death instincts: an investigation into the aggressive aspects of narcissism', *International Journal of Psycho-Analysis* 52: 169—78; also in E. Bott Spillius (ed.) *Melanie Klein Today*, vol. 1, *Mainly Theory*, London: Routledge (1988), 239—55.

Sandler, J. (1976a) 'Dreams, unconscious fantasies and "identity of perception"', *International Review of Psycho-Analysis* 3: 33—42.

—————— (1976b) 'Countertransference and role-responsiveness', *International Review of Psycho-Analysis* 3: 43—7.

Sandler, J. and Sandler, A.M. (1978) ' On the development of object relationships and affects', *International Journal of Psycho-Analysis* 59: 285—96.

Segal, H. (1962) 'The curative factors in psycho-analysis', *International Journal of Psycho-Analysis* 43: 212—17; also in *The Work of Hanna Segal*, New York: Jason Aronson (1981), 69—80.

—————— (1977) 'Countertransference', *International Journal of Psychoanalytic Psychotherapy* 6: 31—7; also in *The Work of Hanna Segal*, New York: Jason Aronson (1981), 81—7.

Spillius, E. Bott (ed.) (1988) *Melanie Klein Today*, in 2 vols. London: Routledge.

Steiner, J. (1982) 'Perverse relationships between parts of the self: a clinical illustration', *International Journal of Psycho-Analysis* 63: 241—52.

Strachey, J. (1934) 'The nature of the therapeutic action of psychoanalysis', *International Journal of Psycho-Analysis* 15: 127—59; reprinted in *International Journal of Psycho-Analysis* 50: 275—92.

—————— (1937) 'The theory of the therapeutic results of psychoanalysis', *International Journal of Psycho-Analysis* 18: 139—45.

Van der Leeuw, P.J. (1971) 'On the development of the concept of defence', *International Journal of Psycho-Analysis* 52: 51—8.

Winnicott, D.W. (1960) 'Ego distortion in terms of true and false self', in *The Maturational Process and the Facilitating Environment*, London: Hogarth Press (1965), 14—52.

Wittels, F. (1938) 'The position of the psychopath in the psychoanalytic system', *International Journal of Psycho-Analysis* 19: 471—88.

Zetzel, E. (1956) 'Current concepts of transference', *International Journal of Psycho-Analysis* 37: 369—76.

Complete list of the published papers of Betty Joseph

(1948) 'A technical problem in the treatment of the infant patient', *International Journal of Psycho-Analysis* 29: 1–2.

(1959) 'An aspect of the repetition compulsion', *International Journal of Psycho-Analysis* 40: 1–10.

(1960) 'Some characteristics of the psychopathic personality', *International Journal of Psycho-Analysis* 41: 526–31.

(1966) 'Persecutory anxiety in a four-year-old boy', *International Journal of Psycho-Analysis* 47: 184–8.

(1971) 'A clinical contribution to the analysis of a perversion', *International Journal of Psycho-Analysis* 52: 441–9.

(1975) 'The patient who is difficult to reach', in P.L. Giovacchini (ed.) *Tactics and Techniques in Psychoanalytic Therapy*, vol. 2, *Countertransference*, New York: Jason Aronson, 205–10.

(1978) 'Different types of anxiety and their handling in the analytic situation', *International Journal of Psycho-Analysis* 59: 223–8.

(1981a) 'Towards the experiencing of psychic pain', in J.S. Grotstein (ed.) *Do I Dare Disturb the Universe? A Memorial to Wilfred R. Bion*, Beverly Hills, CA: Caesura Press, 94–102.

(1981b) 'Defence mechanisms and phantasy in the psychoanalytical process', *Bulletin of the European Psychoanalytical Federation* 17: 11–24.

(1982) 'Addiction to near-death', *International Journal of Psycho-Analysis* 63: 449–56.

(1983) 'On understanding and not understanding: some technical issues', *International Journal of Psycho-Analysis* 64: 291–8.

(1985) 'Transference: the total situation', *International Journal of Psycho-Analysis* 66: 447–54.

(1986) 'Envy in everyday life', *Psychoanalytic Psychotherapy* 2: 13—22.

(1987) 'Projective identification: some clinical aspects' in J. Sandler (ed.) *Projection, Identification, Projective Identification*, Madison, CT: International Universities Press, 65—76.

(1988) 'Object relations in clinical practice', *The Psychoanalytic Quarterly*, 57: 626—42.

(1989a) 'Passivity and aggression: their inter-relationship', published here for the first time (written in 1971).

(1989b) 'Psychic change and the psychoanalytic process', published here for the first time.

Name index

Alexander, F. 34

Balint, M. viii
Bibring, E. 16
Bion, W.R. vii, 5, 7, 14, 24, 72, 96, 103; and containment 50, 86, 112, 141, 169, 206; and projective identification 154, 170, 206
Bromberg, W. 34

Deutsch, H. 34, 76

Feldman, M. 1, 13, 47, 101, 153
Fenichel, O. 34
Freud, S. vii, 25, 65, 106–7, 137, 154, 193; and analytic process 156, 194; and death instinct 32, 128, 205; and defence 108, 116–17, 125; and narcissism 203–5; and repetition compulsion 16–17, 32–3

Gillespie, W. 58
Greenacre, P. 34
Greenberg, J.R. 206–7

Heimann, P. viii, 5, 6, 8
Hendrick, I. 16
Hinshelwood, R. 5, 6

Joseph, B. viii–ix, 221–2; works of, discussed 1–9, 13–15, 47–50, 101–5, 153–5

King, P. 5, 6, 7

Klein, M. 3, 5, 34, 107, 116, 150, 169; and depressive and paranoid-schizoid positions vii, 2, 15, 108–9, 113, 117, 125–6, 168–9, 194, 206; and envy 24, 36, 154; and object relationships 140, 154, 156, 204–6; and projective identification vii–viii, 2, 26, 82, 86, 89, 141, 154, 156, 167, 204–6
Kubie, L.S. 16

Meltzer, D. 76, 131
Mitchell, S.A. 206–7
Money-Kyrle, S. 6

Payne, S. 5
Pick, I. Brenman 6

Reich, W. 34
Rosenfeld, R. vii, 2, 86, 131, 154; and narcissism 49, 76, 103

Sandler, A.-M. and J. 6
Segal, H. vii–ix, 2, 6, 8
Spillius, E. Bott 1, 13, 47, 101, 153
Steiner, J. 131
Strachey, J. 6, 156

Van der Leeuw, P. 116

Winnicott, D.W. 76
Wittels, F. 34

Zetzel, E. 5

Subject index

acting-in 49, 117, 126, 142, 170
acting out 36, 65, 83, 212
   analyst and 80, 107, 111, 147—8,
      159, 208—9; as communication
      77, 87; of perversion 48; *see also*
      transference
addiction to near-death 103, 127—38
aggression 29, 32, 54, 63, 144—5, 195
   defence against 55, 69, 112; passivity
      and 63, 67—74
ambivalence 24, 32, 129, 205—6
   avoidance of 29, 136; and guilt 14,
      101, 107, 108
analyst 27, 38, 40, 62—3, 71—2
   anxiety in 79—80, 176; collusion and
      77, 108—10, 128, 136, 177;
      containment by 36, 50, 109—10,
      112, 206; control of 31, 70, 131,
      141, 175, 196; defensive system
      and 113, 123, 126, 142, 144,
      157—8; dependence on 4, 23, 24,
      31; despair and 61, 104, 122,
      127—8, 133, 148; envy and 59,
      81, 148—9, 200—1; hatred of 129,
      173; idealized 13, 37, 111, 172—4,
      188; invasiveness towards 122,
      148—9, 173—4, 176, 179, 188;
      lack of contact with 4, 81, 102,
      111, 118, 173; listening function
      of 117, 121, 139, 142, 192,
      208—9; manipulation of 79, 86,
      130, 142, 157, 163; patient's

perception of 48, 90—1, 102,
      109—11, 117, 148, 210; as
      phantasy mother 118, 119;
      psychic equilibrium and 142, 208;
      rivalry with 18, 20, 23, 24, 200;
      seductiveness towards 195, 196;
      special relationship with 92, 196,
      199, 200; superior attitude
      towards 53, 102, 201, 213;
      understanding in 4, 140, 209; *see*
      also acting out; identification;
      introjection
analytic process
   defence mechanisms and phantasy in
      116—26; psychic change and 156,
      192—202; psychic equilibrium and
      88
analytic relationship 14, 53, 76, 143,
   207, 211
   analyst in, as whole person 139, 140;
      real 60, 173, 196; sado-
      masochistic 60, 65, 104, 108, 147,
      208; self-destructiveness and 127;
      sexualization of 60, 84
analytic situation 4, 108, 123, 174
   handling of anxiety in 106—16
anorexia 149, 173, 188
anxiety 53, 71, 79—80, 108, 112, 139,
   165, 176, 195
   avoidance of 27, 40, 42, 101, 144;
      claustrophic 48, 169, 178;
      depressive 3, 15, 30, 32, 102,